Empires of the Sky

Empires
of
the Sky

The Politics, Contests and Cartels of World Airlines

Anthony Sampson

HODDER AND STOUGHTON
LONDON SYDNEY AUCKLAND TORONTO

British Library Cataloguing in Publication Data
Sampson, Anthony
  Empires of the sky.
  1. Air lines
  I. Title
  387.7   HE9776

  ISBN 0 340 34931 X

Contents

Introduction

The Air Change

ALMOST anyone who has lived through the air age, watching times and distances contract, must have wondered what this strange new form of transport has done to the world and to them. When I made my first long journey, from London to Cape Town in 1951, the cheapest way was still by sea, taking two weeks while the winter turned into summer, the swimming pools were filled and the decks were opened up to the tropical sun. When I came back three years later it was already cheaper to fly—on a DC-4 plane which took two days, whose propeller-engines seemed to bore into my mind and which landed every thousand miles or so at tiny airports where it stood alone on the airstrip: it circled Victoria Falls and followed the course of the Nile, low enough still to seem part of the continent and the landscape.

Three years later I flew round the world on Super Constellations taking two days and two nights to cross the Pacific and stopping at Fiji and Honolulu. It was still a time when journalists dramatically reported the take-offs and touchdowns of air journeys with awe, and when travel books began by describing the airport. But three years later the jet age had begun, and this extraordinary revolution in travelling quickly became too commonplace, too safe and uniform to provide much scope for description.

I spent more time in the air as I became interested in another aspect of the changing world—the influences of multinational corporations and banks who were using jet travel, together with international telephones, telexes and computers, to provide their own kinds of unity. While I flew between the continents I tried to work out how the airlines themselves, so global yet so national, fitted into the changing economic and political pattern. As the two oil shocks of 1973 and 1979 multiplied their fuel bills and the two recessions cut back their projections, the airlines were caught between two other dominant industries—paying far more to the oil companies and increasingly in debt to the bankers. And by the eighties they were facing the worst economic crisis in their history.

The actual stimulus to write this book came from an unexpected quarter. To my surprise I was invited by the International Air Transport Association, which represents most of the world's airlines, to give a speech at their annual conference. I reminded them that in one of my books I had described them as "one of the most hated cartels in the world". Had they not asked the wrong man? But no, they realised that and they were interested in critical views. After talking with airline chiefs and their critics I became intrigued by the debates that were raging through the airline business about deregulation and competition, and its state of crisis; and I began to trace how the airlines had first grown up in the political framework —and how they themselves had changed the world's political attitudes. This book is the result.

It is not a book about the separate competition of the aircraft manufacturers—which has been vividly described by John Newhouse in his book *The Sporty Game*. Nor is it about the heroic exploits of the early pilots, which have been amply chronicled elsewhere. Nor is it about the domestic American airlines, except insofar that they fly abroad and influence foreign airlines. It is essentially about the politics of international airlines; how they first grew up in a highly politicised atmosphere, how their dazzling ambitions and technology were directed by political decisions and choices, how nations faced new problems as they extended their competition into the air, and how the planes in their turn influenced the politics on the ground.

In writing this book I have contracted no debts or obligations to any airline: I have accepted no free trips or junkets. I am grateful to many friends and acquaintances who have helped me with insights and information, most of whom would wish to remain anonymous. I was much encouraged by a chance meeting on a 747 with Vernon Crudge, the veteran consultant and former British Airways executive. I have had invaluable advice from Stephen Wheatcroft, the aviation economist, and Peter Martin, the aviation lawyer. The staff of IATA, particularly Geoffrey Lipman, have been generous with their time and assistance, whatever my criticisms. Sir Ian Pedder and Alan White of the Civil Aviation Authority in London have been patient with their explanations of the intricacies of air traffic control. I am indebted to many earlier books, which I have tried to acknowledge in the notes, including the important recent history of TWA, *Howard Hughes' Airline*, by Robert Serling, and the two histories of Pan American: *An American Saga* by Robert Daley and *Chosen Instrument* by Marilyn Bender and Selig Altschul. I must also record a special debt to *A History of the World's Airlines* by R. E. G. Davies, the indispensable reference book published in 1964.

In writing the book I owe most thanks to my IBM Personal Computer and the Wordstar word-processing programme. Alexa Wilson has once again helped me through the last ordeals; my wife Sally has been long-suffering as before. I am grateful to my publishers, Bob Loomis of Random House and Eric Major of Hodder & Stoughton, for their encouragement and advice; to my literary agents Michael Sissons and Sterling Lord; and I owe a special debt to Walter Anderson of *Parade* magazine who with characteristic decisiveness first commissioned me to investigate the Korean Air Line disaster.

Prologue

On Top of the World

I'll put a girdle round about the earth
In forty minutes.

Puck, in Shakespeare's Midsummer Night's Dream

Lovers of air travel find it exhilarating to hang poised between the illusion
of immortality and the fact of death.

Alexander Chase, 1966

WAKING in the middle of the night—or is it day?—I ask myself like
so many jet-lagged travellers, "Where am I . . . ? When am I?" It's
harder than usual to guess the answer in this standardised hotel
room. Then I remember that I had flown yesterday from the ghostly
black hangar of Narita airport, after a two hours' drive out of Tokyo;
and that I was talking on the plane to a British businessman who
had flown out to Tokyo for just two days, to look at new robots
which would soon be able to make a complete shirt without use of
human hands. On the JAL plane he'd asked the air hostess about
women's lib and she had sweetly explained that she didn't understand it. Now I remember: I decided to stop in Anchorage in Alaska,
on my way back to London; and in Anchorage the clock says it's
not the middle of the night but breakfast time, and not Tuesday
but Monday again.

After breakfast I try to find out where I really am. Anchorage
has one of the busiest international airports in the world: most of
the big European airlines – British Airways, Lufthansa, Air France,
SAS—stop here twice a day, but they are outnumbered by the
two biggest users, Japan Air Lines—now the biggest international
airline—and Korean. The new Anchorage airport is a triumph of
the nowhere style: the rectangular slabs might have been lowered

yesterday from the sky to fit neatly between the jumbo airliners which are lined up refuelling in rows. The planes seem to have converged on this arctic hide-out like a jumbos' picnic-place, in this snowbound landscape. Inside the echoing airport it is only the airlines which seem to have any real identity, each with its own counter, manager and office decorated with its national flag and symbols, improbably awaiting passengers. In this outpost the staff sound all the more extravagantly French, English or Japanese.

This is America, of course, but it would be hard to guess: at the international airport all the airlines are European or Far Eastern, and the style belongs to the sky. Beyond the customs and security check lies the secret heart of the building, the transit area which is the limbo-land of all airports. Twice every day, after midnight and in the afternoon, the airport suddenly fills up with processions of lost souls from opposite ends of the world, who stare at each other with the familiar glazed dislocated look of passengers who have lost sight of place or time—Koreans on their way to New York, Scandinavians flying to Los Angeles, Japanese en route for London. In the concourse they are greeted by a huge stuffed polar bear standing upright, a menacing arctic wolf and an exorbitant duty-free shop which gives few clues (apart from Alaskan salmon) as to its geography—displaying Korean tape recorders, Dutch cigars and Scotch whisky which have been flown up here to sell to people flying out. Few passengers ever leave the transit area, and many airlines have not been granted what is grandly called the "fifth free-dom"—the freedom for passengers to stop over in a foreign country: the airlines can fly passengers through the place, but not *to* it. Looking at the rows of apprehensive faces of all colours and shapes, each with the same forsaken look, they seem all to have been denied the freedom to belong anywhere, like flying Dutchmen in search of an unattainable love.

But even people like myself who have been allowed to leave the airport to stay in the town of Anchorage find it hard to come to terms with its geography. It is part of the United States, yes, but I soon found that it was far quicker to fly from here to London or Tokyo than to most other American cities: Anchorage is only eight hours' flight from London, while to reach most of the "southern forty-eight"—as they call the rest of the United States up here—you must change planes at Seattle or Salt Lake City. Anchorage, though it calls itself the "polar route", is on the same latitude as Helsinki and not much further north than Stockholm; but it is far more remote, with the Rocky Mountains and the frozen wastes of British Columbia to the south. The time-zones add to the disorientation; for Alaska is five hours out of sync with New York and shares its

"Yukon time" only with Hawaii. The flight from Anchorage to London takes eight hours but crosses nine time-zones, and the British Airways man warns that it is famous for being the most jet-lagged of all journeys. But Alaska is also right up against the international date line; and passengers to and from the Far East have the disconcerting experience of having either two Mondays or none.

Anchorage owes its prosperity to oil but even more to the planes which have connected it both to the world and to the rest of Alaska. The Alaskans are known as the "flyingest people under the American flag" and the little airports and frozen lakes are full of light planes. The sea from the Cook Inlet makes Anchorage comparatively warm, and it has been a popular settling-place for Koreans, Japanese or Scandinavians as well as Americans and Canadians. The town centre of Anchorage, five minutes from the airport, still has a half-finished, accidental look and manages to look tame and suburban in spite of its exotic geography, with few signs of the wild bars of the forties. Only the distant peak of Mount McKinley—the highest mountain in North America—suggests the arctic splendour. The Captain Cook hotel, where I'm staying, has a tower block, a shopping arcade and homely waitresses who can serve brunch all day, excluding any local atmosphere; and the airlines add their own cosmopolitan confusion, filling up the lobby twice a day with pilots and crews from ten countries stopping over. Everyone knows that Anchorage depends on airlines, and they talk with dread about how long-range planes from Europe may eventually cut out this stop altogether on their way to the East, or fly across Siberia instead. Already Pan American, Japan and Northwest Airlines fly non-stop from New York to Tokyo, and Finnair flies direct from Helsinki to Tokyo—connecting Europe to the Far East in one fourteen-hour hop. Will Anchorage follow the fate of Gander or Shannon, which were once so indispensable to flights across the Atlantic, until technology left them behind?

It's odd to be reminded, by the map in the Captain Cook hotel, that this *is* the famous north-west passage which had tantalised and frustrated the great explorers since the sixteenth century. "If I should saile by way of the north-west," said Sebastian Cabot, "I should by a shorter tract come into India." In 1778 Captain James Cook, having discovered New Zealand and Australia, surveyed North-West America right up to the Bering Straits and visited the shores of Siberia. The United States bought Alaska from Russia in 1867, and after that became more interested in the Arctic; but it was not until 1906 that the Norwegian Roald Amundsen finally navigated the passage to the Pacific through the Bering Straits. The result was an anti-climax, like much polar discovery; for the icy route was quite impractical for everyday trade.

But the north-west passage gained a thrilling new significance in the air age. Planes were not hemmed in by land-masses and ice-floes, and they could follow the Great Circles to make their own connections across the world. In 1931 Charles Lindbergh, four years after flying across the Atlantic, set out with his wife in a single-engined seaplane to follow the north-west passage across the pole. "In the twentieth century we have turned to it again," wrote Anne Lindbergh, "not as a myth, a feat for explorers, or an undiscovered path towards an unknown end, but as a practical route to the Orient. For we are again approaching an age of new transoceanic routes, new ways to link countries and continents, this time by air." The Lindberghs' journey was full of hazardous navigation and landings, but they encountered no real political dangers: with their flying-machine they were enthusiastically welcomed by the peasants on the Soviet peninsula of Kamchatka, by Japanese fishermen on Kunashiri island, and by the Chinese in Nanking who asked them to help to survey the Yangtse floods.

Alaska soon became an aviator's paradise. It had only one long road and a 470-mile railway where the frost made the engine jump the track, while the small planes could go almost anywhere. By 1939 its airlines carried twenty-three times as many passengers, proportionately, as the rest of the United States. "Everybody travels by air in Alaska," wrote Jean Potter in her history of the Alaskan pilots in 1945, "fishermen, miners, trappers, Congressmen, prostitutes, engineers, salesmen . . . " During the Second World War seven thousand Lend-Lease bombers and fighters were ferried from Alaska to Siberia, to help the Soviet war effort; while the string of Aleutian Islands with their eerie names—Unalaska, Unimak, Umnak, Adak—which hang like a necklace between Alaska and Russia, acquired a new importance in the war against Japan. It was on Adak that Corporal Dashiel Hammett the thriller writer edited the air force paper *The Adakian*; and from there he flew into Anchorage, thrown out from one drinking place after another until he bought his own bar.

With peace Anchorage found new air opportunities, and by 1947 Northwest Airlines based on Minnesota began flying to Tokyo via Anchorage across the "top of the world". The polar route became a symbol of global unity: when ten years later the Scandinavian Airline SAS made its inaugural flight from Copenhagen to Tokyo via Anchorage, the Danish Prime Minister H. C. Hansen broadcast a message promising goodwill and co-operation between nations as it flew over the pole. The other European airlines soon caught up with the Scandinavians, and business travellers began to take for granted this eerie journey where the sun and the moon seemed to stay fixed in the sky and time nearly stood still. The trade along this aerial north-west passage was very different from what Cabot or Cook had in mind: half the big planes passing through Anchorage are now cargo planes, carrying not spices or gold, but cassette players, watches or computers. The polar route in the end enriched the East more than the West, as it gave the dynamic Asian countries a short cut to their markets in America and Europe.

It was hard to connect such adventurous history with this ordinary town and a placeless airport filled with dazed passengers staring at a stuffed polar bear in a transit lounge. Was this really the outcome of all those centuries of daring exploration?

It is not as commonplace as it looks; for in political terms it is far from nowhere. The air-route to Japan and Korea, which pilots treat as a milk-run, is the now notorious "Romeo Twenty" which at one point flies only thirty miles from the Soviet Union: the pilots can look down with their radar on the American Aleutian Islands one moment, and on the Soviet Kuril Islands the next. The peninsula of Kamchatka where the Lindberghs were welcomed with such friendliness is now bristling with Soviet weaponry: the North Pacific is now a critical frontier of confrontation in the cold war of the eighties. The development of this busy air-route through a highly militarised region was to lead to one of the most horrifying tragedies in the history of aviation. It was a reminder that air travel can still be poised between extreme boredom and extreme danger; but also that the greatest perils today are the political dangers.

"BUMS ON SEATS"

The airline business, having so miraculously circumscribed the world, has reached a kind of limit which baffles and saddens the veterans who can look back to its origins six decades ago. For the first years aviation was a breathless race to reach destinations, to consolidate empires or to forge new trade-routes; and each seat on an airline was a precious prize. Gradually it became a more commonplace commercial service, a business which Eddie Rickenbacker, followed by others, called "putting bums on seats". Then tourists began to outnumber officials and businessmen: there were no longer destinations needing planes, but planes needing destinations—until now there are far too many planes waiting for far too few passengers. Airlines which had been created by barnstormers and high-gambling entrepreneurs were taken over by

marketing men, caterers or stockbrokers who saw their airliners
largely in terms of rows of seats which had to be filled with
bums—like Dick Ferris of United Air Lines who came from Westin
hotels, Colin Marshall of British Airways from Avis Rent-A-Car,
or Donald Burr who learnt about aviation on Wall Street before he
founded People Express. They shocked the pilots and engineers by
talking about airline seats as if they were like hotel beds or restaurant
tables which only needed high occupancy rates and low overheads.

Any romantic passenger would find a contemporary airline conference a disillusioning experience. More mundane industrialists
may sometimes adopt the emotive metaphors of the air—welcoming
colleagues aboard, getting airborne, running into storms or fasten-
ing seat-belts for a bumpy ride. But the airline chiefs are determined
to come down to earth, to discuss their exotic routes and amazing
planes as if they were shopkeepers selling surplus goods in bargain
basements or at January sales. They spend so much time flying
from conference to conference—they give each other free passes to
anywhere—that they long ago ceased to be surprised at waking up
at the other end of the world; and the more businessmen travel, the
more engrossed they become in their own industry. Since they all
have the same basic problem—too many seats, too few bums—they
are all caught in the same dilemma: they want to get together to
fix the same fares, but they can never resist selling cut-price tickets
under the counter, to increase their share of the market. For every
empty seat adds to their losses, and the world airline industry,
whatever its other achievements, is technically close to being bankrupt.

THE SKY CLUB

Every year the airline chiefs fly in from five continents to the
annual meeting of their own club—the International Air Transport
Association or IATA. The full members sit in rows in the conference
hall behind the names of their airline from Aer Lingus to Zambia
Airways, like a miniature United Nations. Only a few countries like
Britain and America send delegates from more than one airline:
most are represented by a single "flag-carrier", ranging from Japan
Air Lines which has forty-eight planes, most of them jumbos, to Air
Ruanda which has one. When they vote, by holding up paddles on
sticks saying AF or LH, they look like a line-up of nations rather
than companies. The non-members of IATA like Singapore and
Aeroflot sit at the back, together with the men from Boeing or
McDonnell Douglas. They all face the platform where their annual

president sits beside the suave director-general Knut Hammarskjöld—whose uncle *was* the UN secretary-general—and who
lends a tone of high statesmanship to the meeting.

But the arguments are far from diplomatic, and the recriminations
have become more bitter as the airlines' predicament has worsened.
When IATA met in its home town of Geneva in November 1982
the industry faced the worst crisis in its history, having lost 1.2
billion dollars the previous year. "We are walking a financial
tightrope," Hammarskjöld warned them, "with the abyss of bankruptcy on the one hand and the slippery slope of subsidisation or
permanent bondage to the loan market on the other." The Swiss
hosts extended their Calvinist morality into the air. Armin Baltensweiler the chairman of Swissair—the bankers' favourite airline—
insisted on "careful husbandry, not reckless abandon". Professor
Guldiman, the former director of Swiss aviation, gave a stern
philosophical address reproving "myopic consumerism" and para-
sitism, and the "degeneration of democracy into democratism" like
the decadence of Athens 2,500 years earlier. He quoted Hegel, Karl
Barth and Valery—"not even the future is what it has been in the
past".

The airline chiefs seemed united against the myopic consumerists,
and determined to stop each other filling up their seats with the
cheap tickets which were being surreptitiously sold through the
"bucket-shops". "No one will help us if we don't help ourselves,"
warned Hammarskjöld, "and no international organisation can be
stronger than its members want to be." The lofty chief executive of
TWA, Ed Meyer, called on them all to stamp out discounting and
monitor any abuses, and others agreed: "The time has come to
show that we're serious," said Vlad Slivitzky of Air Canada. "Our
credibility is at risk," said Sir Adam Thomson, the combative
ex-pilot who runs British Caledonian. But many were sceptical,
having noticed the behaviour of some of the most dignified airlines.
"The most pious airlines are sometimes the worst offenders," complained David Kennedy, the outspoken head of Aer Lingus, with a
dig at his rivals British Airways.

Other airline chiefs were determined to show their own rugged
independence from any agreement. "This is the first IATA meeting
I have ever attended and it will probably be the last," said the
rumbustious new head of Air New Zealand, Bob Owens. "The way
things are going, the next annual meeting will probably be held in
a church." It was left to Umberto Nordio of Alitalia, an intellectual
in the industry, who had started his career in shipping, to sum up
their problem with his typical bluntness. "I first hoisted my sails
in a world of seafaring crooks, and now I spread my wings in a

world of airborne crooks." The airlines, he predicted, could never resist the temptation to offer discounts. "We're selling a product which is not stockable. It's as if a car dealer were told that all his cars would be worth nothing tomorrow morning. Naturally he would rush to sell them—even for a dollar each."

After an acrimonious debate they passed a resolution promising that they would each personally supervise their own airline's "tariff integrity". In the following months IATA sent its inspectors round the bucket-shops to try to catch the airlines cheating, and they did manage to reduce the discounting in some regions. But there were still airlines like Garuda and Korean, not to mention Aeroflot, who were delighted to attract customers on to their half-empty planes; and in the meantime the American movement for deregulating the airlines was beginning to spread across the world. It was an ironic sequel to the collapse earlier in the year of Sir Freddie Laker, the champion of the "forgotten man"—the collapse which the other airlines welcomed as the return to more orderly business. For passengers were becoming more bargain-conscious than ever: Laker's ghost stalked through the conference hall. And the airlines were becoming more desperate than ever to put bums on seats.

It was a come-down for the aviation industry which had begun as the greatest adventure of all, pushing back the new frontiers of the air, forging new trade-routes, transforming continents, girdling the world. It now seemed to be turning in on itself to become one of the most circumscribed of industries and, as Hammarskjöld warned them at Geneva, there were no new miracles or break-throughs to rescue them. The supersonic era had been aborted, and the jumbos, which had been intended as stop-gaps, now seemed to be the last of the great innovations, like the giant steam engines a century ago. The airlines were forced to turn back to the perennial problems of the overcrowded planet: they could fly round the world in forty-eight hours, but they could not get past the traffic jams to the airports. "In the space age," wrote Neil McElroy in 1958, "man will be able to go around the world in two hours—one hour for flying, and the other to get to the airport."

They were now nearly all flying the same giant planes—Boeings, Douglases or Lockheeds—while each trying to claim that theirs were unique. They provided a classic challenge to the advertising agencies to try to detect and proclaim their "unique selling propo-sition"—the "widest seat in the air", "flights so good, you won't want to get off" or "I want to stay up here with you for ever". Their sameness also provided a paradise for economic theorists. As military strategists are fascinated by desert warfare which offers neither side any special advantage of terrain, so competition in the air offers a special purity now that airlines fly the same planes along the same routes. After the United States deregulated the airlines in 1978 the economists could test out their theories and arguments between controls and free entry, between open skies and protection, in the great laboratory of the sky, and the arguments extended round the world. Yet however bright and clear the economists looked inside their own airspace, they became overclouded as they crossed the frontiers into the international arena. For they came up against all the obstacles of sovereignty and national pride, and no nation would allow its own airline to go bankrupt. The arguments between cartels and competition which had been fought out over so many industries reached a caricature in the airline business, which swung from one extreme to the other. The nations, however huge the losses, could not do without their own airlines, while the consumers still clamoured for lower fares.

The airlines, though they seemed to defy geography, are among the most national of industries, inextricably bound up with their home country's ambitions and security. Their competition may look like a contest between smiles or leg-room, but it is chiefly a question of air-routes and frequencies which have been thrashed out in hundreds of tough secret deals between governments; and IATA itself is not just a trade association, but a body established by treaty and endorsed by the governments. The sovereignty of airspace and the law of the air lie behind every agreement and "freedom"; and while airlines can fly across the pole to the end of the world in a day, the great lump of Russia is still more inaccessible and dangerous than ever.

Airlines and politics have collided with each other from the beginning. The airlines, as they changed the shape of the world, were also locked into the ambitions of nations. They provide a kind of visual projection of changes on earth – the shifting political balances of power and wealth, the swings of economic beliefs, the technological developments coming up against political deadlocks and reactions. The politics of the air may sometimes throw light on political problems below; and the story of this extraordinary industry, with its mixture of comforts and dangers, of excitement and bathos, provides its own descant above the pedestrian world.

Part I

The Conquest of the Air

1

Air Imperialism

I fly because it releases my mind from the tyranny of petty things . . .
Antoine de St-Exupéry

It seems to me that the conquest of the air is the only major task for our generation.
T. E. Lawrence

IT was implicit in the attitudes of the early aviators that they were escaping like birds—not only from the workaday lives of earthbound people, but from the ties of nationalism. In 1909 Louis Blériot flew across the English Channel from Calais to Dover—the first international flight in the world, only six years after the first flight of the Wright brothers. He received a £1,000 prize from Lord Northcliffe, the owner of the *Daily Mail,* who welcomed him as the latest in a long line of French inventors. Blériot's flight was seen as introducing a new era of individual aviation. "Roofs will disappear in favour of flat terraces suited to launching and landing stages," wrote Alphonse Berget in his book *The Conquest of the Air* published in the same year. "The flying apparatus will be, without a doubt, combinations of the helicopter and the aeroplane." But both countries also saw the event as the dawn of a new era of Anglo-French understanding, "realising through the atmosphere", as Berget put it, "that *entente cordiale* made between two nations". "Before five years are out," said M. Quinton of the Aerial League in Paris, "England will have ceased to be an island. The sea is no longer a barrier." The British agreed: *The Observer* in London carried a special supplement the following Sunday, with the heading ENGLAND NO LONGER AN ISLAND.

The horrors of the First World War which broke out five years later, when planes first showed their lethal potential, dampened much of the idealism of the air: the aviators could no longer see themselves as flying above mortal conflicts and the air all too clearly had its own frontiers. "The practice of the present war," said Sir Erle Richards, the Professor of International Law at Oxford in 1915, "seems definitely to have established the right of every state of sovereignty over the air space above its territories." But as pilots returned to peacetime conditions in 1919 and began to launch the first commercial "airlines" on the model of the shipping lines, they saw the air once again as the means to travel above the constraints of national territory, and to open up new relationships across the world.

But the pilots and entrepreneurs soon discovered that they could not fly without their governments' support, and that even within their own country they could not make their airlines pay without subsidies or the mail contracts which governments awarded. In every country the soaring ambitions of the aviators and their financiers came up against the controls and military designs of their governments. 1919 was the wonder-year of civil aviation, reborn after the world war, when several airlines were founded and two English pilots, Alcock and Brown—still commemorated by a statue at Heathrow—first flew across the Atlantic from Newfoundland to Ireland. But in the same year the Convention of Paris laid down the first rules for European air traffic (the United States only ratified the Havana Air Convention, which established similar rules for the Americas in 1928). The conventions repudiated the notion of freedom of the air and jealously guarded the new notion of air sovereignty, which limited planes much more than ships; for nations were naturally far more worried by aircraft flying over their territory—whence they could spy, bomb or secretly land—than by ships which under the law of the sea were allowed in theory to call at any port they wished. The first article of the Paris Convention granted each state "complete and exclusive sovereignty over the airspace above its territory".

But European attitudes to the air were very different to those in the emptier and vaster continents. For the European governments were determined from the beginning to harness aviation to their own needs, and particularly to bind their colonies and overseas settlements more closely to the home country. The new "airlines" could not avoid being dependent on the governments which subsidised them, merged them and controlled their routes. The first romantic picture of the aviator as the intrepid individualist escaping from the earth soon faded in the light of the harsher reality: fleets of planes mobilised to serve national interests and ambitions, which were increasingly coming into conflict.

"THE LINE"

The brilliant French tradition of innovation in the air went back to the eighteenth-century balloons, and their role in aviation was commemorated by words like fuselage, aileron, helicopter or aeroplane (which many British pronounced airyoplane) before it was superseded by the American airplane. French governments were much more determined than the British to lead the air world, and to use planes to connect up their empire in Africa and the Far East.

In the first post-war years tiny French airlines, with the help of subsidies, were competing across Europe: one of them, the Farman company which made planes in Paris, could claim in 1919 to be the first international airline, flying its Goliath bi-planes with fourteen passengers at ninety miles an hour between London and Paris and Brussels and Paris. By 1923 three other French airlines had merged to form Air Union, which concentrated on the cross-Channel flights, with connections through France. Another merger in 1930 created Air Orient, which the next year began flying regularly to Saigon, in French Indo-China—via Beirut, Damascus, Karachi, Calcutta, Rangoon and Bangkok.

The most famous of the French airlines was the little company set up in 1919 by a French arms manufacturer, Pierre Latécoère, to fly to North Africa and if possible to Latin America. It became known simply as The Line, immortalised by the writings of the daring young pilot, Antoine de St-Exupéry, who brilliantly expressed the conflict between the sense of liberation among the stars and the stern discipline of The Line. He joined the perilous route flying mails to Dakar in French West Africa, landing in the Sahara where pilots were liable to be captured by the Moors, while other pioneers of The Line were forging new routes in Latin America: the great pilot Jean Mermoz, who had first crossed the Sahara, succeeded in 1928 in crossing the Andes at 20,000 feet. In the meantime The Line had been taken over by a French tycoon with a network of South American interests, Bouilloux-Lafont, who renamed it Aéropostale; but it was still known as The Line, with the same adventurous pilots.

In 1930 Mermoz achieved the most spectacular breakthrough of all, flying a seaplane from Dakar in West Africa to Natal in Brazil in nineteen and a half hours, breaking the long-distance seaplane record and creating the crucial air-link between the two continents.

The south of France was now only two days away from Brazil. Latin American governments clamoured for the services of The Line which was soon operating in eight territories including Trinidad; and the French reached an agreement with the Portuguese to fly to the Azores, as a link across the North Atlantic. But The Line was suddenly undermined by financial scandals involving Bouilloux-Lafont, who was tried for forgery. The company went into liquidation and was sold to Air Orient; but the French government intervened and in 1933 forced the merger of all the airlines into a single company, with Ernest Rhoume as president, called Air France. It was a name—imitated by many of the national airlines that followed—which left no doubt that it was carrying the flag.

The new airline imposed strict economies and quickly withdrew from The Line's operations within Latin America, leaving the two rival companies Lufthansa and Pan American to benefit from the French pioneering; while only the pleading of Mermoz dissuaded them from dropping the service from Paris to Buenos Aires. St-Exupéry, together with his boss, left the new airline in disgust at the transformation into a "soul-less commercial enterprise", and returned to drink heavily in Paris. He later rejoined Air France as a publicity man, flying and lecturing round Europe, and in 1937 he prospected a new route from Casablanca across the Sahara to Timbuctoo. But his days of inspiration were over.

Air France was more concerned with the French empire than with Latin America, and it began competing more hectically with the English, Dutch and Germans in flying to the Far East: by 1938 it was flying as far as Hanoi and Hong Kong, with a system covering 46,400 kilometres. But already its air network was more fragile, as war looked more likely and as the French government concentrated on building warplanes. The French record of innovation and enterprise was being overtaken by the Germans, who now had a much more ruthless sense of national purpose.

THE IMPERIAL WAY

The British and French were able to apply almost opposite attitudes to airlines, as to so many other innovations. The French state subsidised them from the start and the French public saw the air in romantic terms; but British governments were at first reluctant to pay anything, and tended to regard aviators as flying chauffeurs. Winston Churchill, who combined being Secretary for Air with Secretary for War in 1919, was an enthusiastic amateur pilot and excited by the potential for warplanes; but he did not show the same interest in civil airlines and insisted they must not look for subsidies but "fly by themselves". It was, wrote the air historian R. E. G. Davies, "one of the most short-sighted decisions this great statesman was to make". Only a few British visionaries saw an exciting future in the air. "The British Islands are small islands and our people numerically a little people," wrote the scientist and novelist H. G. Wells in his dissenting report to a government committee in 1918, "their only claim to world importance depends on their courage and enterprise, and a people who will not stand up to the necessity of Air Service planned on a world scale and taking over thousands of aeroplanes and thousands of men from the onset of peace, has no business to pretend to anything more than second-rate position in the world. We cannot be both Imperial and mean."

Some British entrepreneurs and politicians shared Wells' enthusiasm, including Lord Northcliffe of the *Daily Mail* who had presented the prize to Blériot, and Sir Sefton Brancker, the air-vice-marshal who left the air force to devote himself to civilian air transport. Most of them were inspired, often hazily, by the desire to link Britain more closely with her huge overseas possessions: while Britain was losing her economic supremacy the air provided a kind of refuge for imperial dreams and fantasies. "In my belief," said Brancker in 1919, "aviation will be the greatest factor in linking up our world-wide empire." (He did not live to see his ambitions achieved: he died on the airship R101 when it crashed in 1930 on its way to India.) Brancker became managing director of a new company, Aircraft Transport and Travel, which had been set up by a bearded entrepreneur George Holt Thomas, who had begun financing planes after Blériot's flight. In August 1919, a plane belonging to AT&T took off from Hounslow Heath—close to the present London Airport—and landed two and a half hours later at Le Bourget, the makeshift airport with a few canvas hangars outside Paris. It was the first *daily* scheduled service between any two countries, much more regular than Farman's in Paris, and the instigator of what was to become the busiest international route in the world.

Thomas and Brancker were determined to extend their air network, but they were too optimistic about the problems of converting warplanes to peacetime travel and both the British public and its government were much less interested than the French. The small British airlines could not compete without government help, and Holt Thomas had to sell his little business to BSA-Daimler. The harsh realities of European air transport were already asserting themselves. Alfred Instone, who had founded his own airline, had warned the British Civil Air Commission in 1918:

"Private enterprise" cannot run successful European air services. Moreover it is impossible to control the air services of Europe on nationalist lines. You cannot have nearly forty sovereign countries each trying to wreck the air services of the other thirty-nine. Europe must be one area for air transport under one control, or there can be nothing but a few ferry services in operation.

It was a plea which would re-echo over the next six decades.

British policies in the air remained confused, and in 1922 seven British companies were flying 7,000 people between the aerodromes at Croydon and Paris, while the French Air Union was still under-cutting them. But the new Secretary for Air, Sir Samuel Hoare, inspired by the adventures of Australian airmen, was more dedicated to air transport. "I saw in the creation of air-routes," he said, "the chance of uniting the scattered countries of the Empire and the Commonwealth." After bitter arguments with the Treasury which (he complained) "did not believe in civil aviation", Hoare appointed a committee under a banker Sir Herbert Hambling, which strongly advocated a single airline, to be granted a subsidy of a million pounds over ten years. It was duly formed in 1924 out of four components and appropriately called Imperial Airways.

The British government saw Imperial Airways as their own "chosen instrument", as they called it, to forge a global service. But the new airline had no proper full-time chief, and British aviation would suffer ever afterwards from amateurs at the top. For the next thirteen years Imperial was chaired by Sir Eric Geddes, as an adjunct to the Dunlop Rubber Company of which he was also chairman. As his successor Lord Reith complained: "The board met in the Dunlop office, employed the same solicitors, auditors, architects; Geddes was the autocrat of Dunlops; his closest associates there, Sir George Beharrel and Sir Hardman Lever, both sat on the Imperial Airways board." Sir Eric was one of the small group of British commercial grandees who moved confidently between wartime government and peacetime industry. He was a tall domi-nating Scotsman who had run railways in India and England and who organised army transport during the war, and in peacetime he became an MP and Minister of Transport. His most famous speech was one in which he demanded that the Germans should be squeezed for reparations "till the pips squeak".

Imperial Airways was emphatically patriotic: it could only buy British planes, which flew the blue ensign as they taxied along the runway. It was much more interested in the Empire than in Europe. "In the eyes of Imperial Airways," wrote R. E. G. Davies, "the continent of Europe seemed to amount to about five miles around the Eiffel Tower and a few lake resorts in Switzerland." The huge extent of the British Empire—including its now-strategic Pacific islands—encouraged the making of an "all-red" route round the world—linking all the possessions coloured red on British maps. There were two missing links. One was the Hawaii Islands which were virtually controlled by the United States. The other was the stretch of the Middle East between Egypt and India—the crucial military route of the Empire—where European rivals had their own ambitions, and flights through Persia (Iran) were very uncertain. But once the British could secure a southern route via Bahrain off the coast of Saudi Arabia, and once they could negotiate Hawaii with the Americans, they would have a unique global network of harbours and bases, knitted far more closely to the mother country.

Their first ambition was to reach India. The planes could stop at airports in Cairo and Baghdad on the way to Karachi—the first Indian terminus. A special fort was built in the oasis of Rutbah Wells in the middle of the desert between Cairo and Baghdad, with an airfield, hotel and emergency supplies. At the end of 1926 Sir Samuel Hoare and his wife embarked on the first Imperial flight to India: "We were both intent upon proving that flying was a normal and dependable way of travelling for women as well as men." Their account of the twelve-day journey provided a useful summing-up of the state of air travel. It was "a stage-coach kind of journey", with leisurely stops; and its importance "was not its speed but its regularity. An ordinary commercial machine with a full load of passengers and luggage had, day after day, carried out its timetable with the precision of a pre-war express train . . . We discovered that we could read and write in an aeroplane better than in a train."

The imperial routes spread rapidly. In 1926 Alan Cobham flew from London to Cape Town, photographing the pyramids on the way, and getting spray from the Victoria Falls into his carburettors. He raced the liner the *Windsor Castle*, which left the Cape at the same time. Cobham had to make twenty-six stops over 8,500 miles, and could not fly by night, while the liner sailed only 5,300 miles, night and day. Imperial Airways began building airfields and rest houses down East Africa, and by 1932 they were running a weekly service from Egypt to Cape Town, linking up the "red route" of British colonies on the way and fulfilling Cecil Rhodes' dream of a Cape-to-Cairo route, by air instead of rail. In the meantime Imperial was pressing beyond India to link up with the Australian airline Qantas (see next chapter).

By 1934 the British parliament had agreed to a new plan for airmail, to subsidise the airline—beginning with £750,000 a year—in return for transporting regular bulk mail across the Empire. Imperial Airways ordered twenty-eight new "Empire" flying boats, and by 1938 they were flying letters to South Africa and Australia, to New Zealand and Hong Kong, providing the most extensive mail service in the world, commemorated by special blue airmail stamps and blue pillar-boxes.

With the help of its subsidies Imperial had been showing a profit since the early thirties. But there was growing political resentment of its monopoly as the sole "chosen instrument", which was not helped by Sir Eric's autocratic style which antagonised his pilots and staff: he built up a system, as the editor of *The Aeroplane*, C. G. Grey, complained, without a personal touch and with "almost inhuman mechanical efficiency". A rival airline called "British Airways" had already been formed in 1935, which was later subsidised by the government to fly mail across Europe, and which unlike Imperial was allowed to buy Fokkers, Junkers and Lockheeds. The government was in a recurring muddle, subsidising rival airlines while having confidence in neither. In 1937 the managers of Imperial, now led by two more Scotsmen Sir George Beharrel and Woods Humphery, sacked the leaders of the new pilots' union BALPA, which retaliated by criticising the directors' high fees and the obsolete equipment, provoking a fierce debate in parliament. "Imperial Airways' service in Europe," complained the union's vice-president Bobby Perkins, who was both a pilot and Conservative MP, "is the laughing stock of the world." The government appointed a committee of inquiry, under Lord Cadman of the Anglo-Iranian oil company, which produced a devastating report. It accused Imperial of being "intolerant of suggestion and unyielding in negotiation", mishandling its staff relations, taking a narrowly commercial view and not co-operating with government departments; and it recommended drastic reforms including the appointment of a full-time chairman.

The British government searched with difficulty for a new chairman—a search that would endlessly repeat itself over the next forty years—and eventually made the extraordinary choice of John Reith, who had built up the British Broadcasting Corporation. Reith was very reluctant—"It was just not the sort of thing I wanted"—and arrived despondently at his shabby office in an old furniture depository behind Victoria Station, to approve the spending of £238 on passengers' lavatories at Croydon: "from Broadcasting House to this . . . "

Reith was soon in dispute with his managing director Woods

Humphery, an old colleague from Glasgow, who resigned in dudgeon. "He accused me of smashing up his organisation," Reith wrote later, "the organisation which I had not been able to find." Reith was appalled by the shortage of aircraft, the late deliveries and the all-British policy, and criticised the basic constitution of the company which was "neither wholly free nor wholly secure". He proposed that it should become a public corporation. The Conservative-led government, now worried by the dangers of war, had their own reasons for nationalising it and in November 1938 they decided to buy both Imperial and British Airways and merge them. In April 1940, when Britain was already at war, Reith became the first chairman of the British Overseas Airways Corporation.

The enterprise of the early pioneers had ended in tragic frustrations after two decades. Britain's only international airline was a state monopoly, run by an outsider with no real interest in planes. All civil air development was overshadowed by the war needs, while building commercial planes was left to the Americans. And the dream of the imperial routes circling the world was soon to vanish for ever.

THE IMPORTANCE OF SMALLNESS

The air everywhere provided a special challenge to the smaller countries to escape from their confines, and to outmanoeuvre their more lumbering big neighbours; and Holland and Belgium were equally determined to use the air to control their colonies or to spread their influence abroad. The Belgians were preoccupied with holding the Congo five thousand miles away and King Albert, whose father King Leopold had so ruthlessly developed the Congo, played a leading part in encouraging African air services. "The civilian air fleet will soon be forging the permanent links . . . " said Major Georges Nelis, who was in charge of Belgian military aircraft in 1919, "increasing ten-fold the economic return from the resources of the world." The next year the Belgian government set up the first overseas air service, flying British Handley Page planes between Leopoldville (Kinshasa) and N'Gombe on the Congo river. In May 1923 a new company was formed whose name clearly explained its ambitions: the Société Anonyme Belge d'Exploitation de la Navigation Aérienne (SABENA). Sabena established its own European network, but its chief ambition was to forge the air-link with the Congo. In 1925 a Belgian air ace, Edmond Thieffry, made a pioneer flight through Africa down to Leopoldville, taking fifty-one days with seventy-five hours' flying-time; and ten years later Sabena began regular flights for passengers and mail in only five-and-a-half days, providing a new surge of confidence in Belgium's African empire.

At the first aviation exhibition in Amsterdam in 1919 a powerfully built young pilot in the Dutch army, Albert Plesman, was inspired with the idea that civilian air services could become profitable, and could be a critical instrument for a small trading nation. Thus began the story of KLM, which claims (like many others) to be the world's oldest continuous airline. Unlike most European airlines it was created by a man, not a government, and Plesman dominated it from the start. But he quickly obtained the support of his government and of Queen Wilhelmina, and he could thus call his tiny airline—like the national oil company—Royal Dutch. Plesman was spurred by the need for faster communications with the Dutch East Indies (now Indonesia) nine thousand miles away, and he had a valuable partner in the plane designer Anthony Fokker, another "Flying Dutchman" who had made famous planes in Germany through the First World War, including the famous triplane flown by the "Red Baron" Manfred von Richthofen. After 1919 Fokker smuggled planes and engines across to Holland, to set up his own company (which still makes planes today at Schiphol, merged with the German VFW company since 1969), and by 1920 he had produced his first real passenger plane, the F2, with four wicker chairs in a closed cabin. For the next twenty years Fokker worked closely with Plesman, designing bigger and faster planes first for KLM, and later for airlines abroad: he set up a factory in New Jersey, and in 1930 he became—if only for a short time—the world's leading plane manufacturer.

Plesman knew that Holland lacked the political clout and the overseas networks of Britain, France or Germany, and he depended on persuasion and free trade to get landing rights for KLM. He was a brilliant salesman and negotiator. As Gordon McGregor, later head of Air Canada, described him: "He spoke accented English fluently when he had a point to make, and could not understand the language at all if he was disagreed with. Basically his approach was that an airline operated by a little country like Holland could not possibly do any harm to anyone." When Hudson Fysh of Qantas met Plesman in his palatial office in Holland in 1937, he was bombarded with free-trade arguments: "Throw the mailbag onto the first plane that goes through." "My reply to these theories," recorded Fysh, "was always that we would have international freedom of trade in the air just as soon as we had free trade on the ground, no customs barriers, and no monetary controls.

Plesman gave me up as a bad job, and when I left said to me, 'When you came here you were Imperial and now you leave you are still Imperial.' "

By 1924 the first KLM plane—a single-engined Fokker F7—had set off for the East Indies, arriving eight weeks later after a breakdown in Bulgaria. Five years later KLM began the longest scheduled flights in the world, to Batavia (now Djakarta), spending eight nights on the way. Plesman's friendship with Fokker did not commit him to only buying his planes, and when in 1934 Donald Douglas in California began making his "tin-can" all-metal planes Plesman quickly bought some, thus outpacing Imperial Airways which were committed to their slow British flying boats: and KLM humiliated Imperial by winning the first prize in the London–Melbourne race with a Douglas DC-2. Two years later KLM was the first European airline to fly the revolutionary new DC-3, soon known round the world as the Dakota.

By 1938 KLM had grown from its small home base to be one of only three airlines—with Imperial and Pan American—that were flying across the world. They had overtaken Air France in their numbers of passengers, and the Dutch seemed to be reliving their old sea-power in the air. The Australians had allowed Plesman to fly as far as Sydney, and KLM, using its new Lockheed landplanes, could arrive a day sooner than Imperial and Qantas. While the major powers were preoccupied with rearming and boosting their own manufacturers, the airlines of smaller countries, including KLM, Sabena and Swissair, were free to buy American planes which were now faster and safer—a pattern that would repeat itself later. "The US aircraft industry," commented R. E. G. Davies, "owes a great debt to the smaller countries of Europe."

LUFTHANSA AND THE NAZIS

But all these European airlines were being eclipsed by the Germans, who were not necessarily the most innovative, but the most ambitious and organised, whether for aircraft or for their speciality, airships. In the year that Blériot flew the Channel they formed the world's first aviation company DELAG, which began the first regular airship service the next year. By the end of the First World War they had built up an unequalled team of aircraft designers, including Dornier, Fokker, Rohrbach and the greatest of them, Hugo Junkers, the engineer from Aachen university who invented the F13, the most popular and adaptable plane of the twenties which carried four passengers at eighty-five miles an hour.

The German airmen after 1919 were encouraged to fly domestic air-routes by the chaotic state of their railways after the war; but by 1923 there were only two major German airlines, one owned by Junkers and the other financed by bankers and shipping companies. In 1926 the government, which was subsidising both, compelled them to merge into a single national company which was given the name of Deutsche Luft Hansa, or German Air Union. It began with 165 planes, many of them converted warplanes, which were painted with the blue-and-yellow symbol of the flying crane which has marked the airline ever since.

Luft Hansa (they remained two words until 1934) rapidly built up a European network, while the British and French were more concerned with their empires; and because the Germans were forbidden to make military aircraft they concentrated on commercial planes. By 1927 Luft Hansa had crossed the Alps to Milan, the next year it was flying regularly to Madrid, and by 1930 it was flying as far east as Istanbul and as far south as the Canary Islands. It pioneered night flying with new instruments and boasted the same kind of reliability, punctuality and comfort as the German railroads before 1914. In 1927 Luft Hansa began advertising "flying sleeping-cars" with convertible bunks and the next year "flying dining cars": a contemporary photograph shows a passenger in a Junkers G.31 sitting behind a neat table pouring wine from a basket, with a steward serving food, looking very like a dining-car on a train. By the mid-twenties Luft Hansa was flying more passengers in Europe than all the other airlines put together, and taking the lead in the new airlines' association IATA (see below) to co-ordinate airline schedules and introduce an air traffic code.

The Germans' most ambitious air plans were in Latin America, where German settlers and traders had already established their own commercial colonies, and looked for closer links with Berlin. By 1919 Junkers had shipped out two seaplanes to Colombia, where an ambitious young Austrian aristocrat, Peter Paul von Bauer, set up a small airline called SCADTA (Sociedad Colombo Alemana de Transportes Aereos). Von Bauer soon wanted to expand across Latin America and the Caribbean, encouraged by an anti-American Colombian government. He went into partnership with Luft Hansa in Berlin, to form the Condor Syndicate which eventually extended right down the Pacific coastline, serving six countries of Latin America. The mountains of Latin America provided a thrilling challenge for French, German and Italian airmen. The French were the most daring, but the Germans were the most effectively organised—all the more after Air France had retreated from Latin America. By 1934 the Condor Syndicate was flying regularly across the Andes—the highest air-journey in the world—and in Brazil it became the biggest shareholder in the new airline called VARIG (Empresa de Viacao Aerea Rio Grandense), which was to become one of the world's biggest airlines.

The real challenge, following the exploits of Mermoz and The Line, was to cross the South Atlantic and connect up with the homeland. It was only 1,890 miles from Dakar on the West African bulge to Natal on the eastern edge of Brazil, ninety miles less than between Ireland and Newfoundland, and with much lighter winds. But it was still too far for the early flying boats, so Luft Hansa and Condor tried different ways of combining planes and ships. In 1930 the airship Graf Zeppelin began carrying mail from Berlin to Rio in five days. Three years later Luft Hansa equipped a ship with a huge catapult to eject a flying boat into the air, which could fly from Gambia—where Luft Hansa had built an imposing aerodrome—to Brazil in fifteen hours. The next year German planes began regularly flying the five-day journey from Berlin to Rio, via Seville, Bathurst and Natal, and a year later night flying had brought the time down to three and a half days. By the time the Hindenburg crashed in 1937, bringing the future of airships down with it, the big German seaplanes were already taking their place. By the late thirties, before the North Atlantic was bridged, Lufthansa and Condor had established a network across the two continents which gave a head-start to German businessmen, diplomats and spies.

Luft Hansa became increasingly important to the German state which subsidised it, and particularly to the Nazis. Its dominant director was an ex-army officer Erhard Milch, the former works manager of Junkers. Milch's father was Jewish, but Milch curried favour with Hitler, letting the Nazi leaders use his planes free, and in 1928 he appointed the former air ace Hermann Goering, who had just been elected to the German parliament, to be the lobbyist for Luft Hansa. When Hitler chose Goering as his air minister five years later Goering appointed Milch as his state-secretary, supervising all the secret plane-production for the Luftwaffe. The two air fleets came increasingly close. When Goering remarried in April 1935 the airline presented him with a private plane upholstered in morocco leather, worth 100,000 marks.

By the end of the thirties Lufthansa was not just a commercial airline: it was a civilian arm of the military machine, providing an invaluable network for the controllers of the Third Reich. "Working in close liaison with the Reichswehr," says a historian of the Luftwaffe, "Milch gradually built up a reserve of trained airmen by incorporating lectures and practical instruction into the Lufthansa training programme that could only be of value from a military point of view." The magnificent new airport of Tempelhof, close to the centre of Berlin, provided Lufthansa's headquarters. Opened in 1939, it was surmounted with a great golden eagle, a monument to the Nazi vision of air power. "Rivalling the great engineering and building feats of New York," wrote Hudson Fysh, "the columns and façades rose skywards and created an impression of grandeur and promise never before seen or attempted in air transport."

AS WIDE AS THE WORLD?

By 1934 air travel had become sufficiently popular for Bradshaw's in London to publish the first monthly "International Air Guide" looking much like a railroad timetable, though appealing to the travelling elite and advertising only luxury hotels, like the Savoy, the Ritz or the Mount Nelson in Cape Town. Air reservations, explained the guide, required a deposit of up to a quarter of the fare, and passengers had to be at the airport fifteen minutes beforehand: "the cabins of the air-liners are enclosed and heated, therefore no special clothing is required". The regular routes included daily flights from London to Moscow via Berlin; weekly flights from London to Cape Town; three separate weekly schedules from Europe to the Far East by Imperial Airways, KLM and Air France; and Lufthansa flights—suspended during the winter—from Berlin to Buenos Aires via West Africa and Brazil. Compared with today's routes only the North Atlantic and Japan were noticeably absent.

Long distance air travel was still rare compared with travel by ships or trains. Flights might cost only a quarter more than a first-class sea voyage, and take less than half the time; but they were too perilous, unpredictable or exhausting for most travellers. The long journeys were an odd mixture of comfort and hardship. Imperial Airways made a great show of luxury on their flying-boat service to the East: passengers were served with lobster or caviar; they could walk on the "promenade deck" and admire the view through portholes, or sit and doze in a special lightweight and adjustable wicker chair—the beginning of the airlines' obsession with their seating. But the journeys were often bumpy and demanding: passengers might be woken at 4.30 a.m. to take off in the cool of the morning, and the mail which weighed down the planes, on which the subsidy depended, always took priority.

Each nationality brought its own attitudes into the air. Americans were the most informal and adventurous, making up three-quarters of the passengers on the early London–Paris flights. Most European

ENGLAND—EGYPT—PALESTINE—IRAQ—PERSIAN GULF—INDIA—BURMA—SIAM—MALAYA
IMPERIAL AIRWAYS (Weekly)
Route 456

Miles	Airports of				
0	LONDON	dep	Sat.	12 30	Sun. 6 0
205	PARIS (Gare de Lyon)	dep		17 15	Even. 6 30
		arr	Mon.	Morn.	Sun. 10 5
1352	BRINDISI ‡	dep		6 40	Mon. Afrn.
1721	ATHENS	dep		11 0	Mon. 10 30
2308	ALEXANDRIA	arr		19 0	Tues. 11 40
2426	CAIRO	dep	Tues.	Even.	15 0
2638	GAZA	dep		5 30	Even. 4 30
3241	BAGHDAD	arr	Wed.	8 50	9 0
3519	BASRA	dep		6 0	Wed.
3594	KOWEIT §	dep	Wed.	9 50	
3859	BAHREIN §	arr	Thurs.		Wed. Even.
4194	SHARJAH §	dep		16 30	Thurs. 6 0
4634	GWADAR §	dep	Fri.	5 0	Thurs.
4934	KARACHI	arr		Even.	15 0
5318	JODHPUR §	dep			Fri. Even.
5620	DELHI	dep	Sat.	10 20	
5865	CAWNPORE §	dep		12 0	
5973	ALLAHABAD	arr		Even.	Sat. 6 0
6445	CALCUTTA	dep	Sun.	5 0	14 0
6778	AKYAB §	dep			Even.
7091	RANGOON	arr		12 45	6 0
7465	BANGKOK	dep		Even.	Mon. 6 40
		arr		7 0	9 30
8458	ALOR STAR §	dep			11 45
	SINGAPORE	arr	Sun.	Even.	

‡ By rail between Paris and Brindisi.   § An intermediate call may be made at this Airport.
§ A passenger spends the night at this port or in the train.

Distance and Time allowance for conveyance between Airport and Town Terminus

TOWN	AIRPORT	TOWN TERMINUS	Miles	Minutes
LONDON	Croydon	Airway Terminus, Victoria Station, S.W. 1	12	45
PARIS	Le Bourget	Airway Terminus, Rue des Italiens	8	45
BRINDISI	Marine	Hotel Internationale	—	5
ATHENS	Phaleron Bay	Hotel Grande Bretagne	4	15
ALEXANDRIA	Ras-el-Tin (Marine)	Hotel Cecil	1½	10
CAIRO	Heliopolis	Shepheards Hotel	4	20
GAZA	Gaza Railway Station	Railway Station	5	20
BAGHDAD	Baghdad	Maude Hotel	1½	25
BASRA	Shaibah	Railway Rest House, Margil	16	50
KOWEIT	Koweit	No Transport	—	—
BAHREIN	Bahrein	Mesopotamia Persia Corporation Office	2	90
SHARJAH	Sharjah	No Transport	—	—
GWADAR	Gwadar	No Transport	—	—
KARACHI	Karachi	Hotels: Killarney, Bristol, Carlton, Central	11	30
JODHPUR	Jodhpur	State Hotel	7	20
DELHI	Delhi	Maiden's Hotel	9	15
CAWNPORE	Cawnpore	Berkeley House	4	30
ALLAHABAD	Allahabad	Allahabad Club	12	40
CALCUTTA	Calcutta	Great Eastern Hotel	2	7
AKYAB	Akyab	Government Rest House	1	30
RANGOON	Rangoon	Minto Mansions; Strand Hotel	5	60
BANGKOK	Don Nuang	Aerial Transport Co.'s Office	15	60
ALOR STAR	Alor Star	Government Rest House	5	35
SINGAPORE	Singapore	Raffles Hotel	13	

SINGLE FARES

	LONDON	PARIS	BRINDISI	ATHENS	ALEXANDRIA	CAIRO	GAZA	BAGHDAD	BASRA	KOWEIT	BAHREIN	SHARGAH	GWADAR
ATHENS	32	30	12										
ALEXANDRIA	40	38	23	14									
CAIRO	42	40	25	16									
GAZA	47	45	30	21	7	5							
BAGHDAD	62	62	47	38	27	25	20						
BASRA	67	67	52	43	32	30	25	6					
KOWEIT	71	71	56	47	36	34	29	10	4				
BAHREIN	78	78	63	54	43	41	36	17	11	7			
SHARGAH	84	84	69	60	49	47	42	23	17	13	6		
GWADAR	90	90	75	66	55	53	48	29	23	19	12	6	
KARACHI	95	95	80	71	60	58	53	34	28	24	17	11	6
JODHPUR	104	104	89	80	69	67	62	43	37	33	26	20	15
DELHI	106	106	91	82	71	69	64	45	39	35	28	22	18
CAWNPORE	110	110	95	86	75	73	68	50	44	40	33	27	23
ALLAHABAD	114	114	99	90	79	77	72	54	48	44	37	31	27
CALCUTTA	122	122	107	98	87	85	82	56	52	45	39	33	
AKYAB	128	128	113	104	93	91	86	68	62	58	51	45	42
RANGOON	135	135	120	111	100	98	93	75	69	65	59	53	50
BANGKOK	155	155	140	131	120	118	113	95	89	85	79	73	70
PENANG													
KUALA LUMPUR													
SINGAPORE	180	180	165	157	146	144	140	123	118	114	108	103	100

Through fares are quoted in English £ and are inclusive of all accommodation, meals, surface transport, and tips en route. As these fares include a proportion of expenditure in foreign currency they are liable to fluctuation without notice in accordance with the prevailing exchange rates.

CANCELLATIONS.—The fare less 10% will be refunded if not less than 14 days notice is given cancelling a reservation. Telegrams or other expenses incurred may be charged for.

RETURN TICKETS
A reduction equivalent to 20% (twenty per cent) of the single fare for the homeward journey is allowed on return tickets taken in advance

LOCAL FARES *

	KARACHI	JODHPUR	DELHI	CAWNPORE	ALLAHABAD	CALCUTTA	AKYAB	RANGOON
JODHPUR	120							
DELHI	220	123						
CAWNPORE	280	190	70					
ALLAHABAD	340	240	120	60				
CALCUTTA	440	350	230	160	120			
AKYAB	550	470	350	330	270	150		
RANGOON	660	580	460	400	380	270	120	
BANGKOK	69	63	54	50	48	40	29	20
SINGAPORE	100	95	86	82	80	73	62	53	34

The fares given are based on the transport of a weight of 100 kgs. (221 lb.) a passenger (including baggage). The average passenger weighs 75 kgs. (166 lb.) and, therefore, normally 25 kgs. (55 lb.) of baggage may be carried free of additional charge. If the personal weight of a passenger be more than 85 kgs. (187 lb.) an allowance of 15 kgs. (33 lb.) of baggage free of charge is made irrespective of the weight of the passenger. Excess baggage at the rate of ½% of single fare per kg. (2·2 lbs.) Fractions of a kilogramme are charged to the nearest kilogramme with a minimum of one kilogramme.

Passengers who wish to break their journey must pay the fares quoted for each section. Break of journey cannot be made on through tickets.
* Local fares in India and Burma are quoted in rupees, but in English £ in Siam and in Malaya. In both instances fares are inclusive of all accommodation, meals, surface transport and tips.

Two pages from Bradshaw's "International Air Guide" in November 1934.

long-distance passengers were businessmen or officials, many of
them colonial servants who brought their social attitudes with them.
The French spent little money on comforts, while the British brought
the hierarchies of the colonial club or the ocean liner up into the
air: one Imperial pilot, at a night-stop in the desert on the way to
India, was reported by a governor's wife for inviting a pretty girl
to sit on his right at dinner. The glamorous image of long distance
air travel was very illusory, and the officials and businessmen were
only gradually leavened by women, children and air hostesses.

As the airlines became more highly organised and more linked
to governments there was less talk about the air as the agent of
new freedoms and friendships. There were still discussions about
internationalising the air. "The road of the air is a free and universal
thoroughfare," wrote Sir Charles Burney in a waffly book in 1929,
"as wide as the world, and almost everywhere navigable, it is
unhampered by any barrier, obstacle or limitation whatever." But
in practical terms the air was increasingly hampered by obstacles
and barriers and the new airlines were following and reinforcing
the old imperial and commercial connections. England was still an
island, and Imperial Airways was much less interested in Europe
than in the Empire. Flights across Italy were banned for many
years by Mussolini. Germany and France had been brought no
closer by the airlines than they had by the railroads which preceded
their war of 1870.

But all the nations realised that air transport would require
exceptional collaboration between them, and as the Europeans were
overtaken by the American airlines (see next chapter) they became
more aware of the drawbacks of a divided continent. As early as
1919, on the same day that George Holt Thomas had inaugurated
the cross-Channel flights of his airline Aircraft Transport & Travel,
he had invited six airlines —British, Danish, German, Norwegian,
Swedish and Dutch—to meet at the Hague. They decided to form
the International Air Traffic Association (IATA) "with a view
to co-operate to mutual advantage in preparing and organising
international aerial traffic". After a fierce conflict with the rival
Trans Europa Union, based on Junkers' planes in Central Europe,
IATA became the single body for airline co-operation, and by 1929
it had twenty-three members including Luft Hansa.

IATA held lavish annual meetings in the European centres, at
the Doge's Palace in Venice or in the Quai d'Orsay in Paris,
welcomed by prime ministers or presidents. Its headquarters at the
Hague tried to standardise timetables, safety systems, statistics—
and above all air-fares. IATA, though it always denied it was a
cartel, was in the pattern of European trade associations which

tried to limit competition. But beyond basic collaboration, each member of IATA—particularly Lufthansa—insisted on its own freedom of action, and opposed moves to internationalise airlines or to take joint initiatives. In 1929 Albert Plesman of KLM pressed in vain for a common advertising campaign to attract American tourists to Europe. "Even farmers do better than we," he complained; "they make propaganda for the sale of their products."

By the early thirties the Europeans were more worried that aircraft would play a much more lethal role, and that civil and military aviation were "two sides of a single coin", as the British Cadman report put it. In 1932 the League of Nations, which the European victors had set up after the first war, called a disarmament conference which included discussions about the control of civil aviation. The French boldly proposed forming both an international air force and an international civil air service—which alone would be allowed to fly larger aircraft, and which would buy the planes and employ the pilots. Other nations including Belgium and Spain agreed. Sweden advocated a modified organisation to run all the airports and supervise national airlines. But Germany and the Soviet Union were opposed, Britain was very sceptical, while Americans, Canadians and Japanese were not interested.

The arguments continued while the prospects of any international policing faded. When Hitler came to power in 1933 Germany left the League of Nations and Europe soon began rearming once again, giving priority to air forces rather than airlines. "How could the governments of a mistrustful Europe," asked the French aviation economist Henri Bouché in a report to the League of Nations in 1935, "allow the indefinite development of a powerful means of transport when aircraft sent on peaceful missions over national territories, and to the very heart of those territories, may also carry out other missions?"

In July 1938 the members of IATA held their annual meeting in the House of Parliament in Budapest to hear optimistic reports: air traffic had increased by nearly a half in the past year; the average cruising speed was now 144 miles per hour; Air France had flown from Paris to Chile in fifty-six and a half hours. The members agreed to elect their first North American member—Pan American Airways—and to hold their next meeting in New York in September 1939, to be chaired by Pan Am's chairman Juan Trippe. The meeting was never held; and all the plans of the European airlines were wrecked by the Second World War.

2

Conquerors of the Sky

Alone, yet never lonely,
Serene, beyond mischance,
The world was his, his only,
When Lindbergh flew to France.

Aline Michaelis: Lindbergh

THE development of air travel within North America seemed to exaggerate the continent's difference from Europe. Planes could open up the interior with far more flexibility than steamships and railroads, turning attention away from the oceans to the land-mass; and pilots and entrepreneurs were at first too preoccupied with the challenge of crossing from coast to coast to take much interest in flying overseas.

Yet the beginnings of American airlines were less vigorous and competitive than the contests between the Europeans. Washington was much less interested than Paris, London or Berlin in encouraging the new form of transport, and unwilling to subsidise airlines except for mail contracts. Nor was there much commercial incentive. The first planes were no faster and much less reliable than the railroads – which were not set back by the First World War like the Europeans—and the early airlines were more concerned with carrying parcels than people. The first regular air service in the United States began as early as 1914 in Florida, where the pilot Tony Janus founded the St Petersburg–Tampa Airboat Line, with a tiny flying boat which carried one passenger at a time across Tampa Bay (fat men over 200 lb paid extra). But it lasted only four months, and other small airlines followed very fitfully.

In 1919, while the first European airlines were being established, Eddie Hubbard began flying airmail regularly from Seattle across the Canadian frontier to Vancouver, in a single-engined seaplane—with the man who built the plane, Bill Boeing, as his first passenger. The next year Aeromarine Airways in Florida started flying four passengers between Key West and Havana in single-engined ex-naval seaplanes. But these short-lived international flights were much less important than the challenge to open up America, and to beat the railroads which carried the mails from coast to coast in three days.

However resourceful the local pioneers, it was the federal government which laid the basis of the serious airlines. At first the Post Office operated its own planes, but the 1925 "Kelly Act" established the system of granting airmail contracts to private airlines; and in 1929 Herbert Hoover's new postmaster-general Walter Brown made the most of his powers of patronage to press the small airline companies to merge. By 1930 four major airlines had emerged, which still survive as the Big Four today. Bill Boeing collaborated with the engine-makers Pratt & Whitney to form the United Aircraft & Transport Corporation—which later evolved into United Air Lines. The Aviation Corporation, created by the railroad magnate W. A. Harriman in 1929, eventually developed into American Airlines. And C. M. Keys, the entrepreneur who was chairman of the Curtiss airplane company, helped to originate both North American Aviation, which was the predecessor of Eastern Airlines, and TAT which later became TWA. By 1930 all four—United, Eastern, TWA and American—were established on the transcontinental routes which would be their mainstay over the next five decades.

As proper airports were built the landplanes became more common than seaplanes, and flying no longer centred on lakes and oceans. The safer, faster planes quickly attracted more passengers and by 1929 America had more air travellers than Germany. In the thirties TWA set a fast pace with Douglas planes, flying first the DC-2, which carried fourteen passengers at 170 mph, and then the famous DC-3, with twenty-one passengers, which revolutionised air travel with its safety and reliability. The tycoons of the internal airlines—Cyrus Smith of American, Bill Patterson of United, Eddie Rickenbacker of Eastern, Jack Frye of TWA—were engrossed in the challenge of opening up their own continent, competing for landing rights and creating networks and "hubs" such as Fort Worth, St Louis, or Kansas City. The airlines were changing the map of America with an abruptness and sense of disconnection which was difficult for either tycoons or passengers to understand; the little airports that sprang up for refuelling on the transcontinental routes had a sense of isolation quite different from the railway stations linked by their permanent way. As Scott Fitzgerald described them, looking back on the thirties in *The Last Tycoon*:

> I suppose there has been nothing like airports since the days of the stage-stops—nothing quite as lonely, as sombre-silent. The old red-brick depots were built right into the towns they marked—people didn't get off at those isolated stations unless they lived there. But airports lead you way back in history like oases, like the stops on the great trade routes. The sight of air travellers strolling in ones or twos into midnight airports will draw a small crowd any night up to two. The young people look at the planes, the older ones look at the passengers with a watchful incredulity.

The American airline pioneers were all competing furiously, but they had their own camaraderie. "I've never known an industry that can get into people's blood the way aviation does," said Robert Six, who founded Continental Airlines in Denver in 1938 and is now one of the few survivors of the pioneer generation, a craggy and forceful old man of eighty-one. "They would fight to the death to get routes, but they could still be friends. They were all boys together. Really, they were like a lot of bar-room gamblers." But they soon became established leaders, secure in their routes. In 1939 Jack Frye of TWA, with the help of his senior vice-president John Walker, set up the aviation club which was grandly called the Conquistadores del Cielo—the Conquerors of the Sky—who dressed up in copies of the old costumes of the original Conquistadores, specially made in Spain. It began as TWA's celebration to thank local leaders in Kansas and New Mexico for helping TWA to get a new route—the "Winslow cut-off" to the West—but the Conquistadores grew into the annual gathering of aviation leaders who still meet once a year on a ranch in Wyoming, to compete with knife-throwing, pistol-shooting, to watch rodeos or reminisce about the old days and sometimes, despite the anti-trust laws, to talk business.

THE LINDBERGH EFFECT

It was not until the historic flight of Charles Lindbergh across the Atlantic in 1927—eighteen years after Blériot crossed the English Channel—that the prospects of international air travel captured the Americans' imagination. The personality of the lone aviator, with his mechanical precision, his Swedish self-containment, his nerve and commercial ambitions, provided a new kind of hero for the "Conquest of the Air". In the next years Lindbergh pioneered a succession of new routes, from Iceland and Labrador to the Azores and West Africa and through Latin America, and achieved the ambition which had eluded so many sea captains, of opening up the north-west passage to the East. He played an important role in advising two major airlines: TWA, which at first called itself "The Lindbergh Line", and Pan American, of which he was first consultant, then a director.

Lindbergh became a hero to Europeans as well as Americans, challenging the glory of French or German aviators. His lonely ordeals undoubtedly gave him a sense of exaltation to which he often referred; but his engineer's discipline and his lonely stamina left little room for broader understanding of the world. When he arrived to a rapturous welcome in Paris he spoke no word of French and had not heard of the Arc de Triomphe. In describing his ordeal, complained the London *Times*, "He packed the whole thirty-four hours into a few drawled sentences." In later years in Germany he showed a naive trust in the Nazi leaders who feted and flattered him, and allowed himself to be used by Goering to misrepresent the power of the Luftwaffe. He was disowned and disgraced by Americans during the Second World War—though later forgiven— and ended his career as a passionate conservationist, disillusioned with the achievements in the air. "If I had to choose, I would rather have birds than airplanes."

Lindbergh's personality seemed to express all the limitations inherent in the association of the air with new freedoms—for man's ability to fly, unlike that of a bird, depended on a careful combination of disciplines which were the opposite of carefree. He liked to give the impression of casualness, and when he first arrived in Paris the London *Times* alluded to him as "the flying fool". But his achievements rested on meticulous thoroughness. As his wife Anne—a more interesting writer than her husband—described it:

> . . . Since flight is not a natural function of man; since it has been won by centuries of effort; since it has been climbed to arduously, not simply stumbled upon; since it has been slowly built, not suddenly discovered, it cannot be suspended as the word "freedom" is suspended in the mind. It rests, firmly supported, on a structure of laws, rules, principles—laws to which plane and man alike must conform. Rules of construction, of performance, of equipment, for one; rules of training, health, experience, skill, and judgment, for the other.

THE PAN AMERICAN MONOPOLY

In the year following Lindbergh's flight across the Atlantic, a new airline called Pan American Airways established the first permanent service from the United States to a foreign country, carrying mail from Key West in Florida to Havana in Cuba, where the plane was tactfully christened after the current Cuban dictator, General Machado. The hundred-mile hop marked the first triumph for the ambitious young chief executive Juan Trippe; and the first stage in the triumphant progress of Pan American southwards through Latin America, which was to provide Trippe's fame and fortune. It also marked the birth of a new kind of transport monopoly.

For the next fifteen years American international air transport was to be interlocked with the story of Juan Trippe. Like Lindbergh, whom he soon hired to advise him, Trippe combined adventurousness and rigid self-discipline which stemmed from his mixed parentage: his father came from a respectable old Southern family, but his maternal grandmother Kate Flynn was an Irish barmaid and his grandfather a bank robber. Trippe was called Juan after his step-grandfather Juan Terry, a rich Cuban who brought money and respectability to his mother's family; but the young Juan Trippe, as he went through Yale, was embarrassed by his first name, spoke no Spanish, and developed a puritanical ambition and self-control, with a stubborn determination to win and no interest in his opponents' views—an invaluable business advantage. He foresaw prospects in aviation after two years working in the Lee Higginson bank, and moved into the business with a banker's cold eye and the support of rich Yale friends. Many wealthy young Americans, including potential investors, were fascinated by this new means of transport and Yale provided a disproportionate share. It was a striking contrast to the British elite of Oxford and Cambridge who were largely bored by the new machines and left them to rugged Scots such as Geddes, Beharrel or Reith. In the air it was the Americans, not the British, who displayed an Old Boy Net.

Trippe began by forming his own company called Long Island Airways which bought surplus warplanes to fly New York socialites to their country retreats; but he soon realised that he could only make money through the airmail contracts which were being awarded under the new Kelly Act. By 1926 he was carrying mail from New York to Boston in a small airline called Colonial, backed by Yale friends including William Rockefeller and Sonny Whitney; but he disagreed with other investors, was outmanoeuvred and had to resign. Colonial expanded and later became part of American Airlines: so Trippe had lost a big chance to be involved in domestic airlines. But with his loyal backers he soon raised the money for a more ambitious company, Aviation Corporation of America, which then took over a small company called Pan American which had won the mail contract between Florida and Cuba. In October 1927 Pan American Fokker F7 tri-motor planes began flying regularly from an improvised air strip at Key West to Havana in an hour, on the airline's first scheduled route.

Trippe was deep in politics from the start. The future of foreign air transport lay in Washington, where the postmaster-general Walter Brown awarded the airmail contracts; and by 1928 President Coolidge was pushing through more generous allocations on routes to Latin America, where the French and German companies were already established. Trippe was well placed to impress Washington with his influential Yale friends and his own persuasive charm: it was said that he deliberately wore shirts with frayed cuffs to impress Washington with his need for new routes. He had already recruited Lindbergh, who publicised the scope for air links by flying 9,000 miles through fourteen Latin American countries. Pan American quickly got the next foreign contract, from Miami to Panama, followed by the first Caribbean route, from Puerto Rico to Trinidad. "While we had been developing an airline in the West Indies," complained the rival bidder, Basil Rowe, "our competitors had been busy on the much more important job of developing a lobby in Washington."

Trippe now rapidly expanded southwards, linking up with local American interests and riding roughshod over Latin American politics. Pan American went into partnership with the Grace trading empire to create the Panagra airline which soon flew down the west coast from Ecuador to Peru to Chile, and across the Andes to Argentina. In Colombia Trippe came up against the formidable Von Bauer running the already well-established airline SCADTA, which was also expanding through Latin America. But Von Bauer was in financial difficulties and was blocked by the US State Department: eventually he and Trippe produced a convenient solution—that Pan American would secretly buy up SCADTA, while leaving Von Bauer in apparent control.

By 1929 Trippe, aged thirty, was already an important aviation figure with an august board which included the chairman Sonny Whitney, Robert Lehman the banker and David Bruce, the Virginian diplomat whose father-in-law was Andrew Mellon; while Trippe himself had married Betty Stettinius, from a wealthy old American family, whose brother later became Roosevelt's Secretary of State.

In the year before the Great Crash aviation stocks were booming, and Pan American was one of the most promising. Trippe cultivated the style of a public service, putting his pilots and crews in naval-type uniforms on flying boats made to look like yachts. Pan Am's overseas monopoly, and its lack of domestic land routes gave it a more dignified image than domestic airlines which had to compete for publicity with gimmicks. Trippe's airline was already being widely attacked by South Americans as an adjunct of the State Department, an instrument of American imperialism. But it was only one example of the prevailing relationship between American companies and Republican administrations which were determined to promote business interests abroad to compete with German, French or Italian ambitions in Latin America.

The Great Crash, followed by the arrival of Roosevelt at the White House, provided new political hazards for the Republican Trippe, and in 1934 Senator Hugo Black began sensational hearings to investigate how the former postmaster-general Walter Brown had awarded airmail contracts. The airline chiefs had to testify about their relations with Washington, and the new postmaster-general Jim Farley accused his predecessor Brown of conspiracy and collusion. Walter Brown, who had virtually invented the big American airlines, was disgraced and his portrait in the post-office building in Washington is said to be still kept hidden behind a door. Pan American, being outside the carve-up of dom-estic air-routes, came through relatively unscathed. Farley showed how Trippe had been specially favoured, and how he had concealed his true profits from airmail by juggling with his accounts in different regions—an early example of multinationals outwitting their governments. But Farley knew that Trippe's expanding network was indispensable, and Trippe knew how to play up his bogey—the foreign airlines whose governments supported them much more directly.

Roosevelt's distrust of the commercial airlines and Black's investi-gations did not permanently damage the power of the American airlines: the Big Four, together with Pan American, all survived roughly intact. Roosevelt spectacularly failed to make the case for government intervention when he rashly cancelled all domestic airmail contracts and called in the army to fly the mails: the army pilots could not handle the emergency and ten of them were killed before Roosevelt had to bring back the airlines. Roosevelt eventually created a new Civil Aeronautics Authority to allocate and supervise air-routes—later re-formed in 1940 as the Civil Aeronautics Board. The new board perpetuated the system of "controlled competition" by which the airlines, behind an appearance of total free enterprise, depended for their routes on government approval—and ultimately on the approval of the president who could and often did overturn his board's judgment. The air was becoming still less associated with freedom of enterprise. The Big Four airlines were granted permanent certificates, or "grandfather rights", to the prime domestic routes; and Pan American enjoyed a monopoly overseas.

But Roosevelt did bring about one critical change when he separated the manufacturing companies—including Boeing and United—from any ownership or control over the airlines. Thereafter the big airlines were able to choose between manufacturers and to play them against each other—a system which almost certainly increased the pace of technological change, while increasing the commercial hazards. The growing aircraft plants of Boeing, Douglas and Lockheed on the West Coast vied for the custom of the airlines which could make or break them, until orders for military planes provided a more powerful patron.

THE CANADIAN IDENTITY

By the mid-thirties the American manufacturers and airlines were already overtaking the Europeans; parcels were giving way to people, and the airlines were becoming less dependent on mail contracts. The American supremacy in the air was beginning to worry neighbouring countries, particularly Canada, whose narrow railroad belt and icy North had provided a special challenge to airmen. In the pioneer years after the First World War the Canadian "bush-pilots", such as Wop May, Punch Dickens or Grant McConachie, had become legendary heroes, landing their planes with skis on the snow, or on pontoons on lakes, and carrying supplies to remote mining camps. But the triumph of individualism soon gave way to the harsh realities of the depression. The government subsidised a few to conduct aerial surveys or to deliver mail; but it could not afford to maintain an air-link between Quebec and the West—as the Prime Minister R. B. Bennett vividly put it—"while desperate prairie farmers, listening below, could hear the planes flying through skies blackened with the blowing dust of their drought-ruined farms". By 1937 Canada was one of the few countries without a national scheduled air service, and Canadians had to use the American airlines to cross their continent: the first Boeing flight between Seattle and Vancouver was paralleled by other flights linking Canadian cities to the United States. The Canadians knew that a national airline was crucial to their identity, as they had decided a railroad was crucial in the previous century. The Liberal government, after many confused arguments about public or private ownership, set up the nationalised Trans-Canada Airline to link the east and west coasts. But the new air age made the forty-ninth parallel seem much less significant; while Canada's railroads had forged the nation's unity from east to west, the new air-routes connected it all too easily to the American states.

THE BATTLE FOR THE PACIFIC

Juan Trippe remained the sole American protagonist of international air transport, and after Pan American's push southwards his greatest challenge was to conquer the Pacific—which, although twice the width of the Atlantic, was speckled with islands which could provide refuelling bases. Trippe had already established a beachhead on the other side, when in 1933 he bought a half-share in the China National Aviation Corporation which flew between Shanghai and Canton. The first hurdle was to cross the two thousand miles to Hawaii, in itself a longer distance than the shortest Atlantic route; but by 1935 Pan American had received the first of the Martin flying boats, with wings like sea birds' and hulls like whales', which could cover that range and fly on to China. The Pacific route was dotted with American naval bases, from Honolulu, to Midway, to Guam, to Manila: the only weak link was between Midway and Guam, where there was only the barren Wake Island, which the United States had acquired but neglected after the Spanish-American war. Trippe petitioned Washington for a five-year lease on the island, stressing the importance of American trade with the East. The State Department was wary of Japan, which was stealthily extending its own Pacific influence; and it was glad to discreetly strengthen American influence through a commercial airline. Roosevelt agreed to put Wake and other islands under naval administration—to the fury of the Japanese—which gave access to Pan American. The airline was beginning to develop its own foreign policy, like the Grace Lines or United Fruit in Latin America, or as the oil companies would soon develop in the Middle East.

With government support Trippe could move deliberately. He set up airfields, equipped radio stations and installed ex-Navy men in the desolate islands. By October 1935 Pan American had won the precious airmail contract for the whole route from San Francisco to Canton, and the next month the flying boat China Clipper took off from San Francisco Bay with an orchestrated fanfare of publicity, including a special post-office stamp, speeches by Trippe and Jim Farley, and massive media coverage. The plane arrived seven days later in Manila, after sixty hours' flying, to find 200,000 Filipinos waiting at the harbour, celebrating a half-holiday. The Pacific crossing soon became the most spectacular regular air-route, with inns built on the islands for stop-overs, and a cultivated sense of romance encouraged by the film *China Clipper*, starring Humphrey Bogart as the pilot. Businessmen, bankers and diplomats saw the Pacific crossing as a crucial means to extend American interests, and to contain Japan's expanding empire. No one could have predicted that forty years later the Pacific flights would become more important as the means for Japan to extend her trade to America.

Trippe came hard up against British interests when he tried to complete the last lap of the route from Manila to China, and he was locked in conflict with Imperial Airways over the right to land in Hong Kong, the obvious gateway to China. But Trippe could bully Hong Kong by threatening to fly instead to the neighbouring Portuguese island of Macao, which he began to equip as a terminal. The British colony, dreading to be left out of the new route, eventually gave in. Trippe achieved his aim of linking up across the Pacific with his Chinese airline. His new empire of the air was already challenging the old "steamship empire", as H. G. Wells called it, of the British; and the Pacific flights westwards were enabling American interests to move closer to Europe's "Far East".

Trippe's next link was to be down to Australia, which by 1934 had just established its regular air service through Asia to Britain. But both the British and the Japanese were becoming more possessive about the Pacific: the South Sea Islands which had been the symbols of innocence and escapism were now looking commercially more desirable to all three powers, and British and American warships vied to occupy the tiny islands.

Trippe was blocked again by the British. The obvious landing place on the way to Australia and New Zealand was the British colony of Fiji; but Imperial Airways had their own ambitions to fly round the world, and were planning to extend their route across the Pacific to Vancouver, for which they needed to land on Hawaii: so they tried to bargain with Fiji for Hawaii. But the Americans insisted on keeping Hawaii for themselves, and in the South Pacific Trippe found a substitute for Fiji in the American Samoan Islands, which included the magnificent naval harbour of Pago Pago. Trippe was able to get his landing rights in New Zealand, as he did in Hong Kong, by threatening to leave it out of his map: like the early railroad barons, he was enjoying his monopoly powers, but dealing with whole territories instead of towns—playing the global bargaining game which would multiply over the next five decades.

The first Pan American plane arrived in New Zealand in December 1937, greeted with hysterical enthusiasm: for New Zealand was the most isolated of all the larger countries, and the trans-Pacific route would be the means to connect up both New Zealand and Australia to the United States. The South Pacific, with its huge distances between islands, proved a treacherous region. Already in July 1937 the aviatrix Amelia Earhart had disappeared without trace north of New Guinea; and in January 1938 Pan American's chief pilot Ed Musick was killed when his plane the Samoa Clipper exploded in mid-air north of Pago Pago, on its way to New Zealand, after which the service was suspended. But by July 1940 Pan American was again flying regular services to New Zealand, via New Caledonia. The political significance of these new Pacific air-routes took many years to sink in. The distances across this "empty hemisphere" seemed to defy any real sense of neighbourhood: it was as far from Tokyo to New Zealand as from Tokyo to Stockholm. But in the Pacific the airlines would create neighbours, by-passing the era of ships and trains, as railroads had made neighbours in Europe and the Americas.

THE QANTAS CONNECTION

Two European airlines in the meantime had been competing to reach Australia, in the most dramatic of all international air-races. Imperial Airways was the most obviously well placed, with British possessions and bases all along the route, and with its flights to India already established. But the Imperial flying boats were slow and committed to the "all-red" connections on the way; while Plesman at KLM had a simpler and more business-like ambition, to link Holland with the Dutch East Indies, without any obligation to buy only Dutch Fokker planes. In 1931 KLM had begun regular weekly flights from Amsterdam to Batavia—then the longest scheduled flight in the world—and two years later it connected up with the key British base of Singapore, the cross-roads of the East, before Imperial had reached it. Plesman was already planning to connect with Australia through its northern port of Wyndham, very close to the Dutch East Indies. In 1934 he bought a new American DC-2 airliner which beat all records in the air-race between England and Australia, reaching Melbourne in less than four days; and by 1938 KLM was using the new DC-3s to fly regularly to Australia, taking only eight days from Amsterdam to Sydney.

The Australians in the meantime were rapidly becoming one of the most air-minded people, for their empty territory provided even greater scope than America. They had been looking to make their own air-links with the rest of the world ever since that wonder-year of 1919, when Captain Ross Smith and Lieutenant Keith Smith had flown in four weeks from London to Darwin in a Vickers bomber, to win a £10,000 prize.

The most remote birthplace of any global airline was in Queensland, the north-east sector of Australia, which was the first home of QANTAS, the Queensland and Northern Territory Aerial Services. The arrival of aircraft affected the inland communities of Australia even more than mid-western Americans. There were very few railroads, roads were impassable in wet weather, and most travel was by horse and cart. The first small planes, however unreliable, transformed rural communications, connecting isolated settlements like country buses to the nearest railhead. "The early Queensland pioneer could only travel eight miles an hour by buggy," boasted Qantas, "but the settler can now travel a hundred miles an hour by air."

The birth of Qantas is now part of Australian folklore. The airline was set up by two young war pilots, Hudson Fysh and Ginty McGinnis, with backing from two sheep farmers and a local doctor. It was based on the corrugated-iron town of Longreach, which was four days by train from the capital Melbourne (before the sheep-town Canberra became capital). The two pilots eked out a living by joy-riding, searching for sheep and kangaroos or shooting wild turkeys, until they realised, like fliers everywhere else, that they could not survive without a subsidy for airmail. They flew round Queensland to raise money—including £250 from an eighty-seven-year-old pioneer, Alexander Kennedy, who insisted on being the first passenger. By 1922 they had won the contract to fly mail between the two railheads of Longreach and Charleville. At sixty-nine mph Hudson Fysh flew the second leg, with Kennedy aboard looking down on the track he had first travelled in a bullock wagon.

Hudson Fysh—The Flying Fish as he called himself—continued flying his own planes while he built up the company, but he was an unusual aviator: he was a more fearful, introverted man (he explained) than his colleague McGinnis, and he always "counted the odds"; he felt unqualified to run a business and preferred writing books to public speaking. He was closely involved with John Flynn, the missionary who conceived the idea of the "flying doctor" who could treat emergencies in the outback; and in 1928 Qantas provided the first ambulance service, which continued for twenty years without accidents. During the "dangerous twenties", when many Australian pilots lost their lives in gambling too far, Fysh combined his daring with caution, and was rewarded by the unique continuity of his airline. He had a longer vision than most airmen, and his personality reassured the politicians in Melbourne who settled the subsidies.

By 1930 Qantas had moved its headquarters to Brisbane, the Queensland capital, and it soon defeated its two rivals, West Australian Airways and Australian National Airways, as the candidate to connect up his country to Britain and the world. The first step was to link up with Imperial Airways, which had reached Singapore in 1933, a few months after KLM. After spiky negotiations the Australians and British agreed to share the long route to Britain, meeting and "changing gauge" at Singapore. They formed a joint subsidiary called Qantas Empire Airways to fly the last stretch from Singapore, and by Christmas 1934 letters from London were reaching Brisbane in twelve days. The Australian Prime Minister J. A. Lyons was bitterly criticised for giving an expensive subsidy to the new airline, but he was unrepentant:

> The establishment of an efficient international airway should not only raise the prestige of Australia in the eyes of the world, but the improved communication arising therefrom should tend to kindle happier relations with the other nations of the world whose friendliness and goodwill is so necessary . . .

The 12,000 mile journey, the longest air service in the world, was a confusing experience for the first passengers. It used five different kinds of plane, and because Mussolini banned foreign flights it included a rail-journey through Italy, to connect with a seaplane at Brindisi. For a time the flight ended at the tiny rail township of Cootamundra, between Sydney and Melbourne, whence the mails went on by train. But when the first airmail was flown from Darwin to Singapore in February 1935, to link up with the plane to London, the Australians became abruptly conscious of their new proximity. "The old isolated and constricted environment of our people," Hudson Fysh wrote afterwards, "was destroyed that day."

By early 1938 the four-engined Empire flying boats were flying twenty-four passengers comfortably all the way from Southampton to Singapore in five and a half days, with another four days to Sydney. The British-Australian partnership—"The Lion and the Kangaroo"—seemed secure, and the new route seemed to be achieving its objective of forging closer bonds across the Empire. The expansion of the Japanese airlines across the North Pacific and into

Manchuria, or the extension of Aeroflot across Siberia, seemed far removed from the self-contained network of English-speaking airlines which now crossed the world.

BRIDGING THE ATLANTIC

The North Atlantic was the richest but most elusive prize, the missing link in the chain round the world. It was a more hostile ocean than the Pacific, with fierce headwinds and no stopping place between Canada and Ireland, except for the icy outposts of Greenland and Iceland or the Portuguese Azores to the south. Lindbergh's solo flight in 1927 had been followed by anti-climax, for no airliners could carry mail and passengers non-stop for two thousand miles; while in the meantime other forms of communication were competing. (On the same day that the London *Times* announced Lindbergh's flight, it published a letter from a reader, R. C. Bartlett, describing how he had received a telephone call from New York "as clearly as if I were speaking on a trunk call, say, to Brighton". The international telephone and the plane were to remain rivals for businessmen's attentions over the decades.)

The South Atlantic had been relatively easy, and as early as 1931 a vast German flying boat with twelve engines arrived in New York via Brazil, and flew back via the Azores to Germany before it was abandoned. The French flying boat Lieutenant de Vaisseau Paris also reached America via Brazil, but was wrecked in a tropical storm and had to be dismantled and shipped back to France. In 1933 an engineer in the DuPont company proposed to build floating islands to allow planes to refuel across the ocean. The Germans put much faith in catapults, to launch their heavy planes: by 1934 they were already flying mail regularly across the South Atlantic, refuelling their flying boats in mid-ocean and catapulting them towards Brazil; two years later a German catapult plane arrived at Long Island via Lisbon and the Azores. The British engineer Robert Mayo invented a still more exotic solution: he devised his "composite" plane the Mercury-Maia which had a smaller plane sitting on top of a bigger plane from which it separated after take-off. The Mercury succeeded in crossing the Atlantic in 1938; but it could not carry passengers, and the British government withdrew its support.

Throughout most of the thirties the North Atlantic remained unbridgeable by air, while the great ocean liners were competing for the Blue Riband and cutting down their time from five to four days. In October 1936 Juan Trippe, with his wife and colleagues, flew round the world: they first crossed the Pacific by Pan American, via Manila and Macao to China; then they flew by the Imperial route to Paris and London. But to cross the Atlantic they had to travel by the German Zeppelin to Rio, and then to fly up by Pan American to Miami.

The North Atlantic was not only a technical hazard: it was also a diplomatic battlefield, the meeting place between European and American ambitions in the air. Juan Trippe had first sought to negotiate transatlantic flights in Europe in 1928, a year after Lindbergh's flight, while he was romping easily through Latin America. But he found the European governments much more formidable, with their imperial ambitions. He faced a battle-royal with Imperial Airways who were determined to complete their "all-red" route by linking Britain with Canada. The British held another trump card in the shape of Bermuda, the British colony 800 miles south-west of New York, which suddenly became the critical link on the southerly route via the Azores. Bermuda witnessed the first agreement between Pan American and Imperial in 1930, when they formed a joint development corporation and both got landing permits for the island. But the subsequent horse-trading brought out all the differences in the airlines' characters. Sir Eric Geddes described Pan American in 1933, as "the equivalent in the US of the Imperial Airways in this country; that is to say, it undertakes for the US government the operation of long-distance overseas American air-transport services". But Trippe had much less straightforward support from his government than Geddes as he began to negotiate with Imperial; the British had crucial bases, and their technical backwardness made them all the more wary of Pan American.

To prepare to bridge the Atlantic the British carefully nursed relations with the two other North Atlantic countries, Canada and the newly independent Eire, which was now a much-wanted stepping-stone. In November 1935 the three nations agreed in Ottawa to form a joint "Atlantic Company", of which Britain would own fifty-one per cent and the Canadians and Irish a quarter each, so that they could jointly control the short route from Eire to Newfoundland. The British after much haggling agreed with the Americans on reciprocal landing rights for their airlines, on condition that Pan American could not begin flying until Imperial was also ready. Trippe went on to negotiate with the other European airlines, including Plesman of KLM, with very tough bargaining: Trippe's aide Ted Wyman told Lindbergh that "the whole thing reminds me of an electric fan. Anyone who sticks his fingers in it is going to get them cut off." Pan American's agreements flagrantly defied the anti-trust laws, but Washington connived in careful wording to conceal the restraints of trade.

The British and Americans chose Foynes, on the river Shannon in Eire, as the eastern terminus, and Botwood in Newfoundland as the western end. Meteorologists spent a year recording winds and clouds until by July 1937 Pan American and Imperial were ready for their first survey flights, planned with impeccable reciprocity. The new Pan American flying boat, the Clipper III, took off in the evening from Botwood and arrived twelve and a half hours later at Foynes; the Imperial flying boat Caledonia took off from Foynes, watched by President de Valera in the rain, and arrived fifteen hours later at Botwood. But neither airline yet had planes which could make regular passenger flights, and Imperial were stalling Trippe, knowing that he was ahead of them.

But the Germans in the meantime were looking closer to success. Their airship the Hindenburg, which had carried a thousand people across the Atlantic in 1936, exploded the next year, bringing the era of airships to an end. But by 1937 Lufthansa was running a weekly airmail service from Berlin via Lisbon and the Azores, whence catapult planes continued to New York; and the next year a new four-engined Focke-Wulf landplane arrived in New York from Berlin, without the help of a catapult, after less than twenty-five hours. The Germans were technically ahead of both the British and the Americans; but they were blocked by Washington from making regular flights.

It was not until 1939 that Pan American was ready to fly its four-engined Boeing flying boat the B314—half as big again as the Pacific Clippers—with luxurious accommodation including sleeping-berths, a dining-room and five passenger cabins. The British government was now too preoccupied with expanding the Royal Air Force to insist on reciprocal flights, and they could only experiment with two flying boats, the Cabot and the Caribou, which had to be refuelled in mid-ocean and never carried passengers. In May 1939—twelve years after Lindbergh's solo flight—the first of the big Boeings, the Yankee Clipper, took off from the Marine Terminal in New York (which still exists, with magnificent murals, alongside La Guardia airport). It carried twenty-two passengers on the first scheduled transatlantic flight—not to London, but via the Azores to Lisbon and on to Marseilles.

The airlines had completed their circumnavigation of the globe and a tireless passenger could now fly round it, with a bit of luck, in ten days—a bewildering change of perspective over the three decades since Blériot had first crossed the English Channel. It was a staggering technical achievement. But the political rhetoric of air transport about bringing peace and understanding was already sounding hollow after warplanes had revealed their destructiveness in Spain and Manchuria. The international air map still had huge gaps where closed systems had no place for foreign planes. Inside the Soviet Union the airline Aeroflot had expanded during the thirties faster than any in Europe, creating a network all the way to the Pacific; but its links with the outside world were slender, and Soviet air policy since Lenin was obsessed by the fear of violation along its long frontiers. Behind their apparently infinite mobility, the airlines were becoming still more bound by the imperatives of sovereignty and national ambition.

Four months after Pan Am's first transatlantic flight Europe was at war. The flights to London stopped short at Foynes in neutral Ireland, while the Clippers from Lisbon in neutral Portugal were soon crammed with rich refugees. Pan American and Boeing had the North Atlantic to themselves. It was not until eighteen years later that British-made planes, the Britannias, would begin to fly regular passengers across the Atlantic. The supremacy of American aircraft would never be broken.

3

Wings for Peace

The modern airplane creates a new geographical dimension. A navigable
ocean of air blankets the whole surface of the globe. There are no distant
places any longer: the world is small and the world is one.
Wendell Willkie, 1943

THE Second World War not only transformed the scope of the
airlines but produced two contradictory political attitudes to the
air. The horrors of air warfare, culminating in the atomic bomb on
Hiroshima, generated a new insistence that both military and civil
aircraft should be separated from national ambitions and put under
international control. Yet every government was more convinced
that it must protect and advance its own airlines, as the lifeline to
its trade and security.

In wartime the European continent soon found itself with only
one major airline—Lufthansa. After September 1939 European air
services at first continued with remarkable normality. Imperial
Airways went on flying from London to Paris and KLM and Sabena
resumed their flights from Holland and Belgium. But when the
Germans overran the continent in 1940 the whole European system
suddenly collapsed and cut off the airlines from the world. French
aviation continued in military aircraft in West Africa. KLM kept
flying in the West and East Indies, as limbs without a head; and
some of their DC-3 planes which escaped from the Nazis flew the
critical route between London and Lisbon, with signs inside their
cabins saying "KLM—still flying". But most of the KLM planes
in Holland were taken over by the German forces. Sabena escaped
from Belgium, and forged new routes in Africa, eventually flying
all the way from Lisbon to South Africa. Lufthansa was denied
most of its overseas routes, and the Americans refused it permission

to fly to New York. But in Europe it was supreme, taking over other fleets including Air France and providing the kind of unified network which planners had dreamt of, until the German oil shortage and the Allied invasion reduced it to a skeleton.

Among the neutral airlines Swissair, surrounded by Nazi Germany, could only keep going by servicing the German planes in return for high-grade steel which the Swiss desperately needed. Spain started its own airline, Iberia, in 1940, part-owned by Lufthansa, and flying as far as the Canary Islands until the Allied invasion of North Africa cut it back. Portugal had its own minimal airline while the airport at Lisbon became a dramatic meeting ground between the enemies—BOAC, Pan American and KLM on one side, and Lufthansa on the other: "The agents of the opposing airlines," as R. E. G. Davies put it, "viewed each other across the airport reception halls, with a strange mixture of defiance and regret." Only Sweden on the top edge of Europe could make any real progress, creating a new airline SILA and ordering new American DC-4 planes: it was even able to adapt American "flying fortress" bombers which had force-landed, in return for repatriating their crews.

The British Overseas Airways Corporation, newly merged and nationalised, was soon overwhelmed by total war. The two flying boats Cabot and Caribou which had been prepared for transatlantic services were flown to Norway to use against the Germans; but they were bombed and machine-gunned and eventually abandoned, while the hopes of civilian transatlantic crossings vanished. Commercial aircraft played their part in evacuating the British from France, but after Dunkirk the British aircraft factories only made fighters and bombers, while the BOAC pilots were used on war service, often pioneering new air-routes. They ferried new bombers from California via Canada across the Atlantic to Northern Ireland, with the help of Trans-Canada Airlines—often in icy conditions across Greenland and Iceland. They flew between Scotland and Stockholm to bring back indispensable Swedish ball-bearings. They flew down to West Africa to make contact with the free French forces, and to link up with American supplies flown across the South Atlantic. And they developed the massive detour of the "Horseshoe Route" to connect up the Empire without passing through the Mediterranean, linking Sydney via Singapore, India and Egypt to Durban in South Africa, where the British built a new flying-boat base.

But BOAC was treated as a junior arm of the air ministry, largely used for transporting troops—until it was further demoted when the air force created their own Transport Command in 1943. The first chairman of BOAC Lord Reith could not conceal his impatience to be promoted into government, where he became Minister of Information. He was succeeded as chairman by an oil magnate, Clive Pearson, while the airline was run by its director-general, the shipowner Walter Runciman. The board of BOAC became increasingly exasperated by their subjugation, seeing Pan American and others planning their post-war expansion, until in March 1943 all but one of the directors resigned in protest. The government appointed yet another amateur chairman, Lord Knollys, a courtier and former Governor of Bermuda, with a golf-playing air commodore, Alfred Critchley, as his director-general, who did little to reassure the demoralised staff. It was not until May 1945, when a Minister of Civil Aviation, Lord Swinton, was appointed to the cabinet, that the British seriously planned their post-war expansion—by which time many European airlines as well as Americans already had a head-start.

THE "EMPEROR OF THE AIR"

The Americans had civil aviation almost to themselves, and overseas that virtually meant Pan American. Juan Trippe seemed almost unassailable, the "Emperor of the Air" as Matthew Josephson called him. His autocratic style infuriated his wealthy fellow directors and for a few months in 1939 they replaced him as chief executive by Sonny Whitney who owned ten per cent of the stock. But they soon learnt that they could not do without Trippe and they reappointed him, unchastened and still more confident.

In wartime Pan American was more indispensable than ever, to the British as well as to the Americans. The transatlantic Clippers to Lisbon, connecting to London via KLM, were filled with refugees, diplomats or spies from all sides, for they were both faster and safer than ocean liners trying to avoid U-boats. They became a critical lifeline for Britain after she stood alone in 1940 and Churchill himself flew from Bermuda to Plymouth in one of the flying boats, after visiting Roosevelt in January 1942. He admitted later to being rather frightened, and had always regarded an Atlantic flight with awe; but he was delighted by his "broad bed in the bridal suite at the stern with large windows on either side. It was quite a long walk, thirty or forty feet, downhill through the various compartments to the saloon and dining-room, where nothing was lacking in food or drink." Pan American's monopoly of these long-distance planes provided huge extra revenues; when they sold three of them to Britain for the West African route they were believed to have made a profit of a quarter of a million dollars on each.

In Washington Roosevelt distrusted Trippe, and saw him (according to his friend Harold Ickes) as "a man of all-yielding suavity, who could be depended upon to pursue his own ruthless way"; while Ickes himself reported that he was "an unscrupulous person who cajoles and buys his way. He has made quite an unsavoury reputation in Latin American countries." In 1941 Roosevelt and his cabinet even seriously discussed buying half the stock of Pan American, to use it as an agent of the government during the emergency. But like other wartime schemes for nationalisation, including Ickes' own projected state oil company, the takeover of Pan Am came to nothing. Roosevelt soon found he could use the airline without directly controlling it, while its private ownership made the airline all the more useful as a cover for the US government while it had to remain technically neutral.

Roosevelt was not surprisingly worried by the Nazi penetration of Latin America, which Lufthansa and its allied airlines had assisted before the war. "The German Lufthansa airlines and the German steamship companies," wrote Cordell Hull, Roosevelt's Secretary of State who had visited Latin America in 1936, "were utilised to the utmost in spreading Nazi philosophy." Early in 1939 the US War Department had warned that the Nazis might actually invade the United States, by seizing the Panama Canal and flying in German troops by the Lufthansa route via West Africa and Brazil. After war broke out in Europe Roosevelt was determined to strengthen his country's presence in Latin America, and he discovered that the Colombian airline SCADTA, still run by German airmen and headed by the intrepid Von Bauer, was secretly owned by Pan American. The State Department insisted that Trippe must help to "de-louse" the airline of Nazis, and after awkward negotiations with the Colombian government Trippe arranged secretly to fly American pilots and staff into Colombia, and then abruptly fired all the Germans in the airline. It was a necessary but embarrassing show of strength, which only enhanced Pan American's reputation as an arm of American imperialism. SCADTA itself merged with another Colombian airline to become AVIANCA, which was eventually taken over by the Colombian government; today it can claim with some justification to be the oldest continuous airline in either of the Americas.

Roosevelt had much more far-reaching uses for Pan American. He became more concerned about American security after the German invasion of Europe, which brought the French Caribbean islands and French Guiana under Nazi control. The War Department wanted to build a chain of airbases down to Brazil as a safeguard, but Roosevelt realised that a private company could do it more tactfully, and he personally asked Trippe to undertake it. Trippe was reluctant to risk further his good relations with Latin Americans, but he eventually set up a subsidiary company to build twenty-five airports, spaced at five hundred mile intervals across the jungles and mud-flats. He could no longer disguise that his airline was being used, not just as a "chosen instrument", but as an arm of his government, like Lufthansa in Germany or BOAC in Britain. But he also saw a glittering prospect of potential Pan American airports.

His opportunity in Latin America was soon followed by an opening into Africa. When Trippe came to London in June 1941 Churchill invited him to dinner to advise him about setting up an air-route to Cairo, and back in Washington Roosevelt asked him to build ten bases across Africa, from the western bulge across Northern Nigeria and Chad to the Sudan, then up to Khartoum and Cairo. The new African air-route, linked up with the east coast of Brazil, became a lifeline for British supplies, and for a brief interim these remote West African bases became the stepping-stones for the South Atlantic. The war network was penetrating deep into the South.

Thus stretching across five continents, Pan American was highly visible as the pre-eminent world airline, not just for foreign airmail but for secret diplomacy and national security. When the attack on Pearl Harbor brought the United States into the war Pan American converted half its planes to military use and gained massive new contracts for leasing planes and building airports. "Trippe embodies, not something called the 'managerial revolution'," wrote Matthew Josephson in 1943, "but the modern version of what used to be called state capitalism. He typifies, knowingly or not, capitalist enterprise nourished and protected by the state, and inevitably assuming a monopolistic form." Josephson was amused by Trippe's ambivalence towards the free-enterprise system. "I have often been puzzled by the apparent contradictions between his espousal of private enterprise," he wrote, "and his unwillingness to accept the competitive disadvantages of the system. But then are not all our modern industrialists full of such contradictions in their thinking?"

But Trippe's rivals were now seriously challenging his overseas monopoly. The Big Four domestic airlines were developing bigger and faster planes as they raced each other from coast to coast. They included the Douglas DC-4 (known abroad as the Skymaster) the four-engined airliner which could carry forty-two passengers at 200 mph, and its dumpy rival Boeing 307, the Stratoliner with forty-four passengers. The old division between landplanes for crossing the continent and flying boats for crossing the oceans was no longer so valid; it was now clear that the long-range planes, unlike ships or trains, could cross over both. The domestic air chiefs were becoming more interested in extending their scope, particularly Cyrus Smith, the hefty Texan book-keeper who dominated the biggest of them, American Airlines. By 1942 American had been awarded the route to Mexico City, followed the next year by the smaller airline Braniff.

The links between airlines and government were working both ways. Trippe's most formidable opponent was the Chief of Staff of the Air Corps, General "Hap" Arnold—who had been one of the founders of the original Pan American airline which had planned to fly down to Latin America before Trippe's group took it over. Arnold not surprisingly was convinced that other American airlines should stretch abroad, and he was also a close friend of Cyrus Smith whom he recruited to run Air Transport Command. In mid-1943, as the tide of war turned, Arnold invited the heads of eighteen airlines, including Trippe, to a secret meeting in Washington on post-war air policy, and asked them to form a committee to ensure effective competition. They all agreed, except Trippe and William Patterson, the President of United, whom Trippe persuaded to stay out. The rest soon issued a statement that overseas air transport should not be left to "the withering influence of monopoly". Many airlines were already flying abroad on military duties—American to Europe, United to Australia, Eastern to Brazil—and Pan American would clearly face much more serious competition. And in the meantime the CAB, under its new chairman Welch Pogue, had announced in October 1943 that the State Department and the CAB, not the airlines, would in future negotiate overseas air-routes. It rang up the curtain, as Pogue put it, for action between governments on the international stage.

FREEDOM OF THE AIR?

The lethal effects of bombers and fighters, which first impinged on America at Pearl Harbor, made many people in both the United States and Britain think seriously about the international security of aviation, including civil aviation. As peace came closer, the notion of "freedom of the air" was seen by many politicians as part of the general pursuit of freedom and security, and Henry Wallace, Roosevelt's Vice-President, pressed for the newly formed United Nations to be responsible for international air services, through its own "air arm". Wendell Willkie, who had been Roosevelt's rival for the presidency in 1940 and became the prophet of "one world", proclaimed a new universality of the air. "The modern airplane creates a new geographical dimension," he said in 1943, in one of his many high-flown speeches: "A navigable ocean of air blankets the whole surface of the globe. There are no distant places any longer: the world is small and the world is one. The American people must grasp these new realities if they are to play their essential part in winning the war and building a world of peace and freedom."

Such dreamy notions about the freedom of the air were easily debunked as "woolly-headed internationalism" by commercial realists like Juan Trippe, or by politicians like the young Clare Boothe Luce who, in her famous speech to Congress in February 1943, attacked Wallace's rhetoric as "globaloney". But more cautious Americans were also anticipating a new kind of world. "The imagination of men's minds leaped to the view," recalled Welch Pogue, "that in the post-war era the airplane would 'shrink' the world so much, both militarily and in a civil sense, as to make every civilisation and its trade and commerce available to every other civilisation on earth. Suddenly, civil aviation had become vitally important." And even the British, in the midst of the war, were looking towards a new air system after the war. "It is perhaps not too much to contemplate," wrote Sir Osborne Mance, in an authoritative British study of air transport in 1943, "that the international organisation necessary for any form of international control on grounds of security should own or participate in the principal air services, and license all other air services . . . "

Roosevelt's own policies for civil aviation were much influenced by his forceful adviser Adolf Berle, who became responsible for aviation in the State Department in 1941, under Cordell Hull. Berle was a brilliant and cocky lawyer who was engrossed in his new field. "I feel that aviation will have a greater influence on American foreign interests and American foreign policy," he wrote to Hull in September 1942, "than any other non-political consideration." He saw himself in the tradition of Hugo Grotius, the great Dutch lawyer who established the law of the sea in the sixteenth century, and he was determined to prevent the carve-up of the airways by national interests. "In the air," he wrote in 1944, "there is no excuse for an attempt to revive the sixteenth- and seventeenth-century conceptions . . . for a modern air British East India Company or Portuguese trading monopoly or 'Spanish Main conception'." From this viewpoint he was determined to confront both Trippe's Pan American empire and the British Empire, with its network of bases and islands.

As early as 1943 Berle was already worried—without much

reason—that the British were forging ahead with their own post-war air policy while the "dunderhead" State Department was helpless. So he set up a committee, including Robert Lovett from the War Department, which recommended an international conference to achieve a general air agreement. By the time of the Quebec conference in August 1943 Roosevelt and Churchill were already discussing post-war aviation policy, and Roosevelt was advocating a "very free interchange" of air and landing rights; and by early 1944 plans were under way for an international aviation conference, to be held at Chicago. All the major countries except the enemy powers were to be invited, but the conference would clearly be dominated by two or three—the United States, Britain and Canada, the "ABC Powers".

It was an uneasy and unequal triumvirate. The Americans were making nearly all the world's civilian planes and so had a head-start in manufacture, with a huge stock of DC-3s, the "work-horses of the air". The British were still only making fighters and bombers, and dreaded the glut of American aircraft; but they still had much of their network of bases all round the world, including the precious refuelling islands which they could use as bargaining counters to safeguard their air interests. The Canadians had the temporary advantage of controlling the key landing place between the United States and Europe so long as airliners could not cross the Atlantic with one hop: the airport of Gander was in the British colony of Newfoundland, which did not technically become a province of Canada until 1949; but it was already part of the Canadian air system, linked with Montreal and Quebec. The "air ferry" of warplanes through Canada to Britain had underlined the dominion's importance, and Canadian diplomats were often seen as conciliators between Americans and British. While Canadians had felt threatened by the American domestic air-routes, they found a new role as the Atlantic bridgehead.

In March 1944 Berle flew to London, stopping at Montreal on the way, to open talks with the British, who were represented by the ex-Canadian newspaper-owner Lord Beaverbrook, whom Churchill had put in charge of aviation. A comic relationship developed between the two autocrats. Berle was fascinated by Beaverbrook's dynamic showmanship, while Beaverbrook set out to flatter and conciliate Berle: he discovered that Berle, an ardent Roman Catholic, was interested in Cardinal Newman, so he gave him first editions of Newman, and even proposed to give him a Cardinal's hat. But Berle retained his suspicion of British imperialism and the European fondness for cartels, and he insisted on "equal opportunities in the air". Four months later Beaverbrook flew to

Washington—flying non-stop in only twenty hours—and pressed for a strong international body to regulate civil aviation, which Berle insisted that the Americans could not support.

The British and Canadians did their best to soften Berle's attitudes, and in his diary Berle recorded his bewilderment at their social style. Beaverbrook invited him for a weekend in his home province of New Brunswick, together with his Minister of State, Richard Law, who was also half-Canadian (his father, Arthur Bonar Law, had been prime minister of Britain), and the Canadian cabinet minister C. D. Howe, accompanied by Beaverbrook's valet called Nockles, who (said Berle) made "Jeeves look like a piker". The whole party visited Beaverbrook's birthplace and went on to stay in a remote camp owned by Sir James Dunn, another Canadian millionaire, who had recently married a beautiful young Greek. Nockles served everyone with caviar and the best champagne and brandy while Beaverbrook reminisced about his youth. Berle managed to talk briefly about aviation with Beaverbrook, complaining that BOAC were already trying to bag the best routes, and proposing that America and Britain shoud exchange landing rights. But it was difficult to make serious points: Beaverbrook seemed to Berle to be "drawing everyone into a kind of maelstrom of warm-hearted and enthusiastic discussion, below which was a discernible flavour of direct political purpose". By the time the party flew back to Massachusetts they were distracted by the news of the American breakthrough in Normandy.

As the Allies advanced on Germany they began discussing the future of the air more seriously. The close co-operation with the Soviet Union encouraged hopes of internationalising the air; and when in August 1944 the Soviets put forward a proposal for an international air force, Churchill regarded the prospect as "an event of the utmost importance", looking back to the lost opportunity after the First World War. "It certainly seems," he told General Ismay, "by weaving the forces of different countries together to give assurances of permanent peace." But the Soviets soon showed resistance to internationalising civil aviation. They made clear to Berle that they must carry all traffic inside their country in their own planes with their own pilots, and that they would only connect up with foreign planes at a few fixed points—a closed system which, as Berle complained, much reduced the prospects of a global agreement. The Soviet Union, as Berle wrote in August 1944, had "made a slight advance, but only a slight advance, in the direction of admitting the rest of the world to her territory in the fashion usual with other countries". In September the Americans invited all members of the newly formed United Nations, together with others, to a great conference on civil aviation in November 1944. Every country except Saudi Arabia agreed to come. The Soviet Union accepted and actually sent a delegation to America, but they withdrew just before the opening day—ostensibly because of the presence of Spain, Portugal and Switzerland. The open skies were already clouding over.

The British arrived in Chicago with an inadequate team. Beaverbrook stayed in London as an overlord, and the Chicago delegation was led by the new Minister for Aviation Lord Swinton, a long-standing crony of Churchill who had only just returned from being resident minister in West Africa. Swinton, as his diplomatic aide Paul Gore-Booth described him, was "a fine, fighting, non-highbrow Conservative political leader", and he was also a convinced protectionist. He and Berle had opposite viewpoints and styles. After Swinton met Berle in Chicago he told his wife that Berle was "easily the most disagreeable person with whom I have ever negotiated", while Berle thought Swinton was "arrogant and inflexible, not having quite appreciated the difference between the atmosphere in the Gulf of Guinea and that of the shores of Lake Michigan". Swinton, as a man of the Empire, assiduously consulted and conciliated his Commonwealth colleagues whom he had met in Montreal beforehand; but he was much less at home among Americans and Europeans. The British took the Chicago conference much less seriously than the Americans: their other leading delegates, Sir Arthur Street and George Cribbett, told Gore-Booth that they were too busy to attend delegation meetings. The British were still inclined to treat aviation as a technical subject secondary to the main stream of grand diplomacy.

> On the threshold of a new era in law of the air [said Roosevelt, introducing the Chicago conference], let us remember our great responsibility to ensure the basis for a lasting peace. Our peacetime arrangements must not be undermined by petty considerations or unreasonable fears. Let us rather, in full acknowledgment of the sovereign rights of all nations and the legal equality of all peoples, work together in order that the skies of the world can be exploited by man for all mankind.

At the opening of the conference Berle, who led the American delegation, proclaimed his belief in "open skies"—which well suited the Americans' technological supremacy, much as the freedom of the seas had earlier suited the sea-power of the Dutch and the British. Berle made his case with a fine historical panache. He explained that the air, like the sea, was:

a highway given by nature to all men. It differs in this from the
sea: that it is subject to the sovereignty of the nations over which
it moves . . . No greater tragedy could befall the world than to
repeat in the air the grim and bloody history which tormented
the world some centuries ago when the denial of equal opportunity
for intercourse made the sea a battleground instead of a highway.

And in his own outline of the American position he explained, "We
are endeavouring to write the charter of the open sky."

Behind the rhetoric much of the conference turned round the
question of whether nations would allow each other some or all of
the "five freedoms", as the airlines were beginning to call the
different stages of liberalising the rights to fly. In the vague idealism
of the time they were sometimes confused with Roosevelt's idealistic
"four freedoms" (the freedoms of speech and worship, and from
want and fear) which he had proclaimed in 1941. But the air
freedoms were really technical arrangements between nations which
defined the limits of air traffic; sometimes more accurately called
the five restrictions. They were:

1. Freedom to fly over a nation.
2. Freedom to land in a nation (without picking up or putting
   down passengers or goods).
3. Freedom to carry passengers or goods from the home nation
   to a foreign nation.
4. Freedom to carry passengers or goods from a foreign nation to
   a home nation.
5. Freedom to pick up and put down passengers or goods belonging to a foreign nation, between intermediate points.

The British agreed in principle to collaborate and exchange landing
rights as far as possible, but they were acutely conscious of their
own shortage of aircraft and anxious to protect their own industry,
and they stood out for a system of quotas to prevent the American
airlines from flooding their routes. The British, supported by
France, Australia and New Zealand, argued for "escalation"
—regulating the frequencies of planes according to the numbers of
passengers—to give their countries time to organise their aviation
industries. But the Americans would not accept it, and the Canadians pressed for a compromise closer to the American freedoms.
There followed a historic British muddle. Swinton tried to get
through to Beaverbrook, his overlord in London, for permission to
drop "escalation"; but when Beaverbrook rang back Swinton replied, "Max, go to hell—it's three o'clock in the morning here."

So Beaverbrook sent a telegram which said, "You may abandon escalation." The British delegates announced the concession to the conference with relief, only to receive a second telegram which said, "before 'abandon', insert 'not'." But it was too late: "A British delegation," said Gore-Booth, "does not go back on its word." "We got totally confused," recalled Sir Peter Masefield who was advising Beaverbrook in London. "We had to cover up and reverse ourselves—it held it up for three days."

Berle was relieved at the British retreat, but he faced a new impasse on the question of regulating traffic between points en route—the so-called "fifth freedom". Berle appealed to Roosevelt, who wrote personally to Churchill to complain:

> Your people are now asking limitations on the number of planes between points regardless of the traffic offering. This seems to me a form of strangulation. It has been a cardinal point in American policy throughout that the ultimate judge should be the passenger and the shipper. The limitations now proposed would, I fear, place a dead hand on the use of the great air trade-routes.

Churchill in reply reminded Roosevelt that Britain had "agreed to throwing open our airfields all over the world to aircraft of other nationalities", and suggested that the conference be temporarily adjourned. Roosevelt replied the next day saying that the British restrictions would be inoperable across many countries, and would make round-the-world routes almost impossible. He promised that American operators would not "so fill the air on long routes that nobody else could get in and survive".

Other countries made themselves felt. The Canadians, led by Herbert Symington, the President of Trans-Canada Airlines, leant towards the American view and insisted that the conference must continue till it reached agreement, to loud applause. The New Zealand delegate, D. G. Sullivan, pleaded eloquently for an internationalised air service under the United Nations. "Any other system must, we suggest, lead to national competition, to an attempt to serve national interests as opposed to world interests, to achieve individual needs at the expense of others. It must lead to the creation of large commercial organisations whose activities must in the long run be based primarily on the profit motive . . . " The Mayor of New York, Fiorello La Guardia—who later gave his name to New York's airport—supported the Canadian speech to Swinton's fury, insisting that "It was pointless to make arrangements for airfields if you had no planes which could fly into them." Other countries, including all the Latin Americans, supported the United States.

The Dutch delegate, Steenberghe, saw the British restrictions as a direct threat to KLM's freedom, and the Swedes had the same fear. Only the Australians, the New Zealanders and the French—very half-heartedly—supported the British.

Churchill kept up his personal pressure. He reminded Roosevelt of America's virtual monopoly of civil aircraft and warned that Berle's proposals would enable American airlines to carry most of the traffic across the British Commonwealth, giving them "the right to everything save sabotage". Can we not reach agreement, asked Churchill, when great battles in which our troops are fighting side by side are at their height? He had no worries, he said, about the domination of the Americans, because he was sure that "justice and fair play will be the lights that guide them". Roosevelt subtly returned the compliments and asked, "Would you like to see a world in which all ports were closed to all ships but their own or open to one foreign ship, perhaps two, if they carried only passengers and cargo bound all the way from Liverpool to Shanghai?" He promised that the US would make aircraft available to Britain on equal terms, provided they allowed aviation to develop "as fast as human ingenuity and enterprise can take it". But he warned that most of the smaller nations took America's side, and if the conference failed the reasons "would be all too clear". At one point one of the American delegation, Ralph Damon, suggested to one of the British delegation, Vernon Crudge, that Britain could have fifty DC-4 planes if she acquiesced. But Beaverbrook in London, advised by British aircraft industrialists, rejected the offer.

The British proposal, Berle reckoned, had been "simply blown out of the water" by the opposition of the smaller countries which it claimed to protect. Berle drafted a simpler plan which theoretically accepted all the five freedoms of the air, while Swinton, backed by Churchill, advocated postponement. Finally a compromise was put forward by KLM which recognised only the first two freedoms, which the British accepted, though Churchill still insisted to Roosevelt that they must be free to review it later.

With this qualified success, the final Chicago convention was drafted. It never achieved the fuller freedom of the air which Berle had once hoped for: basically it was an extension of the pre-war Paris and Havana conventions, which had first agreed to exchange transit and technical stops. The Chicago convention still stipulated firmly, in Article 1: "The contracting states recognise that every state has complete and exclusive sovereignty over airspace above its territory."

Chicago nevertheless laid solid foundations for peacetime air travel across the world. "The conference," concluded Gore-Booth, "was outwardly a failure and essentially a great success." It set up a new body, the International Civil Aviation Organisation (ICAO), under the wing of the United Nations, which provided the means to maintain and co-ordinate the rules of the air. On American insistence it was based not on Paris but on Montreal, and its first president was the American air expert Edward Warner, a modest and scholarly man who had been Professor of Aeronautics and a member of the CAB.

Berle himself was privately humiliated just before the end of the conference by Roosevelt who proposed to sack him from his job—probably after complaints from other Americans on the delegation who thought that he had made too many concessions to foreign airlines. But he kept the news to himself, and ended the last plenary session with a final flourish:

> . . . when we leave this conference we can say to our airmen throughout the world, not that they have a legal and diplomatic wrangle ahead of them, but that they can go out and fly their craft in peaceful service . . . We must remember that these machines that fly are still guided by humans, and, in that connection, we may properly be justified in recalling the words of David—King, Captain, and Poet:

> "If I take the wings of the morning and dwell in the uttermost parts of the sea, even there shall thy hand lead me and thy right hand shall hold me."

What was the lasting significance of Chicago? The historian A. J. P. Taylor, Lord Beaverbrook's biographer, was sceptical. "Great Britain and the United States imagined that they would run the post-war world as autocratically as they conducted the war against Hitler: some concessions to Soviet Russia, but otherwise a 'carve up' . . . none of this came to fruition." Certainly most of the assumptions of 1944 look irrelevant forty years later. The enemy countries which were firmly excluded became major actors. The British lost much of their bargaining power as their empire dissolved and long-range planes no longer needed remote islands and bases. Canada's role became less special after planes could by-pass Gander or Montreal to fly direct to Europe. The Americans soon reversed their position over the "fifth freedom" and resisted foreign airlines flying between American airports. The domination of American airlines became less fearful as the world was criss-crossed by rival Japanese, Dutch or German planes; and only the aircraft manufacturers maintained their emphatic advantage over the next four decades. The Chicago agreement did not represent a fundamental new concept of air freedom, as Berle claimed: it merely reflected the political balance of power on the earth, which was to be transformed over the next forty years. New Zealand's dream of a truly international system soon—as we will note—met with disillusion.

But Chicago and its offspring ICAO did provide the starting-point for the phenomenal development of world airlines and air travel in peacetime, at a speed which few of the delegates had conceived possible. It permitted an exchange not just of landing rights, but of information, safety systems and routine technology which, though soon taken for granted, far exceeded the pre-war arrangements. When Adolf Berle gave a speech to ICAO twenty years later he could justifiably boast about this "vast, if silent, success". The organisation, he said, "realised one small part of Franklin Roosevelt's great dream of organised peace among nations", and the Chicago conference had shown "true international supra-political, even supra-sovereign, law in action".

But one huge obstacle loomed in the midst of the post-war air system—the territory of the Soviet Union and its satellites, which now stretched from East Germany across Eastern Europe and Asia to the Bering Straits opposite Alaska. In the full tide of the wartime alliance with the Soviets the Americans and British held high hopes of peacetime co-operation in the air; the Soviets were anxious to fly their airliners across the world, and the British and Americans wanted to fly into Moscow. But the hopes were soon dashed after the Chicago conference, as the cold war got colder. The Soviet Union, which opposed all five freedoms, was now right out of the international system, controlling its own closed system through its own airline Aeroflot. The vast land-mass on the way between Western Europe and Japan, or between Alaska and East Asia, would remain a blank space on the new air maps of the world.

THE BERMUDA BARGAIN

The global idealism at Chicago was soon followed by realistic hard bargaining, as the Americans negotiated with individual nations to ensure landing rights abroad. By early 1945 Washington had already reached agreement with Eire, which controlled the precious stopping place of Shannon on the edge of the Atlantic. Churchill had bitterly resented the Irish co-operation with Germany during the war and had tried to exclude them from the air talks. "Everyone here is astonished," Churchill wrote to Roosevelt, "that this should have been started without our being told beforehand." Roosevelt sympathised with Churchill's resentment, but insisted that the air agreement was "a post-war matter": he warned Churchill that Britain, having prevented multilateral agreements at Chicago, could not now stop bilaterals. "I think it only fair to tell you," Roosevelt concluded, "that aviation circles in this country are becoming increasingly suspicious that certain elements in England intend to try to block the development of international flying in general until the British aviation industry is further developed."

The British could not block it, and in the meantime their position was weakened by their desperate need for an American loan of $3.75 billion which Washington was reluctant to provide. They suddenly switched their aviation tactics and hastily invited the Americans to a meeting in February 1946 at Bermuda, the traditional meeting ground of the two allies in the air age. "We started poles apart," recalled Sir Peter Masefield who was one of the British team, "but in six weeks we achieved a breakthrough." "The annexe to the agreement was the most difficult drafting I have ever seen," said Sir William Hildred who also participated. "There was a little silver thread between the Americans who wanted everything to be free, and the British who wanted it controlled." The British relented from their extreme protectionism and agreed to exchange the first three freedoms with the Americans. BOAC was allowed to complete its longed-for "all-red" route across the globe by stopping at Hawaii and other American islands across the Pacific, while Pan American were allowed access to British outposts. The dreams of "open skies" gave way to the realities of horse-trading between governments over landing rights, gateways and freedoms.

The Anglo-American agreement at Bermuda became the prototype for all other countries over the next thirty years, and it was followed by a "vast cobweb of bilateral international agreements", as Professor Bin Cheng called it, "linking individual pairs of states". It was also seen (in the words of the air economist Stephen Wheatcroft) as "a general philosophy on the way in which the economic regulation of the industry should be achieved". The regulation was firmly by governments, and in the subsequent bargaining the airlines were only on the sidelines, often never knowing the secret trade-offs contained in the "memoranda of understanding"—which might include deals right outside the airline business, over tariffs or quotas for exports. "The real competition in international air transport," said Charles Stuart, a subsequent British Airways negotiator, "is for national interest. It is played by officials behind locked doors and is deadly serious."

RE-ENTER IATA

It was part of the compromise of Bermuda that the most contentious question, of whether and how to fix fares, should be delegated to the airlines' own club, with the governments discreetly in the background. The International Air Traffic Association, which had supervised the European agreements in the thirties, had lain dormant in the Hague during the war years; but it was revived with a much greater opportunity with peace. At Chicago the Americans, in keeping with their anti-trust laws, had opposed any connivance between airlines; but at the end of the conference BOAC called a meeting, supported by the French and Egyptians, to discuss how airlines could co-operate. They agreed to summon a full conference at Havana in April 1945, where thirty-one nations duly approved the articles of a revived IATA (called a Transport Association instead of a Traffic Association). Its first aim was proclaimed as "to promote safe, regular and economical air transport for the benefit of the peoples of the world".

The airline chiefs each year elected a president of IATA who took the chair at the conference. Trippe wanted to be the first, but he was persuaded that such visible American domination would be tactless and the Canadian Herbert Symington was chosen instead. But the more important figure was the director-general William Hildred, a tough but genial Yorkshireman who had emerged from the British Treasury to become a shrewd air negotiator; and he dominated IATA for the next twenty years. "I was mean-minded, Treasury-minded," he says today at the age of ninety-one, "but I made 'em laugh, and while they were laughing I got my way." He was always a firm believer in the need for regulation and controls. "The open skies failed, and must always fail—they would be deadly."

By the time of the Bermuda conference the next year IATA was fully installed as the machinery to regulate fares, with twin headquarters in Montreal and Geneva. It was a curious hybrid. Like its pre-war equivalent it was basically a trade association with a built-in tendency towards cartels; but it was also sanctioned by governments as part of their bilateral agreements—the more effectively since most airlines were now nationalised. The Americans were very ambivalent. In return for the British concessions at Bermuda they were prepared to accept the machinery to control fares; and their own CAB, which already regulated fares inside America, agreed temporarily to endorse the fares which IATA agreed. But American governments continued to watch and criticise

IATA as a potential restraint on free competition. As more nations joined the fare-fixing, IATA became both the instrument and the scapegoat for the natural tendencies of the airlines to restrict competition; while the United States, as the dominating air nation, uneasily but effectively condoned the global cartel.

IATA was much more than a fare-fixer: it provided the central machinery—which ICAO could not—to co-ordinate and synchronise the growing network of air-routes. Its timetable conferences connected up flights. Its committees on technology and safety maintained common standards. It invented the remarkable IATA ticket, which was to remain the means not only of booking seats across the world, but of changing airlines and switching currencies. A passenger could buy a multiple ticket in New York or Bangkok, unfolding like a concertina, to carry him on twenty airlines in twenty currencies to twenty destinations. Carbon copies were torn off at each stage, to be sent back to the central IATA clearing-house—an extraordinary feat of global organisation and trust.

Hildred was determined that, while ICAO worked in both English and French, IATA should be decisively English-speaking. "Air France used to complain," he recalled, "but I wouldn't have French. No one dared speak French while I was about." Wartime aviation had itself helped to tilt the linguistic balance, and the Americans, British, Canadians and Australians who emerged as the major actors could impose their own language. The expanding vernacular of airports, maintenance, tickets, safety or air traffic control was uncompromisingly English—whether CHECK IN, NO SHOW, the truck on the tarmac called FOLLOW ME, or the final ominous word VOID at the end of the ticket.

To create this co-ordinated world was a massive achievement which travellers soon took for granted until they found themselves outside the system in countries like the Soviet Union—which stayed out of IATA, though it later joined ICAO—which would not commit themselves to fixed timetables or connections. IATA and ICAO provided the technical basis for an unprecedented speeding-up of communications between countries and peoples. But it did not follow—as some idealists of the air were proclaiming—that air travel would lead to any more understanding or peace between nations than travel by trains or ocean liners.

As the airlines spread across the world, with their disciplines, standardisation and often identical planes, the image of the air as the medium of liberation and untrammelled enterprise faded still further. The IATA symbol of the wings across the world, which airliners displayed above their doors, was the badge of reliability and safety but also of uniformity and regular mass travel. And

IATA soon found itself at the centre of stormy controversies about the control of this huge new world industry. Could the airlines achieve any real independence from their governments? Should this critical industry be controlled by agreements, pools and cartels, or could it be thrown open to new competitors?

NEW MAPS OF THE WORLD

Wartime planes had already forged new flight paths across the globe, far away from the ocean routes. American planes were regularly flying between Brazil and West Africa. Qantas introduced a long-distance service from Australia to Ceylon, which had acquired a new importance after Japan occupied Singapore. The Americans, Canadians and British were flying along "great circle routes" to the north, using their huge new base at Goose Bay in Labrador on the way to Iceland and Scotland, or ferrying planes to Russia via Alaska and Siberia.

Aviation experts were predicting a mass expansion of air travel after the war. Edward Warner predicted in 1943 that it would be perfectly possible to build a "leviathan of an airplane weighing 400,000 or more pounds and carrying 400 passengers across the Atlantic". But Matthew Josephson pointed out that "two such planes departing from opposite shores each day could carry twice as many people as ever crossed this ocean annually in cabin and first-class steamers!" And few people anticipated that cheaper air travel would create new markets for tourists and business commuters. "It may with some degree of confidence be predicted," wrote Sir Osborne Mance in 1943, "that for some time to come commercial aircraft will be mainly used for long hauls of mail, well-to-do passengers, and high-grade goods of small bulk."

The huge technical advances of wartime, together with the mood of global idealism, encouraged the misty visions of a world unified by the air. The Pan American emblem, of a globe divided only by latitudes, was the symbol of the new hopes of a world which ignored frontiers. An exhibition called "Airways to Peace" was held at the Museum of Modern Art in New York showing how the new airroutes across the pole would link the world's cities. Five American senators flew 40,000 miles round the world, inspecting the battlefields, and Wendell Willkie flew round the globe before writing his book *One World*.

Mercator's projection, the basis of most maps since the Flemish cartographer first invented it in 1568, was now hopelessly misleading for visualising long flights. It not only distorted the poles and

the equator; it encouraged a "Eurocentric" view, laying out the
world from West to East with the land-mass of Europe and Asia in
the middle. Only the globe—which had become Juan Trippe's
personal symbol—could make sense of the air-routes, and the first
tools of airline planners were a large globe and a piece of string.
Any three-dimensional view of the world provides surprises. The
Arctic, so huge on Mercator, shrinks round a pin-point: Greenland,
which on the flat map looks as big as South America, becomes only
a ninth of its size; the equatorial countries like Brazil or Zaire
show their true vastness. The great circle routes reveal unexpected
parallels: New York and Madrid, or Oslo and Anchorage, are on
the same latitude; Northern Scotland is closer to Newfoundland
than to Turkey; West Africa is closer to Brazil than to South Africa.

In 1944 the Brookings Institute in Washington inaugurated a
series of studies called "America Faces the Air Age". They were
introduced by a booklet called *The Geography of World Air Transport*
by Parker Van Zandt, a forthright airline economist who had been
an aviator in the First World War. Van Zandt pointed out the faults
of Mercator, and then showed how most of the world that mattered
was included in "the principal hemisphere", which contained
ninety-four per cent of the world's population and ninety-eight per
cent of industrial activity. Europe, he suggested, being in the
centre of this hemisphere, would have a new advantage in the air
age—particularly if it could unite to organise its economy. But he
did not foresee that the Far East—on the outer edge of his "principal
hemisphere"—would become a major industrial region, generating
huge new traffic across the Pacific and the pole. And like most other
prophets of the time he did not foresee how thoroughly national
frontiers and sovereignties would stand in the way of air travel.

4

Race Round the World

Unlike the boundaries of the sea by the shorelines, the "ocean of air" laps at the border of every state, city, town and home throughout the world.

Welch Pogue, 1979

By the end of the Second World War there was no doubt that the United States would dominate the world's airways, with its huge manufacturing base on the West Coast which provided the technology for much bigger airliners, and with a network of domestic air traffic which exceeded the rest of the world's. Only Americans could afford to fly abroad in large numbers. The new American era was based on domination of the air as firmly as the British era had been based on sea-power.

But the aviation leaders could have no illusions about their dependence on government, and the first post-war years were hard times for both airlines and aircraft manufacturers, as military orders collapsed and peacetime air travel was slow to pick up. The world was awash with second-hand military planes—particularly DC-3s which some airlines in Africa and Asia would still be flying thirty years later. All the aircraft manufacturers were painfully feeling their dependence on war. The Douglas company which had made 29,000 aircraft during the war produced only 127 in 1946. "The future," complained Donald Douglas, "is as dark as the inside of a boot."

Many of the big American airlines were now looking for new routes abroad; and the development of long-distance landplanes, which were more efficient than flying boats, diminished the division between land and sea. American Airlines, which Cyrus Smith rejoined after his service in government, was allowed to take over

the small American Export Airlines which had begun flying the
Atlantic during the war; and American Overseas Airlines, as it
was renamed, began flying DC-4s to London in 1945—the first
scheduled Atlantic service by landplanes. United, Eastern and
Western were all allocated routes by the CAB down to Mexico.
Braniff extended down to Brazil. National flew to Cuba. One of the
most ambitious airline tycoons was Croil Hunter of Northwest
Airlines, based on the twin cities of Minneapolis and St Louis,
which had pioneered flights to Alaska for the US air force during
the war. Hunter had an influential lobbyist in Bill Stern, a banker
in North Dakota who had befriended the influential Senator
Magnuson; and in July 1947 Hunter inaugurated the new "Flight
to the Orient Over the North-west Passage", flying from the twin
cities to Tokyo, Seoul, Shanghai and Manila, and reaching Tokyo
in only thirty-three hours. It was a dramatic demonstration of how
the air could connect the heart of the continent with distant overseas
markets.

But all the new routes, whether inside or outside America, depended heavily on political influence. "They each had their man in
Washington," said Bob Six; "they couldn't get anywhere without
one. Jack Frye used to play poker with Truman. Northwest had
Bill Stern. Trippe had Stettinius. They all needed the politicians.
But remember, they were all building something, not stealing
something."

At Pan American Juan Trippe still controlled by far the biggest
overseas airline, and he depicted himself as a great American
patriot, enabling his nation through its chosen instrument to spread
its influence round the world. "Think of the English," he said
admiringly, "such a small nation, yet extending the tentacles, so to
speak, of their power all over the earth!" The British, on their
side, intensely resented his obsession with power and money. "He
wouldn't fight," said Hildred, the director of IATA, "he would just
ignore the opposition, and go and do what he wanted."

Trippe's overseas monopoly was already threatened by American
rivals; but he still had political friends and tricks up his sleeve. His
brother-in-law Edward Stettinius who had been Secretary of State
at the end of the war, was wary about his Pan Am connection. But
Trippe also employed Sam Pryor, an old Yale contemporary who
was on the Republican National Committee, who was (said Bob
Six) "the ablest airline lobbyist I ever knew: completely dedicated
to Pan Am". With this help, and with extraordinary chutzpah,
Trippe prepared a plan to consolidate all American overseas airlines
into what he called a "Community Company" which looked to his
rivals very like an extension of Pan American. He restated his

familiar warning: that foreign airlines after the war would again be supported and subsidised by their governments, to the disadvantage of American competition; and that the United States must also have its chosen instrument.

Trippe set about getting a bill through Congress, introduced by his friend Senator McCarran, to establish this "All American Flag Line", and he testified at Senate hearings in May 1945 just before the war ended. He insisted that his proposed Community Company would not be controlled by any one individual, airline or group. He pointed out that overseas air transport made up only eighteen per cent of potential American aviation, and he warned senators that competition would get in the way of lower transatlantic fares. Many senators were sympathetic, but not enough to send it to the full Senate.

The role of Washington was more important than ever. The airlines no longer depended on airmail subsidies for their profits; passengers had become economic and the domestic airlines were soon expanding faster than ever. The returning troops had encouraged a new pattern of mobility, and the airlines were becoming more attractive than the railroads: by 1951 they carried more passengers than Pullmans, and by 1957 they had overtaken both the inter-city railroads and the ocean liners. But however commercially successful, the airlines still depended on the CAB and the president to approve their routes. And Trippe was now coming up against his most formidable political rival for overseas flights, in the shape of TWA which was now owned by a man as stubborn and dictatorial as himself.

THE PLAYBOY'S AIRLINE

TWA originally stood for Transcontinental and Western Air; but by 1950 it had renamed itself more ambitiously, with the same initials, Trans World Airlines. It traced its origins back to Transcontinental Air Transport which had been set up in 1928, a year after Charles Lindbergh flew to Paris and Lindbergh himself was its technical adviser, so it called itself "The Lindbergh Line". TAT had set up the first transcontinental service from New York to Los Angeles with a combination of air and rail travel which took only forty-eight hours; and in 1930, helped by the postmaster-general Walter Brown, it merged with the Western Air Express to win a contract to fly mail across the States. It established its operational base at Kansas City, and vied with the others of the Big Four— American, United and Eastern—to break the transcontinental records. In the thirties TWA set out to attract film stars on their sleeper-flights between New York and Los Angeles, to lure passengers away from the luxury trains like the Super Chief, and they boasted Clark Gable, Carole Lombard and Sonja Henie as regular customers.

TWA was run by a dynamic former stunt-pilot, Jack Frye, who firmly imposed his character on the airline; but he had difficult owners. The airline was first controlled by General Motors, then after 1934 by John Hertz, the former owner of Yellow Cabs; but Hertz was never excited by aircraft, and Frye was exasperated by his caution. After a climactic row in 1939 Frye took a fateful step: he flew to Los Angeles to talk to an eccentric acquaintance, the multi-millionaire Howard Hughes. Hughes loved flying: he had already piloted a TWA plane and had made the extravagant Hollywood film *Hell's Angels*. When Frye explained his problems, Hughes offered to buy the airline. He bought a quarter of it for $1.6 million and went on buying shares until he owned three-quarters. TWA found itself under the fitful control of an absentee owner with a passion for planes but the obstinacy of a spoilt child who had never grown up.

Hughes' first moves were constructive and decisive. He allowed Frye to order Boeing's new four-engined Stratoliner and he secretly commissioned Lockheed to build a new airliner to fly sixty passengers at 350 miles an hour, to cross the US in ten hours. The Constellation, as it was later called, was designed in detail by Lockheed, but it was Hughes' brainchild, one of the most effective and beautiful planes ever built, with its curved back and triple fin like a magnificent dolphin. After the long delay of the war, when the air force took over most of TWA's fleet, the Constellations and Stratoliners gave TWA a critical opportunity to expand across the Atlantic, and thence across the world. By 1944 Jack Frye was predicting that "long-range planes with speeds of 425 miles an hour will shrink the world to the point where travellers can circle the globe in fifty-four flying hours".

7

TWO TYCOONS

The first battles between TWA and Pan Am were not across the Atlantic but in Washington, where Hughes proved more than a match for Juan Trippe. After the setback for his Community Airline bill Trippe tried to merge with other airlines, and began relentlessly pursuing Hughes to try to buy TWA; but when Trippe eventually caught up with him in Washington Hughes put an absurd value on his airline and walked out. Trippe still persisted with his Community Airline and in 1947 he brought his bill back to the Senate, supported by a clutch of senators including Owen Brewster, sometimes called the Senator from Pan Am. Trippe again appeared to be voluntarily relinquishing his own power in favour of the national interest. "The real competition in the field of international air transportation," said his supporter Senator McCarren, "is between nations, not between companies." But his rivals were now well organised, and in a booklet called "The New Monopoly Aviation Bill" they described the dangers of Pan American's power, including how the airline "practically ran their own State Department" in South America. The heads of other airlines, led by Cyrus Smith of American, testified against the bill and it never reached the floor of the Senate.

It was Howard Hughes who dealt the death-blow, by demolishing Trippe's loyal senator Brewster. A War Investigating Committee, which included Brewster, had accused Hughes of having bribed air-force officers including Roosevelt's son Elliott. Hughes retorted by charging Brewster with lying, and with having promised Hughes that he would call off the investigation if he agreed to merge TWA with Pan Am. Hughes appeared personally before the committee, in a dirty shirt without a tie, and swiftly demolished not only Brewster but also the rest of the committee. The hearings were adjourned, Brewster was not re-elected, and nothing more was heard of Pan Am's campaign to remain the chosen instrument.

Trippe's monopoly was not what it was. Jack Frye had been a crony of Harry Truman at the TWA base at Kansas City, near Truman's home state of Missouri; and Truman as a senator frequently flew by TWA to Washington. When Truman became president (the airline's historian Robert Serling insists) "Truman's warm associations with TWA were suspended, naturally." But TWA executives still looked to their friend in the White House, even if he was less supportive than they had hoped. There was a dramatic test of strength in 1950, when Trippe had applied to take over the flights of American Overseas Airlines, which Cyrus Smith no longer wanted to operate. The CAB turned down the merger, but to TWA's horror Truman then reversed the decision, thus greatly strengthening Pan Am's European network. Then (according to one TWA source) TWA swiftly sent an intermediary round to the White House and obtained permission for TWA to compete with Pan Am on valuable flights to London and Frankfurt. Trippe had achieved a very partial victory. He had failed to get any domestic routes for Pan Am; while TWA could now operate with its landplanes both inside and outside America. Other airlines had little doubt that TWA could thank the president for its global expansion which followed.

By the late forties Pan American and TWA, now both with their fleets of Constellations, were extending their contest to transform the shape of the world. The contrast between their two dominating tycoons was like the contrast between two eras of aviation, the romantic and the commercial, the individualist and the corporate. Hughes, for all his self-obsession and paranoia, retained a love affair with the air that Trippe had long ago lost, which mingled with his fascination for Hollywood. Hughes thrived on TWA's association with film stars and insisted on every concession to Hollywood friends, bumping booked passengers if necessary. (When I flew across the Pacific in a TWA plane in the late fifties, half the cabin-space was shut off to make a luxury suite for Mike Todd and Liz Taylor.) TWA filled their inaugural flights with film stars, and always stressed the romance of flying in their advertising, with an image reinforced by the splendour of the Constellation. Hughes contributed his own eccentric panache, sometimes himself piloting inaugural flights: he liked to fly in bare feet "to get the feel of the plane"; and in 1947 he flew a Constellation full of journalists to show off the new automatic radar system. But he never had the discipline or consistency which Trippe maintained, to face up to the technical problems of a modern airline. "TWA was the film-star's airline," said Bob Six, "but American and United concentrated on becoming the businessmen's airlines." And as Hughes became more withdrawn and eccentric his chief executives found his behaviour increasingly impossible.

CROSSING THE WORLD

In June 1947 Trippe inaugurated the first round-the-world service by a single airline, travelling with a group of newspaper-owners. With several stops he took fourteen days—a far easier trip than his pre-war global journey via the South Atlantic in thirty-eight days. This time he flew from New York across the North Atlantic to London, then via Istanbul, Calcutta, Bangkok and Manila to Shanghai and Tokyo, then back across the Pacific via Wake Island —which two years earlier had been a Japanese stronghold.

But already Pan American's Far Eastern empire was being eroded by the invading Communist forces in China. In Shanghai, Chiang Kai-shek's finance minister asked Trippe to pass back to President Truman a secret plan to save China from the Communists, by imposing an American high commissioner: the written plan was pressed into Trippe's hands in the plane's lavatory just before he left for Tokyo. It was a tribute to Pan American's mystique that Trippe should seem a more influential conduit than the American ambassador; but the plan came to nothing, and soon afterwards Shanghai, and the Pan American office, were in Communist hands.

Pan Am's territory had also been invaded by TWA. In February 1946 the first TWA Constellation had taken off from the new La Guardia airport in New York to inaugurate the first commercial air service to Paris, stopping at Gander and Shannon. Six days later another TWA plane, with Archbishop Spellman on board, flew via Paris to Rome, to begin the first transatlantic service to Italy. The next month a new DC-4 plane flew via Paris to Cairo, covering six thousand miles in twenty-nine hours. In August TWA was given permission to fly beyond India to French Indo-China and to China itself; but before TWA could reach China the civil war and the Communist victory had shut out American airlines.

By 1950 TWA was competing more directly with Pan Am, flying into London and Frankfurt and offering an all-sleeper service on the fifteen-hour flight to Paris; and by the end of the year TWA was regularly serving four continents with fifty-five Constellations. To help establish its own global network TWA reached agreements with developing countries—including Iran, Saudi Arabia, the Philippines and Ethiopia—to train pilots and crews, which they called their "private Marshall aid". By 1957 TWA could offer a joint round-the-world service with Northwest Orient (as the Minnesota airline was now called) connecting at Manila, to challenge Pan Am.

But this huge expansion rested on a wobbly base: for Hughes' control was increasingly erratic: he was becoming much more paranoid, often negotiating on the telephone without revealing his whereabouts. While Trippe ran his airline for nearly five decades, Hughes fired five chief executives during his twenty-year rule: the airline was like Belgium, the employees complained, always getting invaded. In 1947, after a spate of losses, Hughes fired Jack Frye who had first brought him in, and put in a stop-gap, LaMotte Cohu. Then he hired the former general manager of American Airlines, Ralph Damon, who survived until he died six years later in 1955 from a heart attack. His successor Carter Burgess lasted only a year, to be followed by a retired chain-store boss, Charles Thomas—"Two-pants Charlie"—who resigned in despair after two years. By then Hughes himself was losing his control.

AIRLINES AND GOVERNMENTS

However commercially adventurous the international airlines, they could not ignore their dependence on Washington. The legendary influence of Pan Am continued to excite its political opponents, and in 1956 the tough old nut Emmanuel Celler, the chairman of the House Anti-trust Sub-committee, conducted hearings to investigate Pan American's monopoly. His report found that Pan American accounted for over half the total route mileage of all American airlines abroad, serving 111 cities compared to TWA's twenty-six; and it complained about Pan Am's "sharp business practices" to exclude rival airlines. But Pan American no longer dominated the air-routes as it once did. In the post-war years each Latin American nation soon insisted upon owning its own airline. Cuba, where Trippe had his first foreign beachhead, nationalised Compania Cubana in 1954. Aeronaves de Mexico, of which Pan Am had bought forty per cent in 1940, was nationalised in 1959. Panair do Brasil was nationalised in 1961—only to disappear in 1965 when its European routes were taken over by Varig. The China National Aviation Corporation (CNAC) which Pan Am had part-owned, saw its routes dwindle as the Communists took over China: eventually its managing director defected to Peking with a fifth of the fleet and Trippe sold out his remaining share. But in the meantime Pan Am was also making new links in other parts of the world, in ways which aroused suspicions that it was acting as an arm of government.

While Trippe was moving out of China he was moving into the Lebanon, giving the newly formed Middle East Airlines three old DC-3s in 1949 in return for thirty-six per cent of the stock; but the Lebanese were not very welcoming to Pan Am, and Trippe soon sold out to the Intra Bank in Beirut. In 1956, pressed by the State Department, he agreed to buy a half-share in the new Afghan airline, Ariana, with the help of a loan from the Export-Import bank. And Pan Am, like TWA, was encouraged to provide technical assistance to other airlines—including the Turks, Thais, Iranians and Pakistanis.

Though Pan American was no longer the sole chosen instrument it retained its special relationship with Washington, doing and receiving favours. Trippe liked to explain that his airline was helping to save the world for democracy, but he was well recompensed for his efforts. Foreigners suspected all American airlines of being closely linked to the CIA, but particularly Pan American—with some reason. Trippe had high-level access to the intelligence world through his well connected board, including David Bruce, one of the original OSS team. The wartime collaboration with the armed forces continued into peacetime: Pan American could provide invaluable cover for agents to watch or trail passengers, and in the key listening-posts like Panama or Miami it could enable the CIA to keep track of political figures. Trippe's lobbyist Sam Pryor, who provided the chief link with the CIA, was involved in plans to discredit President Sukarno in Indonesia, arranging to bug a Pan Am plane chartered to him, and hiring Hamburg prostitutes to dress up as stewardesses.

But other overseas airlines also offered irresistible temptations to the CIA, whether as the means to keep track of suspects or to provide mobility to its agents. Just after the war the American businessman Orvis Nelson set up Transocean Air Lines which was later subsidised by the CIA and which helped to set up a succession of other new airlines, including Air Jordan, Iran Air and Pakair. Thomas Braniff, the right-wing founder-president of Braniff Airways, provided links with the Agency in Latin America. Flying Tigers, the daring airline in China run by General Claire Chennault, had been set up by William Pawley, the ex-head of the Pan Am subsidiary CNAC, and later turned into Civil Air Transport, which was run by the CIA from Taiwan with their other interlocking "proprietary" airlines including Air America and Air Asia. Their pilots and crews, wrote Ray Kline who supervised them in Taipeh, "were true soldiers of fortune and accepted enormous risks on long, clandestine missions over hostile territory".

Later the Vietnam war was to provide new scope for co-operation between airlines and intelligence. Air America was used by the CIA to supply its own private army to harass the North Vietnamese; and Robert Six of Continental Airlines was involved in secret operations, he told me, for fourteen years. In 1965 he was approached "by certain people" to set up a subsidiary in Laos called Continental Air Services to work for the US Aid Agency, with the backing of the CIA. The airline was run by a veteran CIA pilot and operator Dutch Brogersma, and it was supervised by Pierre Salinger, President Kennedy's former press secretary whom Six had hired as his political adviser. The airline's old DC-3s and C-54s flew bags of rice to the encampments, including "heavy rice" which meant guns and ammunition, and Salinger soon discovered that most of the airline's employees were former CIA experts. But their objectives were obstructed by the web of corruption: Continental was supposed to pass fifteen per cent of its revenues to Air Vietnam to help its development, but the money only got as far as the officials of the South Vietnam government; and Salinger concluded that the Saigon government was corrupt from top to bottom. It was not

until after the end of the Vietnam war in 1975 that the CIA finally
phased out its network of secret airlines, and their veterans still
hold reunions of the "Ageing Warriors" in Bangkok.

The spread of airliners round the world, whether American or
others, provided new opportunities for all intelligence agencies to
keep track of their enemies and conceal their own agents. Mossad
used El Al, Boss used South African Airways, the KGB used
Aeroflot. But after Vietnam the CIA abandoned most of its "proprietaries", while the launching of satellites deprived airlines of
their advantage as instruments of surveillance: the Soviets knew that
the CIA and the NSA could map every inch of their ground from the
sky. Intelligence agencies continued periodically to use airlines to
plant disguised hostesses, clerks or co-pilots. "I'd be surprised if
Pan American and British Airways aren't still used by intelligence,"
said Bob Six who still belongs to the Foreign Intelligence Board in
Washington. But as airlines developed into their next stage, as
mass-carriers and flying hotels, they began to lose their sinister
associations as well as their glamour.

5

Imperial Hangover

FACED with this American supremacy, the British were determined
to make the most of their global network of airports and bases which
gave them an advantage over their European rivals. While they
were dissolving their empire they could still maintain influence over
their former possessions, to give them chips in the great game of
landing rights. But that advantage could be misleading; for British
governments were so preoccupied with hanging on to their routes
and rights that they sometimes lost out on the new opportunities,
particularly in the Far East, which were seized by less privileged
airlines.

The nationalised British airline, the British Overseas Airways
Corporation, found it hard to escape from the politicians' control,
and the post-war governments zealously protected their own aircraft
industry, producing a succession of costly fiascos—the Tudor, the
Hermes, the Brabazon, the Princess flying boat. The British stuck
to flying boats long after others had abandoned them as uneconomic,
and in 1947 BOAC had 175 aircraft of eighteen different types run
by a top-heavy staff of 24,000 employees round the world: "too
many people flying typewriters", as the pilots complained.

BOAC still inherited some illusions of grandeur from its predecessor Imperial Airways, which were encouraged when its European
routes were split off in 1946 to form a separate nationalised corporation, British European Airways. BOAC people were inclined to
regard BEA as socially inferior—a class-distinction which still
rankled after three decades. But BEA were much more successful
in commissioning efficient British planes and they resented BOAC's
extravagance and their close links with Americans, which encouraged high living in an age of British austerity. As their chief

executive Peter Masefield later complained, "BOAC were almost in Boeing's pocket."

With all its proud spirit BOAC soon became the most knocked-about of political footballs, under a quick succession of chairmen who were caught between trying to make a profit and having to buy British planes and to fly Commonwealth routes. "There was no really big man, with a vision of the future," as one aviation veteran complained, "no one who could stand up to the ministers." The unhappy history of BOAC revealed all the British politicians' reluctance to take aviation seriously. When the Welsh car tycoon Sir Miles Thomas took over BOAC in 1949 he was appalled by "the cloying sense of lushness, that money did not matter" and by the amateur attitudes to organisation and even maintenance: "more often than not an aeroplane flew far less well after some of those so-called overhauls". After a seven year stint—longer than any successor—Sir Miles had induced some realism, abandoning the extravagant flying boats and introducing serious costing. But he was dispirited by "the failure of successive 'world-beaters' to beat anything at all", and he resigned after a row with his minister, Alan Lennox-Boyd. "Did the government want a strong, financially viable long-range airline or just a political pawn?"

The question was never properly answered by later chairmen. "I never believed it was the Corporation's job to make profits," said Sir Miles' successor, "Pops" d'Erlanger. "The Corporation was there to support the British aircraft industry and to develop routes round the world." "I think the way it is expected to operate is bloody crazy," said *his* successor, Sir Matthew Slattery, when he left in dudgeon. In 1974, as part of the merger-mania, BOAC was remerged with BEA to create "British Airways". But it was never a real merger, most jobs remained duplicated and the "public school airline" continued to look down on the "grammar school airline". Chairmen continued to come and go, alternating between politicians ignorant of airlines and professionals bewildered by politics.

Without the Empire, the British still looked to the air to hold together its successor, the Commonwealth. BOAC's chief political objective (Slattery told me in 1961) was "to try and keep the Commonwealth linked with Commonwealth airlines". In the first flush of internationalism after the war the British had actually created a regional airline, pooling BOAC's resources with Australia and New Zealand to make the British Commonwealth Pacific Airline. The BCPA was planned, as Hudson Fysh of Qantas saw it, to "avoid inter-Empire competition and present a bold front to the great rivals, such as Pan American Airways"; but it soon ran into quarrels. Fysh was always sceptical about co-operating with

other countries and kept asking "Where will the headquarters be?"
Canada would not join, and its airline TCA ran a competing service
from Vancouver to Sydney. When the British Tudor airliners proved
treacherous the airline had to buy American planes. By 1954 both
BOAC and Qantas wanted their own round-the-world flights and
BCPA was dissolved.

The route between Britain and Australia was still the vital chain,
made up of the ex-imperial links. BOAC and Qantas at first kept
their joint airline Queensland Empire Airways, but BOAC persisted
(Fysh complained) "in sticking to British aircraft come hell or high
water", while the Australians were really more air-minded than the
British. After mounting tension Qantas took over its own flights to
Europe and soon grew into a major international airline, flying the
longest routes in the world. By 1958—when Pan Am still could
not fly across America—Qantas became the first airline to run a
scheduled service across the world. The airline with the funny name
which had begun in the outback thirty-five years earlier could well
claim a "qantastic" performance.

British Airways still had its unique legacy of destinations and
partnerships with a shared language and history. But the idea of a
Commonwealth network was never so convincing again as the
grown-up protégés like Qantas, Air India or South African Airways
—each with a much more extensive domestic system than
Britain's—extended their own routes to America or the Far East.
The rapid development of aviation, far from strengthening the influence of the British Isles over these vast territories, encouraged the opposite effect of opening up their new trade and tourist routes to
other countries across the Pacific or the Indian Ocean, by-passing
the mother-country with its small base and its indecisive air policy.

WHO OWNS?

All these English-speaking airlines except the Americans had been
nationalised—though for pragmatic rather than ideological reasons.
It was a Conservative government which had first nationalised
Imperial Airways in 1939, leaving it little scope for autonomy, and
still less under the post-war Labour government. The Canadian
government had created the Trans-Canada Airlines in 1937 in an
ideological muddle; but TCA was stabilised when Gordon
McGregor became its president in 1948 and stayed for twenty years.
"You keep out of the taxpayer's pocket," said his minister, C. D.
Howe, "and I'll keep out of your hair"; and McGregor effectively
dominated the airline—whose name was changed in 1964 to the

more bilingual Air Canada to placate the French-speakers. Even the phenomenal Qantas, with its rugged free-enterprise past, succumbed to the state. The Australian post-war Labour government insisted on buying the national airline, partly to protect it against American incursions; but it assuaged criticism by leaving it under the same durable chairman Hudson Fysh and not disturbing the commercial organisation.

"It is interesting that governments which are reluctant to grant autonomy to other enterprises," wrote Kenneth Galbraith in 1967, "regularly accord it to their airline and often with very good results. It seems possible that public officials, who are among the most important patrons, sense the unique dangers of denying autonomy to this industry." Certainly the concern for safety helped to frighten off politicians and civil servants from interfering with airlines; but the most important element was the personality and continuity at the top. It was BOAC under successive exasperated chairmen which was most hamstrung by governments and took some of the worst decisions, while the unchanging leadership of Air Canada and Qantas was much more far-sighted; and it was the ex-pilots—who had the feel of the air and could defy know-nothing ministers—like Fysh, McGregor or Lord Douglas of BEA, who tended to be most decisive. The airlines all needed a vision of the future which required confident leadership; but as they became complex and more dependent on finance and marketing, the qualifications were much harder to fill.

There was one maverick British exception in Hong Kong which had managed to escape the spread of nationalisation and to carve out its own prosperous territory in the Far East. It began when an adventurous Australian pilot, Sydney de Kantzow, who had been flying "the hump" between India and China during the war, teamed up after the war with an American businessman-pilot Roy Farrell. While the Communists were advancing through China the two pilots began flying DC-3s between Calcutta and Chungking, until in 1946 they set up their own tiny airline in the comparative safety of Hong Kong. To avoid the red taint of the word China, and to suggest their oceanic ambitions, they called it Cathay Pacific. It expanded rapidly, flying immigrants on charter flights to Australia, gold between Hong Kong and Macao or freight from Australia to Hong Kong. BOAC, seeing Cathay's success, soon stepped up its own flights and formed a rival airline called Hong Kong Airways, jointly with the rich local traders Jardine Matheson; while John Swire, who ran the rival local trading company or "hong" and was excited by the future of air travel, saw a chance to buy control of Cathay. A long battle followed between the two hongs, with BOAC moving in and out of Hong Kong Airways and doing their best to squeeze Cathay out of the best routes. But the colonial government became more independent-minded as Hong Kong increased its economic power and there followed, as one of Cathay's pioneer pilots Chic Eather described it, "a gradual escalation of intrigue", with "the home government supporting BOAC, the Hong Kong government manfully standing up for their local Cathay Pacific". Swire's with their shipping contacts and parsimonious Scots tradition were able to make a profit out of their airline from the beginning—"we knew the people, and we knew the routes," as one Swire's man explained it—while BOAC made heavy losses until in 1959 it finally agreed to merge Hong Kong Airways into Cathay Pacific, with Swire's holding control. The maverick private airline, surrounded by its state-owned competitors, was becoming a beneficiary of the great Pacific boom which increased air travel far more rapidly than in the West; while BOAC and its successor British Airways were losing on the one region which showed the most promising prospects.

But whether private, nationalised or subsidised, all airlines were now heavily dependent on their governments for their diplomacy and their routes; and most governments outside America were determined to have their own flag-carrier on which they could rely. The names of the new national airlines—mostly beginning with the conveniently Anglo-French word Air—made the point. The planes painted in their national colours and the glossy showrooms and advertising in the foreign capitals were becoming more visible representatives than embassies or sports teams. And the airlines were all appealing to their countrymen—in the words of British Airways' crude slogan—to "fly the flag".

6

Europe Fragmented

We want the air to unite the peoples, and not to divide them.
Lord Swinton, 1945

WHILE the Americans raced ahead with routes and technology, the Europeans were back with all their problems of political disunity. In their own continent they were more circumscribed than ever. Eastern Europe was cut off, the Soviet Union was still more obsessed by the sovereignty of its airspace. When the Russians tried to cut off and absorb West Berlin in 1948 the Allied airlift revealed how effectively planes could replace trains and trucks, and also gave a huge boost to the charter operators who joined the airlift. But the Berlin crisis underlined the ruthlessness of the division of Europe.

And the Western Europeans soon reverted to their old national competition in the air. They never accepted the flexibility of the Bermuda agreement: they insisted on fixing frequencies and fares rigidly beforehand—which in the US would immediately have brought them up against the anti-trust laws. And they were backed up in their fare-fixing by IATA, which was not inhibited in Europe as it was in America. Its director-general Sir William Hildred insisted on a "firm corset", as he called it, of properly controlled traffic regulations, and he imposed fines on any airline found to be cheating. "There was a team of twenty men, looking for trouble—and finding it."

The European airlines successfully limited their competition through the "pools" which shared the profits between the two ends of the route, and which soon spread to nearly all routes within the continent. The pools had the obvious benefit of allowing airlines to work out a sensible timetable between them, without competing for the same peak-times. But neither side had much incentive to cut fares or improve service; and the pooled airlines could complacently settle down into a network of semi-monopolies. The busiest route, between London and Paris, was carved up between BEA and Air France; the second busiest, from London to Geneva, between BEA and Swissair. IATA regulated not only fares but standards of service and food—which led to the farce of the "great sandwich war" when the Scandinavians were accused of cheating by providing sumptuous smorgasbord instead of the statutory IATA sandwich. The old tradition of European cartels was all the more effective because most airlines were now nationalised. And IATA was backed both by airlines and governments.

Was IATA a genuine cartel? "I made lots of speeches proving it wasn't a cartel," said Hildred. "A cartel exists to keep prices up, but we lived to get prices down." Certainly, like the oil companies—the "Seven Sisters"—during the same period the members of IATA dared not keep prices too high; and periodically the American airlines forced them down across the Atlantic. In the early post-war years IATA succeeded remarkably in bringing order out of chaos, co-ordinating and synchronising the polyglot airlines. Its agreements were little questioned; and in 1949 IATA could claim that it had "at last welded together the services of the world's airlines into an integrated world transport system". But as more Europeans began flying and noticing the lower fares on the other side of the Atlantic they were more concerned about IATA's controls: and there was little doubt that IATA, like the CAB within the United States, helped to limit innovation. By 1968 it could be described as "one of the most hated cartels in the world".

Within their "corset" each national airline tried to increase its share of the market and routes. The new British European Airways had an obvious head-start; and it was decisively led by one of the giants of the business. Air Marshal Lord Douglas was a bulky war-hero with a chin like a spade, whom politicians preferred not to argue with: he had been awarded Britain's fourth commercial pilot's licence in 1919, when he flew planes between London and Paris; and he was much helped by his chief executive Peter Masefield, an unusually articulate engineer and pilot. BEA was uncomplicated by the ex-imperial pretensions of BOAC and it collaborated profitably with British manufacturers, flying first the De Havilland Elizabethan and then the Vickers Viscount—the only really successful British post-war plane. In the fifties BEA carried a quarter of all Western European air passengers and made a profit for five years in succession. "We're the most competitive industry in the world," Douglas insisted, and BEA's motto was *Clavis Europae*, the

key to Europe. London was both the biggest city in Europe and the
hub between two continents.

The ancient cross purposes between Britain and France soon
reasserted themselves, and the airports of London and Paris had
almost opposite conceptions. Heathrow, on Hounslow Heath which
had been the scene of early flights, sprawled its way up from
makeshift huts to brick terminals and hangars which were always
one stage too late, with a mixture of pragmatism and pessimism;
while Orly airport rose up as a glittering symbol of French air
ambitions, later followed by the futuristic tubular shapes of Charles
de Gaulle airport—both monuments to French decisiveness and
planning which kept foreign airlines and competition firmly in their
place.

The French were determined to catch up after the wreckage of
war with all the force of their diplomacy: they still had their network
of overseas colonies, and their lack of colour prejudice made them
better than the British at negotiating with the young countries. In
1948 the French government had bought a majority share of the
old private company Air France, and put all the power of the state
behind it, with a succession of French civil servants in charge. By
1952 Air France could claim to be the world's biggest airline in
terms of its unduplicated mileage, flying all through French West
Africa, the French West Indies and as far as the remote outpost of
New Caledonia between Australia and New Guinea. In the meantime two independent airlines, TAI and UAT, both originating in
Africa, were asserting their political power at home; by 1956 the
French drastically carved up their air world so that Air France
withdrew from the Pacific and much of Africa, and in 1963 the two
independents merged to form UTA, a privately-owned company,
with part of the Schlumberger family as big shareholders. UTA
inherited most of the former French empire, including a share in
the Air Afrique, linking French-speaking territories round the world
with a remarkably self-contained network. "The quickest way to
fly from Malagasy to West Africa," I was told by the present head
of UTA René Lapautre, "is through Paris." The Francophone
routes by which passengers could fly round the world without ever
speaking English were a striking achievement. But the French
language never regained its hold on the wider air world.

The most vigorous European competition was once again between
the British and KLM, still run by the irrepressible Albert Plesman:
he had been first jailed, then confined to Eastern Holland during
the war, and he came under a cloud for having been too friendly to
the Germans; but he was indispensable to the Dutch, and he
returned to the world stage undeterred. "He *was* KLM—though

he never had a seat on their board," Hildred recalled. "He would sit listening for half an hour, and then say 'I vill now tell you vat you vill do.' " Plesman and Lord Douglas were old pioneering friends ever since Douglas flew a De Havilland plane across to Plesman's aviation exhibition in 1919; but this added to their rivalry, and KLM made no "pool" with the British. Plesman came back to KLM to find it with no planes and with its runways at Schiphol full of craters; but he was more flexible than the British, with no obligation to a home aircraft industry and with his government right behind him, and he quickly flew to America and bought thirty DC-3s and eighteen DC-4s: by the end of 1945 KLM was flying again to Jakarta, and in May the following year it was the first European airline to fly regularly to New York. In the same year it flew to Curacao, thus linking up with its West Indies service which had kept going through the war; but KLM lost important bargaining power when the Dutch East Indies became the independent state of Indonesia, and it had to compete more aggressively to attract long-distance traffic away from London to its hub at Schiphol.

Other Europeans competed from the rival hubs to attract overseas traffic. The Belgian Sabena was still enriched by the Congo, while Brussels attracted multinational companies, the European Community headquarters and later NATO. The Italians, though ex-enemies, were allowed by 1947 to have their own airlines—seven of them, eventually merged into one Alitalia. It began under the aegis of British European Airways, which owned thirty per cent until as late as 1961; but it leapt ahead as a national airline heavily protected by the state, linking up with the millions of Italian emigrants in New York, Buenos Aires or Sao Paulo. The Spanish airline Iberia, under the wing of Franco, also expanded rapidly overseas to make closer connections with the ex-Spanish empire in Latin America; though within Europe it was the most protective of all, insisting on a half-share of all traffic in its pools. The Portuguese TAP was sometimes unpredictable ("Take Another Plane") but outstandingly safe, and like Alitalia and Iberia it found new scope in Latin America. The relationships between Southern Europe and South America became far closer by air than they could ever be by sea.

For ten years after the war the Germans were forbidden to own or operate their own planes; and they could only bitterly watch other airlines flying into their country, profiting from their internal traffic. Pan American established its own colony in Frankfurt, the American military headquarters, and its flights inside West Germany accounted for five per cent of the total of all Western European air travel. In 1951 a persistent pre-war Lufthansa executive, Hans Bongers, began pressing the Allies to allow a skeleton German airline, but it was not until 1955 that the Paris Treaties gave back to West Germany the sovereignty over its airspace. In the same year the "New Lufthansa" began flying with the help of TWA, first to New York, then along the old German South Atlantic route to Latin America. The Lufthansa name was still magnetic in spite of Nazi associations and the East Germans also called their airline Lufthansa until they were sued and had to change it to Interflug. In Frankfurt the New Lufthansa, with the familiar symbol of the blue and yellow crane, re-established its name for service and reliability rather than romance. "For too long we've been kidding ourselves," said a Lufthansa advertisement in the sixties, "that anything to do with flying is fun, glamour, excitement. Well, it isn't." It established the busiest internal network in Europe, flying businessmen between the rival cities (though the Soviets to this day forbid it to fly to West Berlin); and since West Germany has no single centre it could claim to be "the capital in the air"—where Germans were more likely to meet each other than anywhere else.

THE NEW MAP OF EUROPE

The air boom of the fifties seemed to make nonsense of the old frontiers of Western Europe. The Alps and the Pyrenees no longer cut off Italy and Spain from the North as millions of tourists flew over them without even noticing, often flying on charters to the Mediterranean sun more cheaply than they could visit parts of their own country. The journey from Athens to London, which took three days by train in 1950, took four hours by air in 1960. Air travel held the promise of transforming the relationships of outlying countries, like Britain and Norway, which had depended on awkward sea-links to the mainland.

The geography of the old Europe was turned inside-out as the expanding airports challenged the dominance of the old seaports. Hamburg, once the terminus of the proud ocean liners and the most cosmopolitan German city, was not only deprived of markets by the iron curtain, but was eclipsed by the inland port of Frankfurt which became the hub of the Lufthansa system, while Hamburg airport became a provincial outpost with far fewer international flights—only partly compensated by Lufthansa repair shops. The Italian seaports of Genoa or Brindisi languished while Milan and Rome airports thrived with cosmopolitan business.

But the density and concentration of Europe soon imposed their own obstacles to easy air travel, and set a pattern quite different from America's. The north-west of the continent—the "golden triangle"—was already criss-crossed with railways and roads. The three airports of Paris, Brussels and Schiphol—each determined to be international gateways—were within two or three hours' drive of each other. And the airlanes were further confined by the restrictions of the military, which compelled airliners to divert along dog-legs. The air which had looked so boundless to Blériot or Lindbergh was now an invisible maze of narrow lanes zig-zagging above the continent.

For a time the concentration of people seemed "a helicopter protagonist's dream": in 1951 BEA planned a service with a Fairey Rotodyne, to carry sixty passengers from the centre of London to the centre of Paris at 200 mph; while in 1953 Sabena launched the first international helicopter service, flying into France, Holland and Germany to pick up passengers for long-distance flights. But by the mid-sixties the dreams of vertical take-off from cities were confined to the rich. And the railroads which had first forged the European city centres together in the previous century could still fight back, as they could not in the United States. After 1957 the new luxury trains of the Trans Europ Express could effortlessly cross frontiers; and the French and British began racing each other to produce high-speed trains. The Europeans were much more committed than the Americans to preserving their inner cities, which were threatened by airports but strengthened by railway stations.

But the chief obstacle to cheap and efficient air travel was undoubtedly the political divisions of Europe. There were some hopes during the war that Hitler's tyranny might be turned to advantage in peacetime. "There can be no question but that European services are now operating under the unified control of Germany," wrote Sir Osborne Mance in 1943, "and hence the moment is particularly propitious for considering the future of air transport in Europe with special reference to unification." Mance even visualised an international air corporation in which existing national airlines would be shareholders, negotiated perhaps by IATA.

But these visions evaporated in peacetime. "Nationalism was soon rising," said Sir Peter Masefield, looking back at his time at BEA, "which retarded European air transport and gave the Americans a huge advantage." The restrictions of cabotage—flying between foreign airports—meant that the British, for instance, could never fly from London to Paris and then on to Nice or Rome—which would have immediately brought down the costs. And the multiplication of national bureaucracies, air traffic controls and supervisors added to both fares and delays.

The governments still had periodic discussions about creating a single European airline, and in 1952 Plesman of KLM founded an air research bureau supported by the six major airlines to try to co-ordinate their plans. But Plesman died the next year, and the bureau made little progress. When nineteen European nations assembled at the Strasbourg aviation conference in 1954 they said little about plans for unification; instead they established the European Civil Aviation Conference (ECAC) to bring together Ministers of Transport, who did little to co-ordinate the airlines. Each airline, backed by its own government, saw its objectives in national terms, based on its own hub airport, its own self-contained crews, staff and maintenance. The most obvious overlaps were between KLM and Sabena, with their headquarters only 150 miles apart. KLM, still partly privately owned—with a large American sharehold-ing—was always profitable while Sabena was consistently subsi-dised and less efficient. There were later serious discussions about merging the two airlines to produce obvious economies; but the Belgians, split between French-speakers and Flemish-speakers, could not agree.

When six European nations signed the Treaty of Rome in 1957, to set up the European Community, there was a new opportunity to integrate the airlines. Article 3 of the treaty proposed "the inauguration of a common transport policy", and "the establish-ment of a system ensuring that competition shall not be distorted in the Common Market". Article 84 of the treaty described the provisions for a transport policy; though it excluded sea and air transport and left the Council of Ministers to decide "whether, to what extent, and by what procedure" they should be regulated by the Community. More hopefully Article 85 defined distortion of competition as including the "direct or indirect fixing of purchase or selling prices or of any other trading conditions" and also "market-sharing or the sharing of sources of supply"—which plainly went against any form of fare-fixing. But the European Community showed little political will to champion the consumer. By 1964 the Commissioners had decided that the common transport policy should apply to both air and sea, but the politicians in the Council of Ministers had no desire to disturb the pools and cartels between airlines.

In the meantime in 1957 Lufthansa had proposed to Air France a closer collaboration to fix quotas and co-ordinate timetables, and the next year they were joined by Sabena and Alitalia. After awkward arguments the four airlines in 1959 established a group called Air Union, partly modelled on Europ Pool, the successful co-operation between railways. Air Union was able to agree on quotas for its members, and more rational timetables, and there were high hopes of its closer integration. "Air Union and the Common Market are surely indivisible," wrote R. E. G. Davies in his study of airlines in 1964. "When all the political barriers are broken down . . . then perhaps a joint European airline will stand a real chance of success." In the same year there was an attempt to push the union further within the framework of the European Community. But both Lufthansa and Alitalia—both latecomers who wanted to catch up—were now opposed to restrictions of quotas; and the airlines could never agree on the most critical aim of any union, the joint buying of aircraft. The national airlines became more entrenched as the idealism of the European movement waned.

THE SWISS SECRET

The most strikingly successful national airline belonged to a neutral country very insulated from the rest; and the air served to separate it further. The Swiss in their landlocked country, could use the air not only to fly over the encircling Alps, but to travel direct to client countries across the world. It was no accident that Swissair became the fastest-growing airline in Europe, and one of the few that were consistently profitable. For air travel called for traditional Swiss skills—whether the strict military discipline, the hoteliers' dedication to service, the mastery of languages, the bankers' internationalism or the mercantilism of the state. If Switzerland, as its many enemies complained, was more like a bank than a country, then the airline was a boon for bankers which they could shrewdly exploit to develop their commercial foreign policy and enrich their money-haven. But politically it distanced Switzerland still further from its European neighbours.

Swissair had been created by the merger of two small airlines in 1931, who shrewdly chose a neutral English-sounding name. But the company had no proper leader, and in the post-war years it faced a financial crisis and had to be bailed out by the state. In 1950 the board appointed the first general manager, Walter Berchtold, a mountain climber and former railway manager who speedily introduced the combination of strict discipline and delegation which he had admired in the Swiss army. In the fifties Swissair followed the most lucrative trade-routes, first to New York, then in 1954 to South America, then in 1957 to Tokyo. From the mid-fifties it doubled its business every five years. It remained privately owned, but always supported by the Swiss government. By 1971 when Berchtold retired the Zurich headquarters was the centre of a global network, linked up with Swissair hotels, agents and banks as a model of mercantilist planning.

Swissair's success soon influenced rivals. Across the Alps the state-owned Austrian airline, set up in 1957, became so hamstrung by the two political parties that it discussed merging with Swissair; but the Austrians dreaded being dominated and eventually settled for a new management with Swiss advice and technical collaboration. Swissair also helped to salvage the Greek airline Olympic which had belonged to the shipowner Aristotle Onassis until he despaired of its unions and sold it to the Greek government. As airliners and airports became more like hotels the Swiss experience of catering gave them an extra advantage, and they provided the food for a whole chain of airports including Karachi, Buenos Aires, Cairo and Vienna. When the Swiss began flying jumbos Swissair linked up with both SAS and KLM to share the high costs of maintenance and adopted the same design for cockpits, galleys and cabins to make them interchangeable.

Swissair still provides a caricature of the new virtues of the air—punctuality, obedience, attention to detail, automatic politeness. It watches over baggage, children and animals with exemplary care: it keeps first-class seats on its short flights while other airlines have abolished theirs: bankers vote it their favourite airline. It relentlessly watches over its staff, listening in to their phone calls to check on their courtesy. It has developed its own all-embracing paternalism, with its own flats, clubs, sports grounds and brass band. Its discipline and dedication take their toll in terms of individualism, and Swissair is widely disliked by other airlines. "Look at their board," said an SAS man, "all engineers or pilots —no one who understands about people." "The much wanted human touch is often lacking," wrote one of its own pilots; "instead the working environment has become more sterile and impersonal." But Swissair knows that its skills are indispensable in the air. "People the world over may picture the Swiss as nothing other than efficient, hard-working, punctual and reliable," said Swissair's historian, Lorenz Stucki. "But there's no denying that these are virtues which do more for an airline passenger's confidence than disparaging clichés about pettiness or a lack of *joie de vivre* or culture."

SASPERANTO

There was one exception to the pattern of European nationalism—
the establishment of the three-nation Scandinavian Airlines System,
SAS. The trio, it is true, had common Viking ancestry and similar
languages, but they also harboured mutual resentments. Norway,
which had once been a province of Denmark, was given to Sweden
in 1814 and did not become independent until 1905. The Second
World War, when Sweden was neutral and Norway and Denmark
were occupied, divided them further. But they had a common
interest in an ambitious air service, both to stretch across the world
and to join up their own scattered communities. Malmo in the south
of Sweden can claim to be the middle of Europe—halfway between
the top of Norway and the south of Italy—and planes gave Scandinavians, like the Canadians, a new opportunity to open up their
frozen north.

They had first considered a joint airline in the thirties when they
all wanted to fly to America, and each had their own airline. The
Danish airline DDL, founded in 1919 and now only a holding
company, can claim like so many others to be the world's oldest.
All the Scandinavians were inspired when the Swedish-American
Charles Lindbergh visited Denmark and Sweden in 1933, after
reconnoitring Greenland for Pan American. The Norwegians briefly
agreed with Pan Am to fly jointly via Iceland to New York, and
even bought their own twin-engined flying boat, but Pan Am
abruptly cancelled the agreement. "The pleasure of eating cherries
with the big ones," as the Norwegian manager Riiser-Larsen put it,
had cost them dearly. They then tried to connect with transatlantic
flights through Ireland, but Pan Am was not interested in carrying
Norwegian mail. "It was Pan Am by its intransigence," recalled
Riiser-Larsen, "which spurred Scandinavian co-operation."

After war broke out in 1939 the Scandinavians could offer an
air-route that flew over the top of the conflict, while the Soviet
invasion of Finland called for closer links with the West. In early
1940 the three airlines talked again with Trippe of Pan Am, and by
April they had agreed jointly to operate flights from New York to
Bergen. But three days later the Germans invaded Norway. The
four years of war and occupation set back any progress, but the
neutral Swedes were determined to forge air links independently of
the Americans and British, encouraged by their powerful banker
Marcus Wallenberg. As the war turned, the Danes and Norwegians
began discreetly talking again with the Swedes about a joint airline.

The Bermuda conference in 1946 put an end to the Swedes'

hopes of "freedom of the air"; and the Scandinavians realised that
they must stick together to bargain for their rights round the world.
They had bitter arguments. Each country wanted its own capital
to be the air gateway to the Atlantic, and each wanted the work-
shops. But they at last agreed that the Swedes would own forty per
cent, and the others thirty per cent, while the headquarters would
be in Stockholm. And all three agreed on the man to run their fleet
operations—Peter Redpath, a Canadian-American who was trusted
to be impartial, and who could use English as the neutral language.
In the summer of 1946 a DC-4 Skymaster plane took off from
Stockholm to New York via Oslo, bearing the English name Scandinavian Airlines System.

In the following years SAS extended round Europe, developing
its own corporate loyalty, mixing up crews of different nationalities,
proudly calling itself a "miniature UN of the air", and even developing its own hybrid language which they called "Sasperanto". Within
Europe SAS had a head-start while the Germans were forbidden
their own airline, and when the New Lufthansa took back their
German traffic SAS fought back with a vigorous tourist campaign
which made the most of the "deviation" clause which allowed
long-distance travellers large detours, luring Americans to Wonderful Wonderful Copenhagen—which for a time had the fourth busiest
airport in Europe. But Copenhagen looked less wonderful to the
Norwegians who found their own Oslo airport out on a limb, and
who complained that "SAS is run by the Swedes for the benefit of
the Danes and paid for by the Norwegians." The supranational
idealism faded, and the nations' politics diverged further when
Denmark without Norway joined the European Community in
1973. Now each country has its own domestic rival to compete with
SAS.

Yet SAS made an impact on air transport which they could never
have achieved in three parts—a lesson to other small countries.
SAS' own collaboration encouraged it to look for overseas partners:
in 1959 it invested unsuccessfully in the Mexican airline Gamsa—
which eventually merged with Aeronaves—but also much more
successfully bought thirty per cent of Thai Airways International
(see chapter 12). The Scandinavians had always been conscious of
being "at the end of the line"; and their greatest triumph was across
the Arctic. As early as 1949 a Norwegian-American pilot, Bernt
Balchen, arrived in Oslo on a US air force plane after a non-stop
flight of twenty-two hours from Alaska, and forecast that this route
would one day be among the world's busiest. Three years later SAS
began actively planning flights across the Arctic, using special
instruments and radio stations for the uncharted route. In 1954 it

first opened up its "north-west passage" with a DC-6 plane flying from Copenhagen to Los Angeles via Greenland; and three years later it inaugurated the regular polar route via Alaska, which was to bear out Balchen's prediction. The polar route made lucrative links for SAS with Scandinavian emigrants, such as the Swedish-Americans on the west coast of America, bringing them within a few hours of their cousins.

THE COST OF NATIONALISM

The fragmentation of Europe provided growing problems for the airlines, as planes and maintenance became more expensive; but it was still more of a problem to the European aircraft industry which before the war had so proudly competed across the continents. Britain and France still had high ambitions and dedicated aeronautical engineers, who were pressed by their governments to compete with the Americans. But as the costs of developing new airliners multiplied the two nations competed for too small a market.

For a tantalising few years the development of jets appeared to give the British aircraft industry the technical lead that it longed for, and to provide BOAC with a unique Commonwealth network. Even before the end of the Second World War a British committee headed by Lord Brabazon had foreshadowed the development of commercial jets, and by 1952 BOAC proclaimed that it had "fathered the jet age in civil aviation" which would halve the travel time across the world. The Comet began flying from London to Johannesburg and aimed to extend "along the main arteries of the Commonwealth".

The Comet gave a huge boost to British confidence, but it was always too small and too short-range to be economic—as Lindbergh had warned Trippe at Pan American. In March 1954 the British hopes collapsed after three Comets had crashed and all were grounded. After recovering the wreckage and making exhaustive tests the engineers traced the fault to the weakness of the skin round the windows and set about designing the new Comet 4. But the grounding left BOAC with a disastrous lack of planes, exacerbated by the delays in delivering the new British turbo-prop, the Britannia. By the time the Comet 4 was flying, it was overshadowed in both size and range by the Boeing 707. The tragedy of the Comet crashes continued to stir up frustrations and speculations of "if only . . . " But it was never probable that Britain with its limited home market could have maintained its jet lead.

The Comet disasters gave all the more prestige to Air France when in 1959 it began flying its elegant jet the Caravelle, through Europe as far as Istanbul. In the next three years eleven other airlines began flying Caravelles, including United based on Chicago, and in Europe they had the same kind of success as BEA's Viscounts in the pre-jet age. The Caravelle continued to attract passengers for the following decade; but like the Comet it carried too few passengers to compete economically with the big American jets which overtook it. Neither the French nor British aircraft industries were big or bold enough to compete in the next jet contest, which was to herald a new phase of American supremacy in the air.

7

Jets and Mass Tourism

Cocooned in Time, at this inhuman height,
The packaged food tastes neutrally of clay.
We never seem to catch the running day
But travel on in everlasting night . . .

John Betjeman, A Nip in the Air

AT Pan American Juan Trippe faced much more competition during
the fifties, both from Europeans and Americans, but he remained
the unquestioned leader of his industry, infuriating his rivals at
IATA meetings by his pursuit of his own advantage. "He was really
only interested in one thing," said Sir Peter Masefield, "which was
money." "He was able but ruthless," said Sir William Hildred,
"with his smooth style and dark Spanish eyes you never knew what
he was thinking. He wouldn't fight: he would just go and do what
he wanted, ignoring the opposition; and no one dared to attack
him." "He was a real dictator," said Bob Six, "and he didn't know
where to stop." But Trippe's lonely determination set the pace for
the others, and it was he who pushed the western world into the jet
age, which transformed both the economics and the sociology of air
transport, making travel not only faster but more reliable and
cheaper and opening it up to a mass market who could never have
afforded to travel by sea.

It was Aeroflot in the Soviet Union which first began regular
long-distance jet flights in 1956—a fact often tactfully forgotten—
with their Tupolev 104 which flew from Moscow to Irkutsk with
only one stop, taking only seven hours instead of twenty. But this
first Soviet jet carried only fifty people, and it was left to the

Americans, learning from the lessons of the Comet, to develop a
bigger and more economic jet airliner. By the early fifties the major
American airlines were all beginning to think in terms of big jets,
but it was Trippe who most clearly foresaw how they could bring
down the cost of travel and enlarge the whole market.

With his usual stealth, Trippe saw a chance to leap ahead of
his rivals. He secretly bargained in turn with the three aircraft
manufacturers—Boeing, Douglas and Lockheed—to make a jet
plane big enough and with sufficient range to be profitable. Bill
Allen of Boeing had already made an air force jet transport, the
707, and he was determined as he said, "to put the 707 on the
airlines". With bullying, persistence and cunning Trippe compelled
Allen to extend his prototype with more powerful engines to carry
150 people across the Atlantic without a stop. He took a bet with
Allen that he could not produce the plane ahead of schedule—a bet
which Allen won—and ordered forty-five of the expensive new
planes to put him ahead of all rivals. Three years later, in October
1958, a Pan American 707 made the inaugural flight from New
York to Brussels, introducing the international jet age. It was,
boasted Trippe, the most important aviation development since
Lindbergh's flight across the Atlantic: "In one fell swoop we have
shrunken the earth."

It was a body-blow to TWA, which had fallen behind in the jet
revolution through a combination of wrong judgments and financial
crisis. Howard Hughes, according to one account, had considered
making his own deal with Bill Allen at Boeing to make the first 707s
exclusively for TWA; but Allen would not risk it, and Hughes
instead backed the more experimental Convair 880, made by General
Dynamics. Hughes eventually had to order the Boeings, but
he was now having difficulties in persuading his bankers to finance
them; and when the jet age first arrived TWA could only fly one
707. Hughes' fitful control was increasingly damaging the company;
it seemed an absurd anachronism for a major corporation to be still
owned by one wilful eccentric. Hughes was overcommitting himself
and getting deeper in debt to his bankers: "He wanted so badly to
retain TWA," wrote the airline's historian, "that he seemed willing
to ruin it." After TWA's chief executive Charlie Thomas resigned
in July 1960 in despair at Hughes' constant interference, the banks
at last refused to lend more unless Hughes gave up his control to a
voting trust. Hughes resisted until the last moment, while the
airline's future hung in the balance, but finally in December 1960
he signed away his control.

Hughes' departure was the cue for a rapid recovery in TWA's
fortunes. The voting trust brought in the kind of chief executive

that pilots dreaded—a lawyer with no experience of airlines, surrounded by accountants. Charles Tillinghast had been running the
international operation of Bendix, the brake-and-bearings company, a quite different business; but like other newcomers who
entered the proud and self-contained airline industry he often saw
its problems more clearly than many professionals. He perceived
that TWA's international routes were its greatest asset, and that
they could rapidly attract passengers if they had more long-range
jets to service them. He quickly ordered twenty-six new 707s with
fan-jet engines; he built up a management team to improve efficiency
and customer service; and he cut costs by beating down his suppliers'
prices. In the booming market of the early sixties Tillinghast turned
round TWA's fortunes until it made profits of $50 million in 1965.
The airline paid its own price: "We liked Tillinghast and admired
him," said an old TWA hand, "but somehow he took away TWA's
soul."

By a final irony Howard Hughes, now that he was powerless,
rapidly became far richer from TWA. The shares which were worth
$7 each after he lost control were worth $86 in mid-1965;
and at that point he finally sold all of them—making him $547
million dollars. His stormy association with TWA had provided a
case history of the awkward transition from one-man rule to the
"technostructure". "Howard Hughes," wrote Kenneth Galbraith
in 1967, "operating from a strong ownership position, long resisted
the passage of control of TWA to the technostructure. And Eddie
Rickenbacker fought a similar devolution of power at Eastern
Airlines. Both companies suffered during this period. Both recovered
promptly when the technostructure took over."

In the jet age, and with Tillinghast in command, TWA's rivalry
with Pan Am became more intense and more equal. By the summer
of 1964 Pan American alone had 214 jet flights each week across
the Atlantic; the next year there were 258. Pan Am's jet flights were
up by fifty per cent over propeller-flights, and they carried three
times as many people. But TWA was luring more passengers and
for a time overtook Pan Am across the Atlantic; after frantically
lobbying President Nixon it began its own jet flights round the
world. In August 1969 a TWA 707 left Los Angeles—blessed by
three Buddhist priests performing a Happiness Ceremony—to fly
round the world via Hawaii, Guam, Okinawa and Hong Kong.
An insatiable traveller could now circle the world in sixty hours
including stop-overs—which came very close to Frye's prophecy a
quarter century earlier. TWA was now a global rival to Pan Am,
including the missing link which Pan Am most coveted, a network
inside the United States.

The huge success of the 707 after the setback to the British
Comets re-asserted the world supremacy of both American manufacturers and American airlines, and no major foreign airlines could
afford not to buy the big jets—whether the Boeings or their rivals
the Douglas DC-8s. The world's airlines were now fighting each
other on a much more limited front than the earlier contests between
different planes or ocean liners. The hundreds of almost identical
707s, with their huge hanging engines, could only be distinguished
from each other by their colour schemes, service or food, and any
successful innovation by one airline would quickly be followed by
the others. When TWA began showing films with headsets in its
first-class compartment—thus reviving a collaboration between
planes and movies which Imperial Airways had pioneered in
1925—they gained a temporary glamour over their rivals, and
some Hollywood producers even used TWA passengers for "sneak
previews" for their films. But other airlines soon followed, and
agreed through IATA to make the same charge of $2.50 for each
headset.

Both the services and the fares across the North Atlantic were
carefully regulated by IATA, which served as the convenient scapegoat for the airlines' own agreements and cartels. IATA, with the
tacit approval of governments as well as airlines, regulated and
monitored all the transatlantic airlines, with the solitary exception of
the Icelandic airline Loftleidir which offered bargain fares through
Reykjavik. The sameness of the transatlantic flights made the
salesmanship and advertising of the airlines increasingly unconvinc-
ing, as each one claimed to provide unique service, comfort or
reliability. In fact, the airlines were all subject to the same remarkable law: the more the traffic, the less the real choice.

The coming of the jets produced a surge in the growth of most
international airlines, at a far higher rate than most other industries,
and transatlantic traffic was increasing by about twenty per cent a
year—doubling every five years. "Only five and a half decades after
Lindbergh flew to Paris," says TWA's historian, "TWA and its
competitors were carrying a million passengers a month across the
Atlantic at a cost considerably less than tourist fares on a 1927
ocean liner." As the airlines extended round the world they were
taking over from shipping or railroad companies as the symbols of
international mobility; and they built up their own diplomats,
embassies and corporate styles. At Idlewild airport outside New
York—later J.F.K.—the airlines vied with each other to receive
passengers in their splendid terminals as if they were nations
themselves. Pan Am built its circular Worldport, while TWA commissioned Eero Saarinen to design its elegant building with soaring

wings like an eagle's. Pan Am proclaimed itself "the world's most experienced airline" while TWA still projected glamour and excitement: "Up, Up and Away with TWA". All the world's major airlines including Aeroflot established glossy façades in the most expensive streets in foreign capitals—along Piccadilly in London, the Champs Elysées in Paris or the Via Barberini in Rome—where chic girls could book flights across the world through the new computers which were growing up as the airlines' real darlings. The old passenger shipping lines which twenty years earlier had seemed permanent were now scarcely in sight—Cunard was taken over by a British property company, and the beautiful liner, the *France*, was eventually laid up and sold to a Norwegian tour operator—and the airlines took their place as world institutions.

But while their growth was spectacular, their profits were not. The IATA cartel had imposed uniformity but it could not assure profits. Between 1955 and 1965 "the international airlines earned an operating return of three per cent on capital" (according to the aviation economist Richard Pryke) "as against a normal return in private industrial investment of six to eight per cent or even more." Even Pan Am and TWA, with all their advantages of equipment and scale and their demanding shareholders, never made profits comparable to those of other fast-growing industries. Why couldn't they do better? They were often needlessly extravagant, as they built up their own palaces, departments and privileges; and they gave way too readily to the demands of unions when they threatened to stop their flights. They could be fooled by some of their own publicity into thinking they were more like institutions than businesses and the glamour of aviation, like Hollywood's, could bemuse shareholders as well as managers. But it was in the nature of a business on the frontier of the future to be almost ruinously expensive. Each new technical advance required more capital while it rendered much existing investment obsolete; and airlines had to re-equip their fleets long before the earlier planes had worn out—so that the second-hand planes, which were often bought for cheap charter flights, could help to undercut them. "There is much to be said for the argument," wrote one historian in 1964, "that air transport would have been better off financially if the investors had been less inventive."

In the meantime competition was constantly hotting up, from airlines which were owned by their governments and which could therefore often afford to lose money on prestigious routes. The North Atlantic was the most competitive of all, as foreign airlines cut into the American share—first the Europeans and then others beginning with El Al, Air India and Pakistan International. In 1947 TWA and Pan Am had carried over eighty per cent of transatlantic travellers; by 1962 they were carrying only thirty-two per cent, while nineteen airlines were competing between the United States and Europe. IATA did what it could to maintain fares, but it could not prevent the pressure from new intruders and from the growing charter flights. The prestige and expansion of the airlines were already attracting too many players to the game.

THE TOURIST REVOLUTION

The big jets redrew the air map of the world with still bolder strokes—all the bolder when they increased their range with more powerful engines. They could fly non-stop from New York to most gateways in Europe, so that travellers could forget about Shannon, Gander or Goose Bay ("No Goose, No Gander," boasted El Al when it began non-stop flights), and the once-crucial airports were only used by local passengers or a few stop-overs such as Aeroflot passengers on their way to Cuba, while the Canadians and Irish lost trump cards in the bargaining for landing rights. The flights from Europe to South Africa, or from New York to Tokyo, could be accomplished in two hops instead of the four or five needed ten years before. Many remote outposts of the third world suddenly lost their diplomatic appeal, while others found a new opportunity in the expansion of tourism. As distance became less related to cost, packaged European tourists could have a two-week holiday in Sri Lanka as cheaply as in Switzerland next door.

Already during the fifties the big airlines had become more interested in the new armies of tourists, who were changing the basis of airline economics by creating a whole new area of demand —particularly across the Atlantic. TWA, as it had added to its fleet of Constellations and Super Constellations, had set out to encourage tourists to travel abroad, and by 1952 they were offering reduced "sky-tourist" fares to compete with Pan Am across the Atlantic, which other airlines quickly copied; and in 1958 the "economy fares" brought a new surge of passengers. The airliners were over-taking ocean liners more rapidly than anyone had predicted; and in 1957 for the first time more passengers crossed the Atlantic by air than by sea. Air traffic across the Atlantic was doubling every five years, and in 1962 over two million people crossed by air compared to only 800,000 by sea. Transatlantic liners would never again become economic, and the airlines were already attracting passengers who would never have had the money or time to travel by ship. Flying had been associated with the rich, but it was now much closer to the masses than sea travel.

The development of the 707, and the huge expansion which followed, provided a far bigger mass market. As Boeing's historian put it in 1966:

A realisation was dawning—the astonishing capabilities of the jets. One 707 could carry as many people as the *Queen Mary* ocean liner could carry in the same time, by shuttling back and forth at jet speed—six and a half hours from New York to Europe. There would be the equivalent of hundreds of *Queen Marys* flying the skies. The capacity of the airlines would be doubled. People of moderate means would begin to think of travel to far-off places not as a fanciful yearning, but as a real prospect in their lives. At jet speed you could circle the globe in forty hours. The world was shrinking to half the size.

Juan Trippe had long ago realised that Pan American's future was bound up with tourism, and at the annual meeting of IATA in 1955 in New York he explained with rare eloquence how for years the tourist plane and the bombing plane had been racing each other. "The tourist plane, if allowed to move forward unshackled by political boundaries and economic restrictions, will win this race between education and catastrophe. Mass travel by air may prove to be more significant to world destiny than the atom bomb." Later setbacks, both in the aircraft industry and in world politics, might throw doubt on that optimism, and the development of civil aircraft was to remain heavily dependent on military prototypes. But Trippe's faith seemed more justified in the booming climate of the fifties.

The speed of the tourist expansion took nearly all airline executives, even Trippe, by surprise. They were conditioned to providing scheduled services, primarily for businessmen; and it was the new charter companies in Europe and the "non-skeds" in America, which could rapidly exploit the burgeoning tourist market, either by flying their own planes or by contracting for seats on the existing airlines. "No one could predict the take-off of mass travel in the mid-fifties," said Alan Snudden, the managing director of Monarch Airlines in Britain which was one of the beneficiaries. "We discovered a broad historic jetstream—the public desire for cheap mass travel. The British traffic went up from a million to fifteen million in fifteen years." The charter companies grew up outside the cartel system, and were able spectacularly to undercut the scheduled airlines. At first, beginning in 1953, IATA had enforced a rule that charter or non-sked flights across the Atlantic could only be permitted for groups and clubs with an authentic "affinity" —whether ethnic relationships, hobbies or staff associations. Some affinities were quite genuine, and the charter flights played an important social role in re-uniting emigrant families in the Americas with Europe. But a whole industry sprang up to devise and advertise dubious clubs which could qualify for bargain fares, and the game reached a farcical climax in 1971 when an American group called the Left Hand Club was raided on their aircraft, and a quarter were found to be spurious members and taken off the plane. The public still insisted on trying any kind of charter, the affinity rules proved impossible to enforce and were abandoned, and the scheduled airlines competed with their own advanced booking fares. "It was a remarkable victory for the public will," said Snudden; "they forced governments to give way."

In the jet age the scheduled airlines realised that mass tourism was becoming an important part of their own revenues. They now had to cater for two quite separate categories, the businessmen and the tourists, together with a third kind of traveller, known in the trade as VFRs, or visiting friends and relatives, who could also be easily packaged on charters.

The distinction between businessmen and tourists became part of every airline's way of life. There was nothing very new about mass travel. Sailing ships in the middle ages were shared by two classes of travellers, merchants and pilgrims. "A merchant was distinguished from a pilgrim," wrote Iris Origo, "merely by the amount of space he chartered," and she quoted a fourteenth-century writer. "What weighs less than ten quintals is not merchandise, and no man is a merchant who pays less than twenty pesanti." Today pilgrimages still provide much of the travel business in the Middle East, including the hundreds of thousands of Muslims who fly every year to the holy city of Mecca, via the vast new King Abdulaziz airport for pilgrims in Jeddah. But elsewhere religious mass travellers have been superseded by lay pilgrims in search of cathedrals or monuments for cultural rather than spiritual uplift, or seeking the simpler pleasures of the sun and the sea.

As the jets multiplied the numbers of mass tourists, the more sophisticated travellers complained that the jet era would rob travel of much of its individuality and adventure and press passengers towards greater conformity. In 1962 the American historian Daniel Boorstin protested in his book *The Image* about the "lost art of travel" and the constraints of mass tourism.

> . . . The newest and most popular means of passenger transpor-
> tation to foreign parts is the most insulating known to man . . .

Recently I boarded a plane at Idlewild airport in New York at 6.30 one evening. The next morning at 11.30 I was in Amsterdam. The flight was routine, at an altitude of about 23,000 feet, far above the clouds, too high to observe landmark or seamark. Nothing to see but the weather; since we had no weather, nothing to see at all. I had flown not through space but through time. My only personal sign that we had gone so far was the discovery on arrival at Amsterdam that I had lost six hours. My only problem en route was to pass the time. My passage through space was unnoticeable and effortless. The plane robbed me of the landscape.

What were the real social benefits of mass tourism? Critics have been sceptical ever since the railroads first opened up the new market, pioneered by the British travel agent Thomas Cook. "Going by railway I do not consider as travelling at all," the Victorian critic John Ruskin complained, "it is merely being sent to a place, and very little different from becoming a parcel." Train travel gradually lost its associations with regimentation and anxiety as tourists found they could travel casually and plan their own schedules and hotels, while the journeys acquired their own romantic mythology of encounters in restaurant-cars or sleeping-berths. But the jet age multiplied mass tourism, extending not just across continents but across the globe, treating passengers more like parcels —as the term packaged tour suggested—than Ruskin could have dreamt. Air tourists, enclosed in their segregated airports, hotels and resorts, were much more constrained than rail travellers, and much more cut off from the natives. While the train station was part of a line, the airport was an isolated point, an image of discontinuity. The economics of jet planes—much more than rail economics—allowed tourists to make long journeys more cheaply than short ones, provided they all travelled together and did not stop on the way; and the equations between cost and distance became increasingly confusing. In the jet age the mass migrations of tourists across the world began to seem as natural—and as detached from the earth—as migrations of swallows or starlings.

Has air tourism added to the understanding between nations or continents? When Louis Turner and John Ash studied its influence in their book *Golden Hordes* in 1973 they concluded that it was essentially retrograde. While Thomas Cook could genuinely believe that his tours contributed to "the advancement of human progress", the authors suspected that modern tourism "actively *impedes* development and progress". And they quoted approvingly the hypothesis of the sociologist Erik Cohen, that:

... the larger the flow of mass tourism becomes, the more institutionalised and standardised tourism becomes and consequently the stronger the barriers between the tourist and the life of the host country become. What were previously formal barriers between different countries become informal barriers *within* countries.

Certainly packaged tourists on foreign beaches, surrounded by their countrymen eating their own kind of food at their own meal-times, do not show much curiosity about their host country. Charter operators and their advertisements are glad to play up to the old stereotypes of amorous Italians, unreliable Spaniards or bouzouki-playing Greeks, allowing tourists to reinforce the prejudices they arrived with; and as the planes got bigger the airlines became more like wholesalers, dealing with prearranged packages who could be kept under control; while the individual tourist became a tiresome complication. While Trippe talked eloquently about the race between education and catastrophe, the airlines were not much concerned with education, or encouraging the understanding of other peoples.

8

Black Sky, White Sky

Coloniser, c'est transporter.

French proverb

JET planes transformed the economics of flying everywhere, not just because they were cheaper and safer, but because they produced a glut of second-hand propeller-planes which the richer airlines sold off at bargain prices to charter companies and to the developing countries. And the jet age coincided with a decade when scores of new independent states were emerging in Asia and Africa, each with their ambitions to expand in the air.

The new national airlines which sprung up all over the third world were the most visible symbols of their nation's independence. Their extravagance was much mocked; but in fact air transport was more essential to the developing continents than to the crowded centres of Europe or the eastern seaboard of America. In Africa or Asia the planes were not just a faster substitute for trains or buses, but the only way to reach remote regions; and it was not only the white settlements which discovered the scope of the air. India attracted some of the earliest aviators, and claimed the world's first airmail service when a Frenchman, Henri Picquet, flew letters from Allahabad to Naini in February 1911.

The most astonishing early achievement of air transport had occurred when gold had been discovered in 1922 in Morobe in New Guinea, one of the remotest of all regions, which was then under Australia's mandate. The gold was eight days' walk from the coast through mountains and gorges—until the entrepreneurial district officer Cecil Levien resigned his job to raise money from Australian investors to buy some Junkers bi-planes. The planes then flew out huge dredges in sections, together with horses, oxen and materials to build a whole gold-mining township. Guinea Airways, as he called it, claimed to be flying four times more freight than any airline in the world: "Passenger fares to the Morobe," it was announced at the time, "will be A£25 for Europeans. Natives will be charged as freight." The gold ran out as the Japanese were occupying New Guinea, and rusting dredges now stand as a memorial. But Papua New Guinea—as it became after independence in 1975—remains one of the world's most air-minded countries: Air Niugini flies as far as Singapore and Indonesia, and its romantic domestic airline Talair flies tribesmen, sometimes with bows and arrows, between seven hundred airstrips—with more destinations, they claim, than Pan American or Lufthansa.

As the colonies gained their independence in the forties, their national airlines acquired an overwhelming importance in the eyes of their governments. They helped to hold the regions together, to reinforce the capital, to forge new routes with neighbouring countries which ignored the ex-imperial lifelines, and to represent their country overseas. As the United Nations in New York evolved into the third world's arena, developing countries felt the need for long-distance planes to show their flags and carry their ministers to New York. Western diplomats criticised the extravagance and pomp of poor countries wasting their foreign exchange, and some blamed the UN for encouraging it. But young nations which felt threatened by imperialist forces not surprisingly saw their airlines as the instruments for their self-determination and their lifeline to the world.

Much of the backwardness of the third world could be ascribed to the difficulty of communications within the land masses, and air transport offered a chance to catch up with history. Latin America was the most spectacular example, where aircraft quickened the economic development, allowed the interior to be mapped, opened up and exploited, and enabled Brazilians, Argentinians or Chileans to overfly their countries in a few hours. The vast internal air network of Brazil, which lies outside the scope of this book, became more extensive than Europe's; the new capital Brasilia was the first major city to be conceived in terms of air travel, with its first building materials flown in by air; the air shuttle between Rio and Sao Paulo became almost as busy as flights between London and Paris.

Yet any air map still reveals the contrast between the hemispheres, north and south. Australians and New Zealanders are now constantly crossing the equator to make contact with North America and Europe, while South Africa can by-pass the whole of its own continent. But the South had few links with the rest of the South, and there are still only a few flights a week between Latin America and Africa: the South Atlantic is a backwater compared with the North Atlantic highway. There have been proposals for scheduled flights across the Antarctic from Tierra del Fuego to Auckland, but the Chileans have no obvious links with New Zealanders; and the migrations of tourists and businessmen still depend on the relationships set up by sailing ships or liners. While the third world countries talk about the common interests of "the South", their long-distance communications betray their dependence on the North —and vice-versa.

AFRICAN DEADLOCK

The new nations of Africa were ambitious to assert their independence through the air, and to break the imperial patterns and routes which had first been established in the twenties. For a tantalising interim during the Second World War the West Africans had found themselves acting as a critical link on the way from Europe to America via Brazil. But the South Atlantic soon almost disappeared from the air maps while flights to Africa stretched from North to South: by the fifties DC-4s were flying in hops from London to Rome to Cairo to Khartoum to Entebbe to Victoria Falls to Johannesburg and Cape Town—still evoking the old British Empire. The chief terminus was still South Africa, while the intermediate airports looked like white spots on a black map. Communications between different regions of Africa were fitful: the main links between East and West were the caravans of Muslim pilgrims on their way from Nigeria to Mecca; the only way to fly from Nigeria to Kenya was via Europe. Between South and West Africa only one unpredictable ship sailed every few weeks.

The new states, beginning with Ghana in 1957, were challenged to connect up with each other. Ethiopian Airlines, which the Emperor Haile Selassie had set up with help from TWA, began flying from Addis Ababa to Nigeria and Ghana, at last linking the two sides of the continent. A Pan American plane even started flying rather erratically once a week from Johannesburg via the Congo to Ghana and Liberia, linking Black Africa with White. By the sixties new air-routes were zig-zagging across the continent, and today eight flights a week—by Pan American, Ethiopian and Nigeria Airways —cross from Lagos in Nigeria to Nairobi in Kenya.

But independence and nationalism produced a jigsaw of competing airlines. The former French colonies managed to co-operate in the air through the uniquely multinational airline, Air Afrique, which was set up in 1961, controlled by the French UAT (later to become UTA); the other shares were held by eleven West African states which managed to hold together despite political squabbles and forged new routes through equatorial Africa and the coast. But the British ex-colonies were at odds, as each wanted their own airline to fly to Europe at any cost. Sierre Leone Airways leased jets from Alia, the Jordanian airline; only Gambia Airways—more accurately known as Gambia Stairways—confined itself to providing services for other airlines. Soon Africa boasted some of the smallest airlines in the world, including Royal Swazi with two planes and Air Botswana with three. The three ex-British colonies in the east collaborated for a time in East African Airways, but by 1977 they broke up to form separate offspring—Kenya Airways, Air Tanzania and Uganda Airlines—of which only the first was seriously viable.

All these national airlines had ambitions to project their countries overseas; but many were soon afflicted by political upheavals and economic crises which made foreign currency scarce. By the late seventies Ghana Airways, which used to advertise on London buses, could only muster one flight to Britain a week, while most others were cutting back to the bone. The African leap into the jet age contradicted many of the assumptions of the white settlers, and of many airline executives. "When they started using black pilots we thought it would be disastrous, using men just off the trees," said one old hand from Imperial Airways. "In fact the safety wasn't really very different." But the gap widened between highly developed parts of a country and the rest. The airports, with their computers, timetables and demands on punctuality and precision, were islands of relative efficiency surrounded by political pressures and upheavals and sometimes literally battlefields—like Entebbe airport in Uganda when it was invaded by Israeli paratroops rescuing hostages.

The confrontation between White and Black Africa put up more obstacles. South African Airways, which had a monopoly over its long internal flights, had far the greatest potential for connecting up the continent; but by the sixties the new black states were forbidding the all-white airline, which practised strict apartheid, to fly over their territory. SAA suffered a costly setback as it flew to Europe by "the dictators' route" via Lisbon and Luanda in Portuguese West Africa, while other airlines flew more directly through Kenya. South African Airways had come to be seen as a pariah airline, an arm of its government's police and propaganda. It provided cover for "spies in the sky" to eavesdrop on passengers ("It's quite surprising," said one ex-employee of the secret service

BOSS, "how loose people's tongues are after they have passed through customs"); and a SAA stewardess was credited with executing the plot which trapped the Afrikaner rebel Breyten Breytenbach.

When Portuguese West Africa turned into the independent Marxist state of Angola, South African Airways was still more isolated. But it could now buy the long-distance "special performance" Boeing 747s which could fly non-stop from Europe to Cape Town, round the edge of the hostile bulge of West Africa. And through secret diplomacy the South African government gained a foothold on the bulge in the Ivory Coast, which gave them landing rights in 1975; while they also began making secret flights to officially hostile parts of Black Africa, including Nigeria, Zaire and Zambia—appearing in no timetable and using military airports—which carried weapons, advisers and crucial equipment. South African Airways also bought the friendship of the tiny independent republic of Cape Verde, off the coast of West Africa, which became independent in 1975 and provided a precious stopping place on the long route from Johannesburg to New York or Buenos Aires. The island airport of Ilha do Sal was built and run by the South Africans for their airline; but in their anxiety to pay for its costs they were oddly indiscriminate in sharing it; and the airport was even observed to be used by Aeroflot flying Cuban troops on their way to Angola, to defend it from the South Africa army.

The map of South African Airways, like that of El Al, showed dramatically how air transport could enable a country to defy its near neighbours: in the seventies SAA flew nowhere in Africa north of Malawi, but it flew to four continents including Asia—with frequent flights to its new ally Israel and a flight via Mauritius or the Seychelles to Sri Lanka, Hong Kong and Taiwan (another member of the "outsider's club"). And the black states' boycott of SAA over their airspace began to look less effective as Pretoria extended its diplomatic embrace further north; while the multiplicity of black airlines, nearly all losing money, reflected the inability of their countries to collaborate.

The aftermath of the empires had revealed all the limitations of nationalism in the air, as small airlines competed with heavy losses. The saddest example was in the Caribbean, where the row of ex-British and ex-French islands, which had been isolated by their long sea-routes linking them to Europe, now found themselves neighbours separated by one or two hours. In the late forties BOAC took over British West Indian Airways, which absorbed the international services of many islands; it was a much joked-about airline ("Britain's Worst Investment Abroad" or "But Will It Arrive") but it provided a valuable unified service. While the British were hoping to establish a West Indian Federation in 1961 they sold off BWIA very cheaply to Trinidad; but the federation was frustrated, Jamaica insisted on its own airline, and each independent state followed with its own. Only one regional service, the Leeward Islands Air Transport ("Leaves Island Any Time"), was able to combine different islands' interests, jointly owned by Barbados, Trinidad and Tobago and other islands. But the bigger territories all competed expensively with their own airlines flying to New York or London.

The coming of airlines to the third world had revealed an apparently paradoxical effect. The air could open up routes through deserts, jungles and oceans which gave new opportunities to developing countries, and the chance to make closer links with each other. But the airlines could play their own tricks with geography as they made distance less important than frequency, and as tourism and trade still favoured the old imperial routes; so that black politicians were more likely to meet each other in New York or in Europe than in their own continent.

Jet planes brought greater mobility to Asia and Africa, still more the jumbo jets which could carry five hundred contract workers at a time to jobs at the other side of the world. But the restrictions on free movement and permanent emigration were tighter than ever.

The jumbo jet airliner enables emigration from Asia to Europe or America on a scale which would make that of the nineteenth century seem modest [wrote the historian Hugh Thomas in 1979]. But no advanced countries, particularly not the USA and Australia, open their doors to unrestricted immigration. Indeed, the age of easy travel has coincided with a period in which the possibility of removal from one country to another has been as a result rendered more difficult than it has ever been.

Part II
The Closing Skies

9

The Age of the Jumbo

These days no one can make money in the goddamn airline business.
The economics represent sheer hell.
Cyrus Smith, on resigning from American Airlines, 1968

WHILE the world was still catching up with this first jet age, the
aeronautical engineers were already planning new leaps ahead,
both in America and Europe, but in different directions. The huge
success of the American jets was a new blow to the pride of European
airlines: they all, even the French, had to buy 707s or DC-8s; the
American domination was celebrated in the French farce of the
sixties, *Boeing Boeing*. The British and French manufacturers were
too late to compete with existing jets, so it was with all the more
ardour that their governments signed a treaty in 1962 to build a
supersonic jet for British Airways and Air France. The Concorde
was one of the most political of all planes: it was seen as a means
to cement Anglo-French unity, just before de Gaulle refused Britain
entry into the European Community, as well as a reassertion of
European technology to capture world markets. It *did* bring English
and French technicians closer together; but during its long gestation
it built up prohibitive costs, and like the Comet it was overtaken
by the new scale of air transport. By the time British Airways and
Air France inaugurated the Concorde, it represented not a new era
of travel but the end of a supersonic dream. The thin beautiful bird
with its sharp-pointed nose continued to cross the Atlantic; but as
an economic proposition it was eclipsed by the new beast with vast
hanging engines which was once again transforming the business
of airlines, and reinforcing still further the American supremacy in
the air.

It was again Juan Trippe who made the bold decision, to commission a giant airliner for Pan Am which would carry more than twice the passengers of any existing plane. It was a decision which was to force all the major airlines into a dangerous new investment, whose price is still being paid. Yet it seemed less rash in the heyday of the airline boom in 1965, when the industry was expanding year after year. Trippe at sixty-six, with forty years' experience behind him, was still the natural leader of the industry, with the triumph of the Boeing 707 behind him. Pan American was still the biggest international airline, making record profits, with a dominating influence symbolised by the new skyscraper crowning Park Avenue.

The Pentagon had already prepared the way for a giant airliner when it commissioned Lockheed to build the Hercules Transport, which incurred the biggest cost overrun in history but then became the indispensable whale of the air, carrying tanks, ships and even planes inside its belly. Trippe naturally wanted a civilian equivalent to carry the massing armies of tourists and to give his airline yet another leap ahead. Lockheed had their hands full, while Douglas was preoccupied with stretching its DC-8. So Trippe again began bargaining with Bill Allen at Boeing and by December 1965, with astonishing speed and confidence, they had signed a letter of intent for a Boeing 747 to carry about 350 passengers.

It was almost equally hazardous for both sides. Boeing had to invest as much as its total net capital, and to build the world's biggest factory while the plane was still being designed. Pan Am would have to pay half a billion dollars for twenty-five planes—more than all its revenues for the previous year. The two men, as John Newhouse described them, "plunged their companies, and the world, into the era of wide-bodied airliners with little hesitation and roughly equal enthusiasm". And in the buoyant atmosphere of the time they both thought that the 747 would soon be superseded by supersonic airliners, leaving it to continue as a mere freighter. "Incredible as it seems," wrote Newhouse, "Boeing and Pan Am were ready to risk all they had on an airplane that each of them, Boeing especially, seemed to regard as an interim . . . " Nor could Pan Am keep the plane to itself very long: Boeing needed another twenty-five orders to finance their expansion, and Trippe needed foreign customers who would provide bigger runways and airports for his jumbos abroad. British Airways and Japan Air Lines, alarmed by the competition, took the lead in ordering the new planes and others soon had to join in the rush. The world's airlines were committed to a transport revolution whose implications were little understood.

The great plane soon faced unexpected setbacks. Its commissioning coincided with a wave of inflation caused by the Vietnam war, when President Johnson asked businessmen to cut their capital spending. Trippe and Allen had to lobby the president personally, stressing the plane's contribution to jobs in Seattle and to the balance of payments, before he gave his approval. The prototype plane got heavier and heavier to comply with Trippe's needs, so that it would have a shorter range than the later 707s. Allen wanted to cut down the passengers but Trippe insisted on redesigning the plane, while he bullied Pratt & Whitney to produce engines with greater thrust. The plane was stamped with Trippe's stubborn personality: inspired by the old two-decker Stratocruiser, he insisted on having passenger space behind the cockpit on the upper deck, connected by a spiral staircase.

Yet while the plane was still building Trippe was secretly planning his own exit. At Pan Am's annual meeting in May 1968 he announced that he would resign as chairman and chief executive— the position he had held for forty years. Nearly all the airline pioneers were now retiring—including Cyrus Smith of American, Eddie Rickenbacker of Eastern and Bill Patterson of United—to be followed by much less confident leaders. "We all picked the wrong successors," said Bob Six when he retired as chairman of Continental. "Mine committed suicide. Trippe's successor didn't even want the job."

Trippe remained an enigma. He could look back on an enterprise which had transformed the world's communications and brought the capitals within a day's travel of each other. Yet his recorded remarks revealed curiously little interest in the political or social consequences. His cold banker's mind seemed preoccupied with maintaining technical supremacy and financing his fleets—which he insisted was the most interesting part of Pan Am's story. The jumbo, as it turned out, was close to being a financial disaster, and it marked the end—or at least a pause—in the long era of growth. And in bequeathing it to his successors Trippe left them problems which not even he could have mastered.

By the time Pat Nixon had christened the first Boeing 747 in January 1970, to fly its inaugural flight to London, Pan American was already facing the hangover. Trippe had been temporarily succeeded by his president, Harold Gray, who was already ill with cancer, and Gray was soon succeeded in turn by *his* president Najeeb Halaby, a stylish lawyer and former test-pilot who had only joined Pan American in 1965. Halaby had no illusions about Pan Am. It was, he said, "locked in a shrinking box, with the top, bottom, and sides all closing in at once". The financing of the new fleet of jumbos was costing $10 million a month and the new markets were not growing fast enough. Pan Am still had no domestic flights which could link up with its international service. It was, complained Halaby, "an airline without a country". Halaby put some hopes in the prospect of a merger with TWA and had long talks with its chief Charles Tillinghast; but TWA was now the more economical airline, and when its domestic traffic improved it lost interest in a merger. Halaby brought in management consultants and fired many of the Pan Am veterans; but the losses continued. "I was the right man at the wrong time," he lamented afterwards, "somewhat like the 747 in the world's airline industry . . . It would have taken a man with much greater airline-operating experience and a successful student of Machiavelli to run a company as big as Pan Am, one so involved with self-satisfaction, prior arrogance toward the public and the government, and one internally full of divided loyalties and prejudices."

By March 1972 the board turned against Halaby, declining a vote of confidence: "Trippe's Yalies," Halaby told me afterwards, "could always pull the rug from under his successors." He resigned and set up his own aviation business in the Middle East—dealing among others with Alia, the airline of Jordan, whose king became his father-in-law—and Halaby was succeeded by *his* president, William Seawell, a former air force brigadier-general who had been through Harvard law school. Seawell wielded the axe still further around Pan Am's empire: he cut out the loss-making routes to the Caribbean and made deals with TWA, abandoning Paris and Rome but keeping Frankfurt, and he shared the proud Worldport at Kennedy airport with other airlines. Pan Am's air map which had first stretched across the world twenty years earlier was now shrinking again. But Seawell's cuts still could not turn the airline back into profit; for the whole industry was now suffering its biggest shock since the Second World War.

THE OIL SHOCK

The oil embargo of 1973, followed by the quadrupling of the oil price, hit the airlines even harder than most other businesses. Their whole expansion had been fuelled by cheap oil, and the energy crisis revealed their desperate dependence on it. In the icy American winter of 1973–4 the domestic airlines cancelled and merged their flights to economise on fuel; and by next year all the free world's airlines faced much bleaker economic conditions, as their fuel bill rose while the recession was discouraging passengers. The airline chiefs, as one of them complained, were increasingly pigs-in-the-middle, caught between the oil companies who provided their life-blood and the banks who were bailing them out, with little room for manoeuvre.

Long-distance flights made the biggest losses, and Pan American soon faced a real prospect of bankruptcy. In desperation Seawell got in touch with the Shah of Iran, one of the chief beneficiaries of the oil shock, who offered a ten-year loan to Pan Am to buy six per cent of the stock. The State Department, though appalled, did not obstruct it; but the Iranians backed down and Pan Am had to borrow still more from the banks and cut back its routes further. At TWA Charles Tillinghast faced a similar crisis, and he too looked to Iran: in 1975 TWA sold six of their 747s to the Iranian government, and six months later three more. The glittering new airports of the Middle East, filled with the half-empty jumbos of Iran Air, Saudia or Gulf Air, became the most showy signs of the huge transfer of wealth; and Saudia, which TWA had set up less than thirty years earlier, was now richer than its old master.

The Boeing 747s were soon followed by other wide-bodied jets, and by 1973 the world's airlines were flying 211 Boeing 747s, 70 Douglas DC-10s and 51 Lockheed 1011s. The giant planes had already become the normal means of travel across the oceans. The curved domes of the 747s towered above the airport buildings and their painted fins stuck up like huge flags, dwarfing the 707 which only a decade earlier had seemed unimaginably large. The wide bodies imposed their own strict conditions: only the bigger airports, with reinforced runways and extended buildings, could unload three or four hundred passengers—enough to fill a whole train. The costs of maintenance and spare parts strained all the small airlines, pressing them to standardise or merge. And most worrying to the airlines, this proliferation of jumbos coincided with the worst recession in twenty years, when all the projections of future tourism and travel had to be revised, and when more airlines were competing for less custom.

Many of the great planes were soon flying across the Atlantic with only a handful of passengers, losing a small fortune on each flight, while still discounting their fares. For lucky passengers it was a new golden age, as they found themselves in an airborne room with rows of seats and a stewardess to themselves. For the airlines it was the ultimate absurdity, at a time of exorbitant fuel costs and financial crises, to be flying huge empty planes round the world at 40,000 feet.

JUMBO CULTURE

But in the peak seasons the jumbos offered a much bleaker experience for passengers, which removed them still further from any sense of individual adventure. Four hundred people—about the same number as the slaves in an eighteenth-century slaver—are packed equally closely. The passengers inside the "tin sausage", most of them far away from a window, are cut off from any sense of the earth or the sky—an experience almost opposite to that of the early aviators. As the seats crept still closer together the airliner looked still less like an ocean liner, more like a crowded cinema or fast-food counter. It became an extension of the consumer society, with a submissive captive market all conditioned to eat, to watch films or to buy duty-free goods at the same time.

The jets and jumbos brought new standards of reliability, punctuality and safety; but they also abolished almost any sense of travelling. There was little meaning now to R. L. Stevenson's proverb: "It is better to travel hopefully than to arrive." The headsets, the in-flight movies and the constant meals were designed to obliterate the experience of travelling, and the definition of a good trip was one which had hardly been noticed. The regimented rows of passengers left little scope for the romance of the earlier flights, or the mythology of the "mile-high club" of airborne seducers, or of air hostesses asking "coffee, tea or me?" The jumbos could accommodate a train-load, but they could never conjure up the association of a long-distance train. Only when something went wrong, when a plane was delayed or had to land somewhere else, when passengers had to meet, talk and escape from their schedule, did travel regain its old sense of "travail".

Earlier advertisements for airlines had proclaimed exotic destinations, fashionable passengers or luxurious new planes; but now most of the advertising concentrated on a single unglamorous object, the seat. The hoardings displayed contented businessmen snoozing on slumberettes or sleeperettes and boasted about leg-room and reclining angles, while the cheap operators worked out how closely together they could pack their bodies. Airlines, with their need to keep down weight, had always been obsessed by special seats: in the thirties Imperial Airways had designed a famous light wicker chair for their flying boats. But wicker had long ago been banned as a fire hazard, and the seat turned into a complex aluminium and plastic apparatus which included a table, seat-belt, call-button, headphone, switches, ashtray and recliner. Some airline executives insist on conducting their own "fanny test": TWA's President, Ed Meyer, six foot three inches tall, is reported to make his executives sit in a mock plane cabin in his conference room, while Pan American employs an orthopaedic surgeon as its consultant. But the fat or the tall can never be satisfied unless they fly first class or book seats near the emergency exits which by law must be wider. The most critical seats of all are the lavatories, the focus of passengers' anxieties as they line up at the end of the journey; and no airliner ever has enough of them. To the airlines they are above all a fire hazard, in which determined smokers can set light to paper towels or toilet paper.

The jumbo era brought still more conformity to the airline business: the bigger the plane, the less choice it offered to passengers. Most jumbos across the Atlantic, though owned by twenty different airlines, showed the same kind of films and served the same kind of food from the same mass caterers with much the same kind of service. (Even an Air France jumbo has been observed at Heathrow with a Trusthouse Forte food van slinking away from it.) The times of departure came closer together as airlines competed for peak hours and tried to keep their planes airborne for as many hours as possible, within the limits of curfews. Every evening more than ten planes leave New York for London, while only two—plus two Concordes—fly in daylight; the airlines prefer the night flights which can be turned round in London next morning, without wasting time on the ground; while passengers become obsessed by saving time, whatever the discomfort. The "red-eye specials" represent all the conformity of the jumbo culture, keeping passengers awake with meals, films and duty-free sales, and emptying them into London, Paris or Frankfurt all at the same time at dawn. But the barbarity of night flights suits both the restless passengers and the airlines determined on "maximum utilisation" of planes. Veteran fliers reminisce about early night flights on planes like the Boeing Stratocruiser, with its rows of bunks and a bar in a downstairs cabin; and KLM before the war advertised passengers being served tea in their bunks; but today only a very few airlines, like Singapore Airlines across the Pacific or Philippine Airlines to Manila, can offer beds in their planes.

The giant planes inevitably affected dimensions on the ground as they demanded airports with long arms to reach out to them. Airports moved still further away from city centres—Malpensa is twenty-nine miles from Milan, Narita forty miles from Tokyo—and these distant airports had become "newly ambiguous points of arrival" as Boorstin described them: "when the visitor 'arrived' on the ground he might not even see the city to which he had come."

The jumbo-loads also demanded bigger hotels. In the thirties the flying boats had often been exaggeratedly called "flying hotels", but now airliners carried far more people than most hotels; and their needs brought the airlines and hotels closer together. The two big American airlines had set the pattern by building up their own chains of luxury hotels. At Pan American Trippe had first begun with a few "Intercontinental" hotels in Latin America, which he later expanded to make a chain round the world, most of them owned by local capital, but all linked to Pan Am's reservations system. At TWA Tillinghast had decided by 1965 that (as he put it) "the airline business had certain ingrown economic problems and that the strongest airline would be the one with the strongest capital structure." He looked into possible diversification, and began talking with Barron Hilton, the son of Conrad Hilton who had set up the chain of luxury hotels. Hilton at first hoped to become controlling shareholder of TWA, but instead TWA bought the Hiltons for $17 million, making them operators of forty-two hotels in twenty-eight countries.

Most big airlines followed the example of Pan Am and TWA—all the more in the jumbo age. British Airways collaborated with four other European airlines to build up the Penta hotel chain which succeeded in conveying an almost identical sanitised atmosphere in each foreign city. Air France built up its chain of Meridien hotels, forty-three of them by 1984, dedicated to exporting the French way of life with the help of French food flown out by Air France. At the same time they reassured their guests in France that they had not really left home: "This is London," says an advertisement for the Hotel Meridien in Paris, promising "direct satellite relays of English TV programmes"; while another advertisement for the same hotel says "An American in Paris . . . CBS News, direct your room". Swissair had its own global hotel network. The airline hotels could exclude foreign influences much more effectively than the earlier railway hotels in the city centres; they were much more self-contained and insulated from the cities, with their own shopping arcades, cosmopolitan restaurants and coffee-shops and English-speaking staff.

Thus the jumbos exacted a price for their benefits in terms of conformity and obsession with time. A century earlier the railroads, "the iron horses", had imposed their regimes of punctuality and timetables on rural peoples who had kept time by the sun. Jet planes brought a much greater sense of haste and impatience, together with an overwhelming need for safety which pressed passengers into submission. The pervasive phrase "for your comfort and safety", used by nearly all airlines, spelt both paternalism and warning: "this is your captain speaking" carried more authority than any sea-captain's. The mime of lifebelt drill, though long ago ritualised and largely ignored, still served to remind passengers of their vulnerability; and behind all the airborne jollity there was always a suppressed sense of fear which seemed to dry up the creative spirit. "The facts of aviation have been so harsh," wrote the historian Hugh Thomas, "that there is as little good writing about aeroplanes as about cars." And the airlines were only too glad to take advantage of the anxieties to treat passengers as sheep—as the hostesses often called them—leading them from one pen to the next.

The mass tourism and uniformity of the jumbos helped to reduce the status, as well as the adventure, of flying. Many of the frequent travellers in long-distance jets are now ordinary businessmen and salesmen equivalent to the commercial travellers in the earlier railway age: flying round the world no longer commands awe in the boardroom, while other means of communication are catching up. International telephones had been competing with transatlantic air travel ever since Lindbergh's first flight, becoming both cheaper and easier: the spread of direct dialling in the seventies allowed businessmen to have relaxed conversations across the ocean without talking face to face. Other new technologies followed. "Teleconferencing", which allows businessmen a few thousand miles apart to confront each other on video screens, can cost companies much less than flying executives across the world, while optical lines and satellites will make transmission cheaper. The airlines claim that international telephones encourage more air travel rather than compete with it, and that businessmen will always want to "eyeball" with each other. But "there are those in the communications industry," the *Financial Times* has warned, "who believe that, given modern transmission techniques and 'chips', business travel will soon be the exception rather than the rule." It would be an ironic outcome to the long honeymoon between businessmen and the air. After the airlines have made travel far more convenient but more commonplace, linking it up with telecommunications and computers and depriving it of any real sense of arriving, will they find that their business customers can dispense with them altogether, in favour of the video screen, satellites and computers?

The development of the jumbo, following the false dawn on supersonic travel, brought airline technology on to a plateau with no new spectacular heights in sight. The manufacturers would make quieter and more fuel-saving planes, and they could "stretch" the hump of the 747 to accommodate up to 800 passengers. But the engineers could promise no great new breakthrough after the extraordinary increases in speed, size and economy over the previous sixty years; and even the most spectacular achievement of the aerospace industry, the race to the moon, faced a kind of anti-climax after Neil Armstrong stepped on to the moon's surface in July 1969. The scientists and politicians were forced to turn their minds back to the problems of the earth below, and the airlines had to settle down to more workaday problems of marketing, packaging and maximum utilisation. The next generation of airline chiefs—the hoteliers, marketers, financiers or car-rental men—would appal the engineers and pilots by their lack of interest in the planes themselves.

The arrival of the jumbos coincided with the most serious financial crisis in the airlines' history, which would need all the salesmanship and ruthlessness of their chiefs and which brought new fears for their future. Would their industry follow the fate of so many railroads, when they ceased to be profitable and were nationalised, merged or went bankrupt?

10

The Deregulators

Wherever competition is feasible it is, for all its imperfections, superior to regulation as a means of serving the public interest.

Alfred Kahn

THE crisis facing the American airlines came not just from the recession and the surplus of jumbos, but from a fundamental change in the political weather. The politicians began demanding that Washington withdraw its protection and regulation, and the airlines became the most spectacular test case in the crusade to deregulate America, which soon affected airlines all round the world.

The American airlines were an obvious target for the deregulators. The Civil Aeronautics Board which Roosevelt had set up in 1938 had defended their interests, and for nearly forty years had refused to approve any of the applications for new airlines to fly major routes. The Big Four—United, American, TWA and Eastern—kept their "grandfather rights" to the profitable transcontinental routes. The system was deep in political patronage. The president not only appointed new members of the CAB, but retained the right to reverse its decisions about new routes or mergers without appeal; so that the airline chiefs were constantly seeking political influence and friends.

Robert Six, for instance, the founder-head of Continental Airlines, hired Pierre Salinger—who was on good terms with President Johnson—to run his international division, at a time when Continental was trying hard to get the rights to compete with Pan Am and TWA across the Pacific. But Johnson gave his permission too late, just before he was succeeded by Nixon, who denied the route to Continental and eventually, via the CAB, awarded it to American Airlines. Six believes that it was Robert Haldeman, who was then Nixon's aide, who refused to give him the route. "He had been account executive at J. Walter Thompson who were my advertising agents," he told me, "and I got rid of him. He bore me a grudge." But Salinger strongly suspected that Johnson had made a secret agreement with Nixon to favour American, whose durable Texan boss Cyrus Smith was an old friend of Johnson's.

The relations between presidents and airlines remained murky, but in 1973 the Watergate hearings threw a brief sudden spotlight on them, as on so many other dark political corners. The airlines were not surprisingly anxious to be on the "inside track" of the White House, and the campaign to re-elect Nixon naturally looked to the airlines, whose ticket counters and offices abroad made it easier for them to conceal secret cash payments in their accounts. Braniff Airways raised $40,000 through Camilo Fabrega, their regional vice-president in Panama, who collected the cash by selling special Braniff tickets, and then flew the money to Dallas. ("Some men are like the Lord in one respect," commented Senator Ervin: "they move in mysterious ways their wonders to perform.") But the more revealing case was that of American Airlines, then run by Cyrus Smith's successor George Spater, an unusually literary tycoon who was an authority on Virginia Woolf. Spater, as he later told the senators, was specially anxious to influence the White House because he wanted to consummate a merger with Western Airlines which required Nixon's approval. He was approached for funds by Herbert Kalmbach, who was both Nixon's personal lawyer and counsel for American's chief rival, and who told him: "We want you to be a member of the special class." Spater was fearful of being left out of this charmed circle, "It was something like the old medieval maps," he told Senator Ervin, "that show a flat world and then what they called 'terra incognita' with fierce animals lying around the fringes of this map. You just don't know what is going to happen to you if you get off it." He decided he must make "a substantial response" and arranged to raise $75,000 dollars in cash through a Lebanese agent, André Tabourian—who collected the money in $100 bills, brought it to New York and was then reimbursed. But American Airlines got no reward for their risky gift, for soon afterwards the CAB turned down the merger with Western.

"Is it not fair to say," Senator Ervin had asked at the hearings, "that if there is any industry in the United States which is peculiarly susceptible to express or implied pressure from people exercising governmental powers, it is the airlines?" "Yes, sir," replied Spater.

"You are absolutely right." The corruption endemic in the relations between the airlines and the White House was itself a good reason to try to reform the system of regulation. But the powerful pressure came from a different quarter.

By the early seventies the opponents of "big government" were becoming much concerned with the lack of competition between airlines. Successive chairmen of the CAB had very visibly taken the side of the airlines against the consumers and American regulation appeared tighter than that of many other countries including Britain. The board insisted that airlines must maintain regular jet services between every pair of major towns in America, while in return it tried to protect airlines from heavy losses or bankruptcy. Secor Brown, the chairman of the CAB from 1969 to 1973, was an advocate of "intelligent oligopoly" and dreaded destructive competition, while his successor Robert Timm was strongly criticised in Senate hearings for fraternising too closely with the airlines and later resigned. In the oil crisis of 1974, when many airlines including Pan Am and TWA faced the prospect of bankruptcy, they were allowed to connive about capacity across the Atlantic as well as at home without trouble from anti-trust laws.

But the airlines' political climate became stormier as both Democrats and Republicans, including both consumer lobbies and business interests, pressed for greater competition. The academics were in the forefront. The air, the most visible marketplace filled with identical products, was becoming an economists' playground which offered a unique opportunity for bold experiment.

The high priest of deregulation was Alfred Kahn, a quick-firing Professor of Economics at Cornell University, who had regulated energy industries in New York State. Like Milton Friedman, he was both an economist and an evangelist: a witty talker with a long nose and a sharp chin, he popped up like an irreverent imp determined to unleash new forces; and he had no great respect for the giant airlines. "I never thought that the TWAs or Pan Ams would be happy with more competition," he told me. "I always complained that the government regarded itself as representing the interests of the incumbent airlines." Kahn was backed up by another very articulate academic Mike Levine, a supercharged economics lecturer from Los Angeles, who could point to California's success in keeping down air fares by minimal regulation. Kahn and Levine were both prepared for the market to show all its ruthlessness, including expensive mistakes and bankruptcies. "Maybe it's sex appeal," Kahn said later, "but there's something about an airplane that drives investors crazy. That's the notion behind regulation. You can't leave it to the free market because it will do crazy things.

But that's the purpose of the free market—to let people do crazy things."

The first major assault came from the Democrats, when in 1974 Senator Edward Kennedy took up the issue in hearings in Washington, assisted by his aide David Smith and a young anti-trust lawyer Stephen Breyer, who had recently been assisting Archibald Cox in investigating the ITT corporation. The hearings, where Levine gave eloquent evidence, presented the CAB and Timm as the cronies of the airlines and Kennedy as the consumer's champion (he rewarded Breyer by making him a judge in Massachusetts). Several of Kennedy's team, including Smith and Breyer, later had misgivings about deregulation; but in the meantime the momentum was growing. On the Republican side President Ford took up deregulation in his 1976 campaign as part of his general policy to liberate free enterprise, while at the CAB Timm was followed by John Robson, who decided that the airlines "were uniquely suited to deregulation" and claimed to have turned the agency round by 180 degrees. "Basically we said, 'Look, what the CAB has been doing for the last forty years has made the aviation system less efficient and more expensive'."

But it was President Carter, to many people's surprise, who became the ultimate deregulator. He asked Kahn to become the new chairman of the CAB, where he was soon joined by Mike Levine; and thus began the greatest upheaval in American air transport since the thirties. At the CAB Kahn soon stimulated a rush of applications for new routes within the United States, and could point to lower fares on the busiest routes. "I have only to open my mouth," he exclaimed, "and the fares come tumbling down!" His policy was soon reinforced by the Airline Deregulation Act in 1978 which laid down a six year programme, to end in January 1985 with abolishing the CAB altogether—though still allowing subsidies for "socially essential services".

The first effects of deregulation were dramatic. A new breed of air entrepreneurs saw the chance to expand small companies or to establish "instant airlines" which could undercut fares on local routes; they could dispense with much of the superstructure and bureaucracy of the big airlines and could use their flexibility to hit the giants at their weakest points where they could make quick returns. Allegheny Airlines, which ran short-haul "puddle-jumper" flights out of Pittsburgh, took up new routes to Texas and Florida, changed its name to US Air, sold off some short routes to pilots and soon made much bigger profits. New York Air was set up in 1980 as an offshoot of Texas International, to compete with Eastern and others from La Guardia in New York. It tried without success to find a special niche and made huge losses until it got a new president, Mike Levine, the young apostle of deregulation, who moved into the bleak offices at La Guardia with all the enthusiasm of an academic turned tycoon. "There was a lot of scepticism about whether an airline could be run profitably in a deregulated environment," he said, "and I kind of wanted to have a part of showing it could be." Levine moved it upmarket, "from a backpackers' to a businessmen's airline", providing a more stylish image, with "wines of the month" and superior service. By 1983 New York Air was making profits of $4.5 million; but its prospects were still uncertain, and in April 1984 came a bare announcement that Levine had resigned to return to academia.

The most publicised "darling of deregulation" was Air Florida, which was transformed from a staid local airline by its chairman Ed Acker, a tall and confident Texan with a cryptic smile who had been president of Braniff. Acker had graduated in both economics *and* psychology, and he epitomised the aggressive cunning of the new-style airline boss. "Once you get hooked on the airline business," he explained, "it's worse than dope." At Air Florida he saw how to use aggressive marketing and bargain fares to expand out of Florida as far as Europe and he was a master of gimmicks like "Free Rides for a Kiss" and serving champagne "Sunshine Sparklers". His chief target was Pan American, which since deregulation had been allowed to buy National Airlines, which gave it—at prohibitive cost—a domestic network including Florida: in a classic fare-war Acker rapidly undercut Pan Am's Florida fares, forcing it to reduce its flights. Then in 1981 the board of Pan American, which was facing mounting losses across the world, took the drastic step of luring Acker to be *their* chairman. Acker moved into the Pan Am skyscraper bringing all his aggression and combativeness to the global contest, precipitating a deadly price-war across the Atlantic. In Florida the fight was reversed as Acker fought back at his old company in a "grudge match" with rough tactics on both sides, until in July 1984 Air Florida collapsed into bankruptcy.

The most innovative of all the newcomers was Donald Burr, the young entrepreneur who had founded his own airline People Express with an almost messianic zeal for his own version of capitalism. He had first learnt about airlines as an analyst on Wall Street, and he then joined Texas International, which was going through a financial crisis, "that taught me what it's like when the rubber hits the road", he told me. "I saw how people could be misused and abused, and what it's like close to bankruptcy." He turned round Texas International with the help of "peanut" fares and then left and looked for another job; since he was offered none, he decided to set up his own airline to take advantage of deregulation; and he called it People Express. He had no romantic illusions about airlines. "They're a low-end commodity," he said. "They're capital-intensive, labour-intensive, fuel-intensive. You can't sell the seats with sex or caviar: the highest value is the price."

Burr concentrated everything on cheap fares, reducing costs to a minimum, and building up a new "hub" from the unfashionable airport at Newark on the wrong side of New York. "I learnt not to fight the high ground, which gets the politicians against you," he explained. "In Newark I could avoid confrontation." He avoided advertising, relying on word-of-mouth among students and the fame of his fares. With his skeleton staffs he could undercut every other airline, and his costs in 1984 were 3.25 cents per seat-mile—the lowest, he claimed, in the history of air travel. And his ideas on management, profit-sharing and motivation were beginning to re-echo through the industry.

The new airlines by 1983 had only captured 7.8 per cent of the American market. But they had compelled the established airlines to reduce fares and become more aggressive, at a time when they were already buffeted by the second oil shock of 1979 and the subsequent recession. None of the airline chiefs dared publicly oppose deregulation in the political mood of the time. "Competition is a wonderful thing," proclaimed Dick Ferris, the new President of United Air Lines in Chicago. Frank Borman, the astronaut who had taken over Eastern Airlines in 1975, first opposed deregulation and then supported it. "At the time of deregulation we were all thrown to the wolves," recalled a Vice-President of Eastern, Al Brescia, "but we were the wolves and the chickens, all at the same time, and we were all looking for a free lunch. We've learned there is no free lunch."

Most of the big airlines were in serious difficulties after three years of deregulation and recession. While the local airlines were able to maintain profits of $160m in 1980 and $177m in 1981, through the depths of the recession, the airlines on trunk routes were showing mounting losses—from $350m in 1980 to $544m in 1981 to $636m in 1982. The industry as a whole was sinking deeper into debt to the banks. Many airlines were using second-hand or leased planes rather than investing in new ones, and in the Arizona desert there were still longer rows of "whitetails"—the planes which could find no buyer.

The biggest victim of deregulation was Braniff, the airline founded by Tom Braniff in Oklahoma in 1928 which had been taken over by Texans including Ed Acker. In the sixties it had become the fastest-growing of all, based on Dallas, which advertised "the end of the plain plane": it even commissioned Alexander Calder to design two DC-8s with his signature blazoned on the front. But realism caught up: Braniff was hit by the second oil crisis of 1979, its losses mounted over the next two years of deregulation and in 1981 the board brought in a tough young chairman, Howard D. Putnam, to turn the airline round. Braniff was locked in a deadly battle with American Airlines who flew competitive routes from the same hub airport at Fort-Worth Dallas, and Putnam was convinced that American — which had its own financial problems—was unfairly gunning for Braniff. When in February 1982 Putnam was telephoned by the President of American, Robert Crandall, he warily consulted his attorney and then returned the call with a tape recorder running. Crandall told Putnam that the two airlines were "dumb as hell" to pound each other on the same routes when neither was "making a —— dime". Putnam replied that it was American's fault for entering Braniff's markets: "I can't just sit here and allow you to bury us without giving our best effort." There followed a historic exchange:

Putnam: Do you have a suggestion for me?

Crandall: Yes, I have a suggestion for you. Raise your goddamn fares twenty per cent. I'll raise mine the next morning.

Putnam: Robert, we . . .

Crandall: You'll make more money and I will too.

Putnam: We can't talk about pricing.

Crandall: Oh, —— Howard. We can talk about any goddamn thing we want to talk about.

Crandall was wrong, and the suggestion which would be common-place in Europe was heresy to American trustbusters. Putnam turned over his tape to the Justice Department who later charged Crandall with attempted price-fixing and released part of the tape. But in the meantime Putnam had not solved his problems: he offloaded 800 employees and tried to turn Braniff into a cut-rate airline, but by May 1983—after only eight months as chairman—he was compelled to file for bankruptcy. Braniff's rivals including American could hardly conceal their relief; but the respite was only temporary. Several of Braniff's planes were soon bought cheaply by other airlines: "You just can't wash those planes out of the system," as one airline lawyer put it. And by March 1984 a "New

Braniff" was flying, now owned by Hyatt hotels, to try to recapture some of the old routes—though on a much smaller scale. The collapse of the Old Braniff was seen as a sign that deregulation was going too far, but Kahn was unrepentant: "Yes, it's my fault, in part," he told the *Wall Street Journal*, "but this is an economically healthy process—painful but healthy." Certainly the Braniff story suggested that a major airline could collapse without doing any serious damage to consumers or the national interest.

The arguments about regulation continued to rage. "The year or two after deregulation," Kahn later claimed, "witnessed many more improvements in service, for towns in all size categories, than deteriorations, as measured by frequency of departures and the convenience of their schedules". And in 1984 Kahn insisted to me that, "By far the greater number of travellers and communities have benefited." His successor at the CAB Marvin Cohen could point to the fact that many big airlines including Pan Am, Western and United, had reduced their expenses per ton-mile during 1982; and he was proud that deregulation had enabled each airline "to find its own niche", ranging from the luxury flights of Air One to the rock-bottom prices of People Express. But by mid-1984 many of the niches were still very insecure. "I think the big airlines and the small airlines can do all right," said Robert Six, surveying the deregulated scene. "It's when the small ones try to get much bigger, when they get to challenge the real gorillas, American or United, that they'll have troubles."

Deregulation was certainly changing the basic concept of an airline. The big corporations like Pan Am or TWA had seen themselves in the fifties and sixties as historic institutions which could command a special loyalty from their passengers. But deregulation soon revealed that most passengers only cared about two things—price and convenience. As the upstart airlines competed on both these fronts the older airlines tried artificially to try to regain "brand loyalty" by offering free flights to frequent travellers. American Airlines began the giveaways in 1981; soon TWA were offering two first-class round-trips to anywhere after 95,000 miles while Pan Am promised thirty days of unlimited first-class travel for two after 175,000 miles. The attractions tended to cancel each other out; and busy passengers were still inclined to take the first cheap available flight. It was a hard knock to the airlines' pride: they were beginning to look still more like shops or bazaars, or like middlemen between the customers and the planes who had constantly to adjust to the shifting market.

Deregulation was also drastically changing the American air map. The cut-throat competition on the most crowded routes—like

New York to Florida or New York to Los Angeles—had brought some fares rapidly down. But many passengers on the less-used local routes soon found themselves paying higher fares for less regular service, often without jet planes. Distance and cost were becoming still less closely related, and it was cheaper to fly from coast to coast than to many cities in between. And the hub airports, which provided the junctions of the air, were becoming much more attractive to the airlines. Many hubs had been long-established—like Minneapolis the home of Northwest Orient, Kansas City the base of TWA, or above all Atlanta which became the hub for both Delta and Eastern, providing the hectic changing-place for passengers from southern and mid-western states. "When you go to heaven," it was said, "you must go via Atlanta." Deregulation encouraged the airlines to link up more flights through their hubs: the more passengers they could herd through a few airports, the more easily they could fill up their planes. In the first three years from mid-1978 American Airlines' departures from Dallas/Fort Worth went up by thirty-two per cent, Delta's departures from Atlanta went up twenty-four per cent and US Air's departures from Pittsburgh up by twenty-six per cent.

The air map was looking much more like a cluster of overlapping spiders' webs with long threads stretching out. The hub cities gained strategic advantages, attracting new companies and industries to make use of their range of direct flights; while communities on the edges became more dependent on hubs. When planes had first opened up the continent fifty years earlier, many smaller communities welcomed them as providing a new access, after the ruthless centralisation that followed the railroads, with their junctions and termini. But now the airlines too were looking like centralisers, enforced not by iron tracks but by the harsh laws of competition.

PILOTS AND CRASHES

While passengers and economists argued about the benefits of deregulation few pilots had many doubts about what it had done to *them*. The first instigators of deregulation had not foreseen the consequences for the unions. "We didn't see it as union-bashing," Kahn told me. "The unions were right to oppose deregulation, but none of us were aware what intense opposition they would face." "We didn't realise they'd be so vulnerable," Mike Levine confirmed in 1983. But the new policy coincided with a world recession and an economic climate which had already undermined the bargaining position of the employees, particularly the pilots.

Over fifty years the pilots had built up a position which other professional unions watched with envy. In the United States the Air Line Pilots' Association (ALPA) working from its Washington palace, had successively increased the salaries and leisure-time of pilots as their planes got faster and bigger until by 1975 the pilots' average flying-time was only fifty hours per month, and they could insist on having a crew of three in the cockpit. They effectively exported their union power through the pilots' international federation IFALPA and foreign pilots were quick to follow their example. In Britain the pilots' union BALPA had been able to delay the flying of the Boeing 747s while they stuck out for higher salaries, and pilots who had once been regarded as chauffeurs had achieved the same kind of status as the captains of ocean liners, with valuable perks including first-class travel for their families: sometimes the whole first-class cabin seemed filled with the airline's employees. Pilots were ex-officio members of the new "international upper class", and other airline employees were able to reflect their glory: in 1980 airline typists in America earned forty-one per cent more than average typists, and aircraft cleaners earned eighty-two per cent more than average janitors.

The pilots' bargaining power was soon undermined by the combination of deregulation and recession, which hit them even harder than other unions. The first blow came from the strike of air traffic controllers in August 1981, which antagonised the public and demystified attitudes to safety before it was broken by President Reagan. The airline chiefs as they faced mounting losses naturally looked at their pilots' salaries. The scenario became painfully familiar, as the President of ALPA, Henry Duffy, complained: first the management would invite the pilots' leaders to share the airline's problems, then threaten to put pilots on furlough, then talk about invoking Chapter 11 of the bankruptcy law to renegotiate all agreements. By 1983 fifteen per cent of the 34,000 members of ALPA were on furlough, many with little prospect of being re-employed since "job-hopping" is rare among pilots; while in the meantime new airlines could often attract younger pilots for half the salaries. "The trouble is," as one of them said, "we like to fly." Some of the new pilots were much more individualist than the traditional company men. "We're not country club boys," said the chief pilot of the new Phoenix airline America West. "We're expatriates and scabs, war heroes and cargo jockeys."

The orthodox pilots took refuge in the ultimate justification of their high status—like that of surgeons—their hold over life and death. At first there was little real evidence that deregulation was reducing safety standards: the American Transport Association which represented the airlines could show that between October 1979 and January 1982 there was no fatal accident on any turbo-jet plane in the United States. But over the next year there were five fatal air crashes, killing a total of 236 passengers in America; and the most worrying of them gave credence to the pilots' warnings. A plane of Air Florida, the "darling of deregulation" which did not recognise unions, took off from Washington national airport in icy weather, flown by two young pilots who sounded—from the transcripts later made public—remarkably casual and indisciplined. "Slushy runway", said the first officer just before take-off. "Do you want me to do anything special or just go for it?" And the captain replied, "Unless you got anything special you'd like to do . . . " Two minutes later the plane crashed into the Potomac river, killing all but four of the seventy-seven passengers. The pilots insisted that such crashes were being precipitated by economic pressures and union-breaking: and Henry Duffy warned that desperate airlines would press pilots to land in marginal weather conditions—what was called "pilot-pushing" in the thirties.

As the airlines cut down their pilots' salaries and privileges their union naturally looked out for signs of reducing safety standards. In September 1983 Continental Airlines, under its aggressive new chairman Frank Lorenzo, filed for bankruptcy and quickly restarted the "New Continental", offering the pilots only half their previous pay. But the pilots went on strike against the new terms, and Lorenzo rapidly had to promote co-pilots to captains to fill the gaps: the Senior Director of Flying, W. S. Laughlin, resigned in protest. In November one newly promoted captain Mike Wood was flying seventy-three passengers, including Lorenzo himself, to Denver where he landed by mistake on a taxi-way instead of the main runway. It caused no damage or injuries, but the pilots' union could not resist publishing an advertisement headed: ROOKIE CAPTAIN MISSES RUNWAY. It was only one example, they insisted, of "why they warned passengers not to fly 'The New Continental' ".

There *was* a danger that fierce competition and dismantling regulations could lower the standards of safety: it was the exceptional danger of planes, after all, which had first caused them to be so exceptionally regulated. Some of the more extreme early proponents of deregulation in Chicago in the sixties had advocated that air safety could be left entirely to the marketplace. When that argument was put by a Chicago economist, Professor George Stigler, to Sir Ronald Edwards, the British chairman of the important committee on air transport in 1969, Edwards made a classic response: "Are you telling me," he asked, "that I should let airline A kill me to prove to you that you should travel by airline B?"

Deregulation was never so total, and Washington still retained its independent body, the National Transport Safety Board, to ensure proper safeguards. But there were some signs of greater carelessness by 1984. And some of the first proponents of deregulation, including Kennedy's team, were now worried that the pressures to cut costs among smaller airlines were seriously affecting safety standards.

The deregulators were determined from the start to extend the new competitiveness round the world, wherever American airlines were flying. But their campaign, which looked relatively straightforward inside the United States, became far more confused in other countries where airlines were owned by their governments and deeply interlocked with national policy, and where the appearance of free competition was never quite what it looked. The CAB in Washington, which had for so long uneasily co-existed with IATA, now came into headlong conflict with it. "With the exception of the US-Europe service," said a later general counsel to the CAB, David Kirstein, "international air transportation is probably the most regulated and least competitive industry in the world."

The first suggestions of deregulation abroad met with rapid resistance from foreign airlines, and in 1977 ICAO summoned a special conference in Montreal—the most important gathering since Chicago—where a hundred governments supported the IATA system and the US was almost isolated. But Fred Kahn at the CAB had anticipated heavy opposition from protectionist countries, and he pressed ahead, issuing an order which required foreign airlines and IATA—which it called an "illegal cartel"—to "show cause" why they should remain immune from American anti-trust laws. There was fierce lobbying on a global scale. "Airline chief executives started flocking into Washington to express their misgivings," said Umberto Nordio, the head of Alitalia who was one of the most adamant for regulation. "We warned that the proposed policy would not work in the international air transport field." In Washington the great departments were as so often divided: Justice took Kahn's side against IATA, while Transportation called for caution and the State Department summoned a succession of conferences. The big American airlines including Pan Am were not keen on extending deregulation, but they could not be seen to lobby against it.

Kahn first concentrated on the North Atlantic route with its forty different airlines, which became the chief battleground of

deregulation; and in 1980 the US government forbade their airlines
to take part in any IATA conferences to fix rates between Europe
and the United States. Kahn's chief opponent was Britain; for
almost two-thirds of North Atlantic passengers passed through the
London airports, and any agreements with Britain set a pattern for
others. Soon after Kahn's arrival, the British and Americans had
signed a new 'Bermuda 2' agreement, to supersede the first Bermuda
agreement signed thirty years earlier, which tried to liberalise fares
across the Atlantic, but still maintained strict controls and was
angrily attacked by the deregulators. The British and Americans
began playing tit-for-tat. The CAA in London allowed British
Caledonian to Houston, and the CAB allowed Braniff to fly from
Dallas to London; but the British complained that Braniff competed
unfairly with low fares to other Western American cities, so after
Braniff had made its showy inaugural flight they refused to let it
continue until it dropped its cheap fares. Kahn was exasperated:
"I said, let's stick it to the Brits—let's put pressure on the Germans
through Amsterdam." He began helping the Dutch—who always
want Schiphol to be "London's Third Airport"—to lure traffic
away from Britain, and promised them new destinations in America
if they accepted the Americans' fares, which they did. Lufthansa
became worried by Germans flying from Schiphol instead of Frankfurt, and soon accepted the same rules. Faced with these rivals the
British were forced to interpret Bermuda 2 more liberally and to
allow more American airlines into Heathrow and Gatwick.

The American intervention in Europe continued to exasperate
the European airlines, particularly the Italians and French. "If
reality did not fit their theories," complained Nordio of Alitalia, "it
had to be stretched or chopped up, like Procrustes' visitors were
until they fitted Procrustes' bed." "The national interest of any
country," said Pierre Giraudet of Air France in 1981, "prevents it
from entrusting the responsibility for its foreign trade to foreign
carriers motivated solely by profit." "We tend to get confused,"
said Jan Carlzon of SAS, "when American policy is urging for
transport by sea the very same policy which is denounced for
transport by air." "The plain fact of the matter," Patrick Shovelton,
the British air negotiator, told the Americans, "is that both of us
believe in mercantilism—that is to say in promoting and developing
our own commercial interests."

The Europeans were highly suspicious of the Americans' real
motives. "The rest of the world, now as in 1944, tends to distrust the
motives behind America's 'open skies' policy," wrote the Swedish
political scientist Christer Jonsson in 1981. " 'Survival of the fittest'
in international aviation inevitably entails 'survival of the fattest',

and there is widespread apprehension that the American preaching of laissez-faire really means 'laissez-nous-faire'." While many American export industries had been declining, the United States remained by far the most prosperous country in the air: it still dominated aerospace technology, and its internal air traffic was still equal to the rest of the world's put together. "The notion of waning American power does not apply to international aviation," as Jonsson wrote, "where the United States is by far the strongest nation and does not hesitate to exploit its issue-specific power."

But the export of deregulation did little to help the American airlines. "For Pan Am, the effect was negative," said Ed Acker. The Reagan administration began to have second thoughts. The House Subcommittee on Investigations and Oversight had exhaustively reviewed international aviation policy, and produced a report in August 1983 which described how foreign governments discriminated against American airlines, and how some foreign airlines such as KLM had benefited from deregulation more than the Americans. It showed how the American Export-Import Bank was lending money at low rates to foreign airlines buying American airliners: so that the US was "subsidising foreign competition against its own carriers". And it complained that the agencies in Washington had not been forceful enough in dealing with foreign governments' discrimination. "Our carriers' viability," it said, "has been adversely affected by an open skies policy which has extended domestic deregulation to the international arena."

As foreign governments and airlines mobilised themselves to meet the competition, Washington once again faced the question which had dogged it since Trippe first built up Pan American, and which was recurring in many other industries faced with new challengers from East Asia. How far could they combine an aggressive policy of competition and trustbusting inside their country, while they confronted highly organised foreign states which put all the force of their government behind their favoured airline, their chosen instrument?

11

Laker versus the Cartel

The trouble with predators is that they don't know who's the prey—
until he's dead.

Sir Freddie Laker, 1984

As the deregulators extended their campaign across the world they
brought to a head the old arguments about competition and cartels
—particularly across the North Atlantic, where all kinds of ideology
collided—and the argument for free enterprise was dramatised to
the point of melodrama by an engaging British airline tycoon.
Freddie Laker set himself up as the champion of the "forgotten
man" who wanted cheap travel across the Atlantic, and as the
challenger of the cartel of giant airlines. But he was always less in
command of his own fate than he looked. "He was carried along
by currents," as his chronicler Howard Banks put it, "that at the
time he seemed not to comprehend and that he rarely controlled."
But the economic and political currents were below the surface
while Laker was always highly visible; and he appeared as a
folk-hero on both sides of the Atlantic. His story was not just an
individual epic: he turned into a pied piper who rallied not only
passengers but bankers, manufacturers and politicians in his long
train; while his crusade showed up the manipulations, hypocrisies
and political props behind the apparent free competition.

Laker's style suited the part. He is a big, loping Englishman with
a common touch and the gift of the gab who talks with a sarcastic
South London voice like the film actor Michael Caine and who likes
to call all women dear. Today, from a small office in Croydon, he
looks back on his extraordinary rise and fall with wry humour.
"What else can I do? Shoot myself?"

His early career epitomised the entrepreneurial, buccaneering spirit which airlines were fast losing. He came from a working-class home in Kent and learnt about planes as an engineer and pilot in air transport during the Second World War. In peacetime he dealt in aircraft spare parts and then bought some old planes from BOAC just in time to use them for the Berlin airlift of 1948 which provided him and other lone operators with a sudden bonanza. He later sold his business, which in 1960 became part of a newly formed airline called British United Airways, which the Tory government encouraged to compete with the state airlines. Laker became the chief executive of BUA, where he learned much about how to raise money and how to bargain with the government—which provided half the airline's revenue in troop-carrying contracts.

But after five years he had a row with the chairman and at the age of forty-three he set up his own Laker Airways to cater for package holidays. He borrowed from the Scottish Clydesdale Bank (which was later taken over by the Midland Bank) to buy planes including two cheap Britannias from BEA which had been outdated by the new jets: his crucial advantage always lay in buying second-hand bargains as the big airlines were forced to buy new planes. He was unlucky with his timing, as package tours slumped and tour companies went bankrupt. But he was always looking out for new markets and in 1969 he leased two Boeing 707s—which had belonged to the bankrupt airline British Eagle—and began flying charters across the North Atlantic.

He soon found himself in the midst of the comic but bitter controversy over the IATA rules for the so-called "affinity" fares (see Chapter 7) which accounted for much of his charter business. As airlines and governments became more watchful about the charters Laker saw his Atlantic business shrinking and looked round for a better way to attract passengers. He found it in the idea of the "Skytrain"—a basic service which would allow passengers to arrive at the last moment, to fly cheaply on planes with "no frills". It was a doubly attractive idea which attacked the higher fares and the overblown bureaucracy of the giants while appealing to the public's growing resentment of the air cartel; and it brought the cheap fare principles of charters or non-skeds into scheduled flights. But Laker was up against much more than British Airways or Pan Am: his prospects depended on influencing governments on both sides of the Atlantic, and on the very changeable political mood in Britain.

The British Labour government had surprisingly encouraged competition in the air after it published Sir Ronald Edwards' report in 1969 which stated boldly that "the private sector should be encouraged to create a 'second force' airline"; and free enterprise got a boost with the new Tory government under Ted Heath, who had once worked as a civil servant in the aviation ministry, where he conceived a dislike for the cartel system. The Tories passed a new Civil Aviation Act in 1971, which brought into being the Civil Aviation Authority (CAA) to arbitrate on air-routes, theoretically insulated from political pressures. But the main beneficiary was the newly merged airline British Caledonian which had bought up BUA, run by a formidable Scottish ex-pilot Adam Thomson who was more than a match for Laker. Thomson had brilliantly exploited Scots loyalties and lobbies on both sides of the Atlantic; and he soon obtained licences to compete with BOAC by flying from London (Gatwick) to New York and Los Angeles, as well as to the Far East. Like many new members of select clubs, Thomson was strongly against admitting any more, and he fiercely opposed allowing Laker to share the increasingly crowded North Atlantic; while BOAC was now proposing its own scheme to compete with charter flights through the new "APEX" system which allowed passengers cheaper fares if they booked several weeks ahead.

But Laker persisted, and he saw yet another chance to buy planes on the cheap: he rashly bought two giant DC-10 airliners from the Japanese Mitsui Bank, thus committing himself to the war of the big jets. Laker now seemed to be in luck: he gained the sympathy of the first chairman of the CAA, Lord Boyd-Carpenter, to whom he put his theory of the "forgotten men"—the supposed millions who would fill up his cheap seats without significantly damaging the other airlines—and the CAA awarded Laker a licence for his Skytrain, with some restrictions. But the equivalent body in Washington, the CAB, had become highly sceptical of Laker's record as a charter operator with dubious "affinities"; they first fined him $101,000 dollars, and then in June 1974 refused him a licence. It was the British who were now pressing for more competition, while the Americans were more restrictive.

Laker's luck was again running out. The first oil crisis had precipitated the new airline crisis across the North Atlantic, threatening both Pan Am and TWA with bankruptcy. In the oil panic the American government had dropped its anti-trust objections and allowed Pan Am and TWA to meet with both British Airways (as BOAC had now become) and British Caledonian to agree on cutting down their flights to reduce their losses—on condition that no new intruder like Laker was let in. In Britain the Labour government came back, committed to appeasing the unions who detested the free-booting airline; and the Secretary for Trade, Peter Shore, soon overruled the CAA and revoked Laker's licence. It was a bitter moment for Laker: "Shore decided we wouldn't fly even though ninety-nine per cent of the people would have voted for me," he complained to me later. "Consumers don't have any impact—like voters. The governments and the regulators don't take any notice of 'em. We could only screw 'em through the law."

But Laker was mustering some powerful legal support. In Washington he had hired a superlawyer, Bob Beckman, an expert on aviation law and anti-trust who was to become a star actor in the long dramas that followed: he had a genius for publicity, a theatrical style and a glamorous English wife: his law office looked more like a scene from *Charlie's Angels*. "If you left Beckman in a room by himself," said one British lawyer, "in ten minutes there'd be an argument." Beckman promptly sued the airlines for conspiring to delay Laker's Skytrain, compelling them to recast their agreement excluding the reference to Laker. In Britain some Labour politicians as well as Tories sympathised with Laker's populist appeal— including the unpredictable new Secretary of Trade, Edmund Dell. And when Laker appealed against his lost licence he received unexpected support from the judges, culminating in a stirring judgment by Lord Denning, the scourge of the bureaucrats, who found that the minister had exceeded his powers.

In early 1977 came a new turn of fortune. The Labour government conceded Laker's right to fly Skytrain; while in Washington Alfred Kahn at the CAB was pledged to liberalise air travel and soon granted Laker his permit, seeing "a golden opportunity to encourage imagination and innovation in the North Atlantic air travel market". By June 1977 Laker was free to start his Skytrain. The established airlines in IATA held a worried conference to try to counter his cheap fares, and the British CAA allowed other airlines to have their own "stand-by" fares, while in return it allowed Laker to fly the Skytrain, not from the remote Stansted airport, but from the more accessible Gatwick. It had taken Laker six years of negotiation, but his battles and showmanship had made him a unique popular hero—playing the role of the lone entrepreneur of the air battling against a cartel of corporations.

Laker launched the Skytrain with a folk-festival which combined Spartan economy with razzamatazz in a way that was irresistible —particularly to the British with their nostalgia for queues and wartime discomfort. The Atlantic Big Three—Pan Am, TWA and British Airways—did their best to steal his thunder with their own bargain fares; but Laker could still undercut them with the help of his cheaper planes, and he pared his costs to the bone with improvised booking offices, no meals or drinks, and publicity provided free by the media. He was soon able to attract passengers who would otherwise have flown on charter planes, and 1978 was boom year. At the end of the first year, Laker was triumphant. He reckoned he had made a profit of £2 million on his New York run; he was knighted by the Labour government which had so long obstructed him; and his face was on the cover of *Time* magazine. Students from Holland and Scandinavia were flying via Laker across the Atlantic, and in the United States Laker was also a hero to Kahn and the deregulators.

But Sir Freddie was bent on further expansion. "I had to keep moving," he now says, "because they kept moving at me." He began flying to Los Angeles and talked about flying round the world with a "Globetrain". He staggered his rivals by announcing plans to buy five *more* DC-10s for long-distance routes—for which he later borrowed from American banks, led by the Export-Import Bank —together with ten of the new European airbuses, to cater for Laker holidays in Europe. In fact Laker's scope for expansion was still severely limited. The flights to Los Angeles lost £2 million in their first year; Australia and Hong Kong were resistant to the round-the-world trips; and competing with European airlines was, as Laker put it to me at the time, "like farting against thunder". But Laker had always believed in buying planes before he knew he could use them, and he was encouraged with amazing rashness by the Midland Bank, which was anxious to make money out of loans for future airbuses; while the new Tory government under Margaret Thatcher—whose husband had been Laker's business colleague— treated Laker as a mascot of free enterprise. It was hardly surprising if Laker, after his first dazzling success, was fooled by his own ballyhoo and forgot the harsh facts of the business.

By the middle of 1979 Laker faced two serious setbacks. The second oil crisis and the following recession hit all the airlines with higher costs and set back all projections of air travel. And in May the crash of a DC-10 in Chicago killed all 274 passengers, and led to the grounding for six weeks of all DC-10s including Laker's, forcing him to cancel Skytrain and costing him, he reckoned, £13 million in lost revenues. Laker appeared undeterred and remained stolidly loyal to the DC-10. But the tide was now beginning to turn against him.

By early 1981 Laker was operating nine different scheduled flights between Britain and the United States, carrying one in seven of all passengers between the two countries and ranking sixth out of the forty-three airlines which crossed the North Atlantic. He was attracting businessmen as well as tourists, causing the established airlines much heavier losses. But his own problems were mounting as the recession showed no signs of improving. The value of the pound sterling, which provided most of Laker's revenues, was sinking, while the dollar, which accounted for most of his debts, was rising. Already by the spring of 1981 Laker behind his brave face was in deep financial trouble. The possible bankruptcy of Laker was worrying the bankers and the government, while the competing airlines now appeared determined to put him out of business. The resulting saga, whose details only emerged later, dramatically lit up the workings of both the airlines and the banks.

"THE DESTRUCTION OF LAKER AIRWAYS"

By early May 1981 Laker realised that he would not be able to repay the loans due at the end of the year, and he warned all his main lenders, without gaining any concessions. By August the Bank of England—which was facing an avalanche of bankruptcies in the midst of the recession—was seriously worried about a possible Laker crash. Their adviser Lord Benson, the veteran accountant and troubleshooter, invited Dennis Kitching, the head of corporate finance at the Midland Bank, to an emergency meeting. Kitching was warned that Laker was about to default on his American loan, and asked to try to refinance him. Kitching was very aware (as he recalled in an affidavit) that Sir Freddie "was a very popular figure in the public eye" whom the Tory government had publicly commended. He also knew that he "was grossly overextended, and it would have been a sensible commercial decision to withdraw any further banking support . . . " But the Bank of England urged him to persevere.

In September Laker met with his bankers in London and told them bluntly that he could not continue in business unless they postponed repayments for a year. Kitching patiently set about restructuring Laker's debts, with the help of the merchant bank Samuel Montagu which belonged to the Midland. McDonnell Douglas, who had in effect loaned their DC-10s to Laker, sent their own team of financial analysts who prepared projections for Laker's future: they showed that he would lose £4 million in 1981 and £12 million in 1982, but that he should make a profit of around £14 million in 1983. Reassured, the Midland agreed to maintain Laker's overdraft and persuaded other lenders to postpone the repayments.

But in the meantime Laker's competitors—as Sir Freddie's lawyer Bob Beckman saw it—"smelled blood and closed for the kill". They had not been too worried as long as Laker had been mainly competing with charter flights, and helping to kill them off. But now he was confronting the big airlines head-on, with first-class seats as well as cheap ones. The attitude of the Big Three had become noticeably more ruthless since September 1981 when Ed Acker from Air Florida had become chairman of Pan American, and was all set to compete with Laker's low fares. British Airways at first warned that drastic fare-cuts would be "mutual suicide"; but on 16 October—only a month after Acker's arrival—BA agreed with Pan Am to ask the British government to approve lower fares. Was this a predatory act, designed to kill off an intruder in the method favoured by Rockefeller or Vanderbilt? The question was to re-echo through the subsequent lawsuits. Acker claims that he didn't even know BA's commercial director, Gerry Draper. Laker claims that he warned the Tory minister responsible, Iain Sproat, that if he approved BA's low fares he would be broke by the end of March; but Sproat went ahead and the Big Three airlines all brought their minimum fares down to $249.

Certainly it was a costly move for the airlines which were already heavily in the red, which they could not sustain for long. Pan American had only survived by selling assets for $800 million, and British Airways was kept going by huge loans from its government. Laker was convinced that the low fares were predatory and that he was the prey whom the giants were determined to destroy. He knew, as he put it, that "there was no way I could survive if they matched me". To compete effectively, he reckoned, he had to have his own hub at Gatwick, with connecting flights to the Continent, which he was planning to operate with his new airbuses; but this was already stirring up enemies among the European airlines.

Predatory or not, the low fares soon took effect. In the first two weeks of November, Laker claimed, his transatlantic traffic went down to fifty-nine per cent of his projections, worsened by rumours among travel agents of his impending collapse. He realised that he urgently needed still more help to tide him over the bleak winter months, and his bankers led by Montagu's worked out a new plan to raise money including an additional overdraft. At the same time the two manufacturers, McDonnell Douglas and General Electric, offered to convert debts into preference shares in Laker's company. It was a rash promise. Manufacturers would always try hard to avoid bankrupting an airline, for the two industries' fortunes were interlocked, and the last thing McDonnell's needed was to get their planes back. But by offering to take Laker shares they clearly risked the fury of his competitors.

Laker was now offering his own first-class "Regency" service which was a long way from his original appeal to the small man and which still further antagonised Acker and the others. He insists that he was only trying to negotiate a deal with the other airlines: "you stay out of the back, and I'll stay out of the front". To try to

reach an agreement he actually secretly approached his old bogey
IATA about becoming a member, to obtain immunity from anti-
trust laws; but it came to nothing. When IATA held a meeting in
Florida in December 1981 Laker sent his representative, John Jones,
who in theory was not allowed to talk directly to the other airlines,
and could only do so through the British government's representative. But the elaborate exchanges failed to reach an agreement, and
Laker was on his own. Just before Christmas Montagu's announced
that the rescue plan had been agreed, and Laker promised travellers
that his future was assured. But his giant rivals all faced their
own financial crises, and were determined to prevent any special
treatment for Laker. They entered the most ruthless phase of the
battle.

The most evidently incensed of the airline chiefs was Sir Adam
Thomson of British Caledonian, who had recently been chairman
of the Association of European Airlines (AEA) which put him in
touch with other operators. Behind his courteous low-key style Sir
Adam was capable of sudden gusts of emotion and anger; and he
never concealed his intense resentment of Laker. In January 1982
he sent a New Year message to all his staff describing the industry's
desperate situation. 1981 he said had been "the year of the lemming"
for the airlines. "Never before have the forces, both external and
internal, been so stacked up against our industry." British Airways
had made record losses during the year, while Laker could only
survive through "massive support from a number of quarters".
British Caledonian's staff had to make sure that "in their efforts to
assist the other two British long-haul airlines, those responsible do
nothing to undermine British Caledonian".

Thomson was outraged to learn that McDonnell Douglas and
General Electric—for whom British Caledonian were very good
customers—were helping Laker by converting their debt into
shares, and he soon put pressure to stop them. The easiest target
was the aero-engine division of General Electric, whose boss Brian
Rowe, a former Englishman, had never been keen on investing in
Laker. On 2 February Adam Thomson sent a curt telex to Neil
Burgess, GE's general manager, saying that, if the information was
correct, BCAL HAS NO FURTHER INTEREST IN MCDONNELL DOUGLAS
AIRCRAFT.

Other European airlines, which were less obviously threatened
by Laker, were now worried that he would barge into their markets
and wreck their agreements; and they joined the attack with the
appearance of a concerted campaign which would soon be the
subject of intense legal inspection. The Belgian airline Sabena had
an old friendship with Laker back in the fifties when he flew car

ferries for them; but Sabena's chairman Carlos Van Rafelghem now telexed Brian Rowe to protest against GE's support and to warn him that SUCH PRACTICES WOULD ADVERSELY AFFECT OUR PRESENT GOOD BUSINESS RELATIONSHIP. René Lapautre, the chairman of the French airline UTA which was not obviously threatened by Laker, had been quite critical of the rigid European controls; but he too was now spurred into protest. He telexed GE to say that he was "extremely upset" and that it was IRONICAL THAT YOU WOULD PROVIDE DIRECT SUPPORT TO THE ONE WHO OPENLY AND KNOWINGLY GENERATED THE DISASTROUS CRISIS WHICH WE ARE IN. Other airline chiefs joined in, including Sergio Orlandini, the President of KLM, who telexed that his company was "deeply concerned". Faced with this bombardment General Electric not surprisingly retreated, and Brian Rowe soon made clear that General Electric would not be putting equity into Laker.

The airlines' chief target was not GE but McDonnell Douglas, who had much more reason to be loyal to Laker. Sir Freddie had gone out of his way to praise and endorse their DC-10 after its disastrous crashes, for which the chief executive John Brizendine —who took most of the fire—was lastingly grateful. McDonnell's still looked to Laker as an important customer and their loan was modest compared to the high stakes of their future production. But the airline chiefs were determined to stop Brizendine and his chairman, Sandy McDonnell, from becoming shareholders in Laker. On 27 January Yvan Goosens of Sabena, who was regarded as close to the chairman Van Rafelghem, called McDonnell's (as their man Geoffrey Norris reported it) to "register his airline's amazement and disappointment that McDonnell Douglas should try to prevent what appeared to be the natural demise of a man who had caused other airlines so many problems". Sabena soon emerged as the most vindictive of all. "There should be ways of saving Laker," they said later, "without preserving the man himself and enabling him to continue his unhelpful career throughout the airline scene."

The following week a succession of airlines fired remarkably similar salvos. On Monday, 1 February, Bo Stahle of SAS called Warren Kraemer of McDonnell's London office to say that his management viewed McDonnell's move "with grave apprehension". The next day produced an angry chorus, with Adam Thomson again the most vociferous. He cabled both Brizendine and McDonnell saying that he would "absolutely forbid" any further negotiations for DC-9s, calling Laker "the most disruptive airline on the North Atlantic", and then read out the cable to Warren Kraemer apologising for "being almost incoherent with anger" at the thought of McDonnell's insensitivity. Martin Junger, Swissair's Vice-President for Finance, also called Kraemer to express his company's "gravest concern"; then Reinhardt of Lufthansa, who had already talked to Sandy McDonnell for forty minutes, called Kraemer to "strongly chastise" the company and to explain the difference between "reasonably mature and responsible air carriers" and one that had "chosen the path of violent disruption".

On the same day James McMillan, the President of McDonnell Douglas' finance company, was visiting Frankfurt and Zurich and heard the complaints first of Lufthansa, then of Swissair; and the next day the stern head of Swissair, Armin Baltensweiler, cabled McDonnell and Brizendine to express his "deep concern" about the equity plan and to warn that it would be "detrimental to our current good business relations". Lapautre of UTA told other airline chiefs that it was "totally unacceptable" that McDonnell's and GE should help someone "who very openly and knowingly generated the disastrous crisis which we are in". Could it be that the protests, which sounded so remarkably similar, had been planned in a single conspiracy?

Certainly McDonnell's were becoming unnerved. When Kitching of the Midland Bank returned from three weeks' holiday on 25 January he found that McDonnell's "had not made any cash injection and were showing reluctance to proceed with the debt to equity conversion". By 4 February Geoffrey Norris, one of McDonnell's men in London, was reporting to his headquarters what looked "suspiciously like the start of phase two—more pressure from other carriers, this time exerted through the press". He recommended keeping a low profile. "Whether we appear as FJL's saviour, or his executioner, we will have problems."

The next day Sandy McDonnell sent a placatory telex from St Louis replying to all the airline chiefs who had sent "nasti-grams" —as Brizendine called their angry telexes. McDonnell explained that his company always tried to remain neutral between customers, but that they had a fiduciary responsibility to their shareholders to try to safeguard their loans to Laker; and he asked them not to hold that against them. But he added that the protests had anyway "been superseded by subsequent events". For in the meantime Laker had met with the fate that his competitors had wished for.

Laker's terms of trade during January, always the cruellest month for airlines, were even worse than expected. At the Midland Bank Kitching, back from holiday, soon decided that "the position looked almost hopeless"; and on 28 January the Midland told Laker that they would appoint new accountants, Ernst and Whinney, who were both aviation specialists and prominent liquidators. But the

Bank of England, under some political pressure, still sought a solution and on Monday, 1 February, they called a meeting with the bankers and McDonnell's men who later had a friendly dinner with Laker. Sir Freddie seemed cheerful: the next day he flew by Concorde to New York, and at London airport he gave an ebullient interview saying "all my financial worries are over". In New York he prepared a TV commercial in which he confidently proclaimed his new "Regency" first-class service which had so antagonised his rivals, standing in front of one of his planes. He was telephoned from London by David Sedgwick, another McDonnell's finance man, and warned of the growing pressure from airlines including Lufthansa who were asking the German banks to foreclose on him. But Sedgwick (according to Laker's account) assured Laker that Lufthansa would relent if Laker promised to abandon his cheap flights within Europe—which he did. Sedgwick (Laker insists) gave him no clue of the disaster to come. But back in London his last supports were crumbling away.

THE KILL

While Laker was in New York his time was running out. In London Ray Colegate, the civil servant who ran the Civil Aviation Authority, faced his most testing ordeal as umpire of the air. He was watching Laker's progress from day to day, for he had a statutory duty to withdraw his licence if he could not meet his obligations; and the figures he saw on 2 February showed Laker flying even fewer passengers across the Atlantic than predicted. David Walker of the Bank of England was now very pessimistic, and asked Colegate to explain the situation to the people most involved; so on Wednesday, 3 February, Ian McIntosh of Samuel Montagu invited the bankers and McDonnell's men, including Sedgwick, to dine with Colegate at the Waldorf-Astoria, close to the CAA offices in Kingsway. Colegate explained that Laker would need still more money—£10 million rather than £4 million—but none of the others offered help. The Midland Bank sent a message to Laker asking to see him in London the next day, without saying why. After the dinner Sedgwick realised, as he noted, that there was "no chance for Freddie", but when he phoned his boss Sandy McDonnell in St Louis they agreed not to tell him that. So when Freddie called Sedgwick from New York, just before catching the overnight Skytrain, Sedgwick only told him that the CAA "wasn't satisfied with the cash availability".

When Sir Freddie arrived at Gatwick the next morning he went straight to the Midland Bank with his solicitor, where he was promptly told that his overdraft would be withdrawn within the hour. They were joined by Sedgwick, to whom Laker complained about "not having told him of disaster", and then by Dennis Kitching, who told Laker that he could have until 9 a.m. the next morning to raise the money.

Laker made a desperate last bid. He called the minister, Iain Sproat, who told the Prime Minister, Margaret Thatcher, who had her own political stake in Sir Freddie's survival: only three months before she had explained to the Conservative conference that it was "thanks to Freddie Laker that you can cross the Atlantic for so much less than it would have cost in the early 1970s . . . Competition works." It was not the first time that Laker had appealed to Mrs Thatcher, but this time she acted: she summoned an urgent meeting including the chancellor, Treasury officials and Colegate from the CAA. They discussed at length whether the Treasury could guarantee another final £5 million "with a ring fence round it"; but the Treasury were negative while the prime minister, contrary to her public image, dithered. When she was warned that £5 million might still not be enough she said (as one participant vividly recalled): "Oh dear, I couldn't impose an open-ended situation on my poor taxpayers." Competition, it seemed, didn't work.

Laker also telephoned Harry Goodman, an old rival who was chairman of the tour company Intasun, who was then in Spain, to try to sell him his tour business. Goodman immediately flew back to Gatwick and met Laker at the Hilton hotel at midnight. They could not agree. By 4.30 a.m. Laker and his directors decided to cease trading. At 8 a.m. the board met formally. Half an hour later Laker's solicitor told Kitching at the Midland Bank that they had agreed to call in a receiver.

The newspapers carried the headlines LAKER GOES BUST. The public, even though many had lost their holidays with his crash, mourned him as a fallen hero, and subscribed to a fund to save him. For a few days it looked as though the Orion Bank, or the wily entrepreneur Tiny Rowland, might salvage the company; Laker still believes that his rescue was sabotaged by his rivals. But the liquidators—Christopher Morris from Touche Ross and Nigel Hamilton of Ernst and Whinney—moved in promptly to begin selling the thirteen planes, the hangars and equipment. Five DC-10s were repossessed by the American Export-Import Bank and flown to the Arizona desert; two more were taken back by the Mitsui Bank and then re-leased to British Caledonian; two airbuses were sold to Air Jamaica. The big airlines sighed with relief at the end of this "disruptive force" and the "rampant consumerism" which Laker had encouraged. "Laker became the victim," said Knut

Hammarskjöld of IATA, "of the open market he was preaching himself." In the industry only McDonnell Douglas were very serious mourners: "Laker has made a unique contribution to the airline passengers of the world," wrote James McMillan afterwards, "and had a lasting impact on the fare structure. It is a tragedy that, after forty years of effort, he was not able to realise more from his many contributions."

But the recriminations were bitter and long-lasting. The banks, who had once been so eager to lend, faced a barrage of criticism. The Midland, which had led the big airbus loan that had hastened Laker's demise, were the most fiercely criticised. "It is hard to escape the conclusion," said the *Financial Times* the day after his collapse, "that if the bankers had taken a more hard-nosed approach yesterday's sad story might have been averted." "I thought that forty-three banks couldn't be wrong," Laker said afterwards. "The banks were no smarter than anyone else," he told me. "Why do people think I was stupider than anyone else?"

But the political repercussions were still greater; for the free-booting businessman who had been Thatcher's hero had failed just when the nationalised British Airways, which had helped to destroy him, was making record losses paid by the taxpayers; and on the same day that Laker announced his bankruptcy, the British government announced a large loan to British Airways. In the year 1981–2 BA lost a staggering £144 million, partly as a result of their reckless fare-cutting against Laker. "BA got into a box by chasing me," Laker said afterwards. "The losses went through their whole network."

THE LAWSUIT

But it was not the end of the story, for in Washington Bob Beckman saw the opportunity of a lifetime. Only a month after Laker's collapse he was retained by the liquidators to investigate how it happened, and he came up with a sensational response: Laker Airways, he maintained, had a valid claim against the big airlines —including British Airways, Pan American, TWA, Lufthansa, Swissair and British Caledonian; as well as the Midland Bank and McDonnell's—for conspiring to violate the American anti-trust laws. He estimated the compensatory damages at $350 million, which under anti-trust laws could be trebled to over a billion dollars. The way was open for one of the biggest anti-trust suits in history, a lawyers' banquet.

Nine months after Laker's collapse the liquidator, Christopher

Morris, decided "after giving the matter the most careful consideration" to go ahead with the lawsuit. On 24 November 1982, having first warned Dennis Kitching not to destroy any documents, he sent the Midland Bank an eighteen-page document with the horrifying title:

THE DESTRUCTION OF LAKER AIRWAYS LIMITED

or

HOW THE MIDLAND BANK AND BRITISH AIRWAYS COMBINED WITH FOREIGNERS TO FORCE A PROFITABLE BRITISH COMPANY OUT OF BUSINESS

Drafted by Bob Beckman, it described in gruesome prose how the airlines had conspired to discipline Laker and had "closed in for the kill", while McDonnell's had "cracked under the pressure" and the Midland had joined the conspiracy. The bankers were suitably appalled. The next day they told Morris that the document was defamatory, outrageous and misconceived and that it contained "monstrous allegations" against the bank, without "a shred of evidence". Morris' partner Michael Blackburn tried to soothe them by explaining that it had been prepared by an American lawyer, and "was not necessarily couched in the same courteous terms as perhaps employed by English counsel"; but without much effect. There was a more cordial meeting between the Midland and Morris the next day, when Dennis Kitching was away making a speech; but Morris held to his threat to sue the Midland as a co-conspirator. Antony Willis, the Midland's solicitor, set about examining the files and interviewing bankers and swore an affidavit saying that, "There was no form of agreement or pressure which could possibly be described as a conspiracy." Dennis Kitching in an affidavit insisted that, "We needed no conspiracy to keep Laker in business; equally we did not need a conspiracy finally to decide that Midland could no longer support Laker."

In the United States the mammoth case was taking two divergent directions; or as the *Economist* put it: "Laker's bones were boiled in two separate cauldrons." While Judge Greene was hearing the civil case for damages in a federal district court the Justice Department had taken up a criminal case against the principal airlines for alleged price-fixing across the Atlantic in contravention of the anti-trust laws.

British Airways and British Caledonian hastened to stop the suits going any further on the grounds that they went beyond American jurisdiction; and by January a British court had granted them an injunction to prevent Christopher Morris from suing them in the United States. The case soon became a classic test of American strength in the law: Judge Harold H. Greene, who was trying the case in Washington, insisted that the British courts could not grant this relief, and in May Justice Parker in the British High Court also overturned the injunction. But the British government had now invoked the Protection of Trading Interests Act, which had been passed three years earlier. British Airways took the case to the Court of Appeal, where in July Sir John Donaldson and two other judges reversed the High Court, explaining that invoking the new Act made the case "wholly untriable". Christopher Morris then appealed to the Law Lords, the highest British court, who lifted the injunction and decided that the cases could after all be tried in the States. As the affidavits, opinions and memoranda piled up on both sides of the Atlantic, enough to fill whole rooms, the prospect of huge fines still loomed over the international airlines.

Whatever the outcome in law, Laker's crusading career had caused tremors which still reverberated through the industry. "Laker did not directly change much that wasn't already happening to international aviation," concluded Howard Banks, "but he was a marvellous catalyst. His presence made those changes happen faster." The contradictions in regulating airlines had been implicit since the Chicago conference and the rebirth of IATA, but they were now coming to a climax. Consumers were clamouring for cheaper fares and the break-up of an international cartel; yet unrestricted world competition could cause ruinous price wars with no end in sight; for most airlines were state-owned and could never be bankrupted; and all the governments—even the American government—were lurking in the background as their ultimate protectors.

Some fervent advocates of free enterprise were having second thoughts about price wars after the losses incurred in the fight against Laker. As Ed Acker of Pan American put it in October 1982:

Reckless price wars, while offering the public some temporary bargains, can lead to the financial ruin of many companies in the industry. The main reason for this self-defeating behaviour in our industry was the airlines' lack of experience with unregulated price competition. Unlike, say, department stores and super-markets and appliance manufacturers that have been competing on a price basis for many, many years, the airlines didn't even have to think about price competition until very recently. And so learned the hard way that ill-conceived price policies usually fail even to meet their own goals, including improvement of market share.

But Laker and the deregulators had released a public clamour which, like a genie out of the bottle, could not be put back. The political mood in America was already infecting Europe, the heartland of pools and cartels; while both American and European airlines were feeling a colder wind of competition from the booming countries of the Far East.

12

The Wind from the East

"You're so obsessed with the North Atlantic," an Asian airline chief warned his western rivals in 1983, "that you don't notice what's happening in the Pacific." While Pan Am and British Airways were battling with cheap fares and ideologies across the Atlantic, Japan and Singapore Air Lines had been growing much faster, much less affected by oil shocks and recessions. The Pacific and Indian oceans opened up wider opportunities and political consequences than the Atlantic; for the Asians could defy their traditional geography to create new trade-routes and speed up their industrial development; and their young airlines were encroaching on the old preserves of the West. While the North American share of world air traffic had gone down from thirty-one per cent to twenty per cent in the ten years to 1981, the Far Eastern share had gone up from eleven per cent to twenty-two per cent.

It was not only the highly industrialised countries whose airlines were racing ahead. Air India was one of the most remarkable successes, for it had constructed an efficient organisation in the face of heavy political pressures and traditions—in contrast to the frustrations of Indian industries on the ground. Air India could trace its origin back to October 1932 when the young Indian pilot Johangir Tata flew a Puss Moth from Karachi to Bombay. Tata was one of the heirs to India's biggest industrial group in India, which was set up by his Parsi grandfather J. N. Tata, and he established Tata Air Lines with the help of an English ex-RAF pilot Nevill Vintcent who had come out on a barnstorming tour. They began by flying their two planes themselves, picking up mails from Karachi—where Imperial Airways dropped them—and flying them to Bombay.

After the war Tata re-established the airline in 1946 as Air India, equipped with surplus DC-3s and boldly introducing Indian air hostesses trained by TWA: by the time India became independent in 1948 Air India was already flying to London. But India was soon flooded with many more DC-3s which encouraged competing airlines with chaotic finances, and in 1953 the Nehru government nationalised all air transport, creating Indian Airlines for domestic flights while allocating all international routes to Air India, still with Tata as chairman. In spite of the shortage of dollars Tata persuaded Nehru to let him buy new American aircraft, and by the sixties Air India was flying Boeing 707s, decorated with the tourist-conscious symbol of the "Little Maharajah", as far as Moscow, Sydney and via London to New York. It was the first third world airline to fly regularly across the Atlantic, much resented by its British and American competitors.

The smooth working of Air India seemed almost opposite to the Indian tradition on the ground—not least at its home base Bombay airport, with its chaotic huts, shouting porters and primitive equipment, which was one of the least alluring gateways to the East. Tata, a domineering but far-sighted tycoon, could effectively insulate Air India from the domestic obligations to make jobs and dispense favours: he could impose strict discipline and employ highly trained engineers, of whom India has a surplus; and Air India could make more intensive use of its jets than most major airlines. Tata continued as chairman until 1977, the most long-lasting of all the pioneer aviators: in 1982 at the age of seventy-seven he flew the same Puss Moth again from Karachi to Bombay to celebrate his airline's fiftieth anniversary.

While the Indian economy suffered setbacks from the high oil price in the seventies, Air India could still make a profit (with the help of ingenious accounting) thanks largely to new revenues from flying to the Middle East, where Indian workers now flocked and where fares were kept high. The present chairman Raghu Raj, a conservative banker, remains cautious of the future: as President of IATA in Delhi in 1983 he warned that developing countries were facing growing threats from western technology. But Air India may yet have a more promising future than many European airlines. "The smaller developed countries like Britain," said one former executive, "don't realise that the giant developing countries, with their own technology, can become quite a menace to them."

It was the oil countries of the Middle East not surprisingly which saw the most spectacular growth in their airlines. While Pan Am or TWA were painfully staving off bankruptcy Saudia, Iran Air and Kuwait Airways were ordering fleets of jumbos without worrying too much about passengers.

Iran Air was encouraged by the Shah to become a global airline, and quickly bought jumbos from TWA—which flew half-empty to Europe and New York laden with caviar. The airline became Iran's prime status symbol, with its extravagant advertising, elegant booking-halls—and a fine safety record. But after the Ayatollah Khomeini took over in 1979 Iran flew to Peking instead of New York and flew only once a week to the European centres—where their lush premises were heavily guarded and occupied by black-clad women, grappling uneasily with the austere Islamic timetables and computer-terminals.

Other oil-rich airlines had a more lasting impact. Kuwait Airways now flies its teetotal 747s from London to New York three times a week, and to the Far East every day. Gulf Air has been one of the fastest-growing: set up by the Sheikh of Bahrain in 1950 and still based on Bahrain's huge echoing airport, it now has four wealthy and co-equal shareholders — Bahrain, Qatar, Oman and the United Arab Emirates (another rare case, with Air Afrique and SAS, of a multinational airline). Saudia, representing the richest oil nation of all, has never been altogether commercial: it dates back to the DC-3 which Roosevelt had promised to give King Ibn Saud when he visited him on his way back from Yalta in 1945, which TWA flew out to Saudi Arabia—and which now hangs in a museum in Jeddah. The national airline was formed in 1946, with a few more DC-3s which TWA helped it to fly to and from Cairo. Saudia at first existed primarily to carry the royal family, and it still keeps a fleet of executive planes for the princes. But the oil boom soon turned it into the businessman's airline, and Saudia grew at the rate of thirty-four per cent a year over the next decade. The Saudi international airports at Jeddah, Riyadh or Dhahran (one of the world's most beautiful airports) are monuments to conspicuous wealth, with elaborate entrances and waiting halls for princes and VIPs and marble vistas undisturbed by passengers—except when the annual pilgrimage to Mecca brings millions of Muslims from three continents into Jeddah, which now claims to be the world's largest airport.

The booming airlines of the Middle East increasingly attracted the Boeing salesmen from Seattle, particularly after successive oil shocks had cut down their custom in the West. They worked hard to turn the whole Middle East into Boeing-land, assisted by generous commissions and reinforced by top-level representatives including the billionaire Mahdi Al-Tajir, the ambassador for the United Emirates in London: he helped to persuade Arab neighbours to buy Boeings whether they needed them or not, and Syrianair even bought long-range Boeing 747SPs—though it flies no further than Moscow and Delhi. The Europeans fought back to sell their airbus with the full weight of their diplomacy, and when President Giscard visited Kuwait he persuaded the government to order a fleet of them. But Kuwait Airways had no idea what to do with them, while Boeing was counter-attacking to sign up orders for their new 767. By 1984 Boeing, in their last costly bid, agreed to buy back the airbuses from Kuwait in return for selling them Boeings. It looked absurd, but it gave Boeing a precious foothold to sell their new generation to the Arabs.

In spite of their lavish airports and fleets the oil-rich countries were not much interested in attracting mass tourism; Kuwait and Saudi Arabia were apprehensive of visitors who might turn out to be subversive to their sensitive regimes, and their high air-fares effectively discouraged most travellers except businessmen. The ordinary return fare from Western Europe to the Gulf countries was actually more expensive than round-the-world fares, so it was cheaper to fly from London to Riyadh by way of Los Angeles, Honolulu, Hong Kong and Bombay. The high fares together with the heat and lack of alcohol effectively kept the Gulf countries off the tourists' brochures.

The airlines of poorer Arab states bore the brunt of political tensions and rivalries. Syria and Egypt for a time had their joint United Arab Airlines—which was famous for its unpredictability and would not commit itself to times of departure. But it soon broke up into separate components, Egyptair and Syrianair, which are now both eager discounters. For many years the most favoured of the Arab airlines was Middle East Airlines based in Lebanon— originally part-owned by Air France. It provided the chief link between the Arab world and Europe, and the escape route for Saudis or Kuwaitis to the delights of Beirut: grave figures swathed in burnouses would disappear into the lavatories and emerge to drink cocktails as dapper playboys in western suits. But MEA, as the flag-carrier for the Lebanon, was soon intimately involved in its collapse, flying into Beirut airport when no other airlines dared, and seeing five of its Boeings destroyed on the ground. It made the point forcibly that any nation needs its own airline in a time of crisis. The Arab airlines learnt all too painfully that technology and wealth could not buy security, and that their networks depended above all on political stability.

THE PACIFIC EXPLOSION

The most fundamental air change was further east, where airlines were both boosted by the industrial expansion and helped to boost it. In the expanding economies of East Asia the airlines played the same kind of role as railways and steamships had played in the take-off of Western Europe a century earlier, helping to cross-fertilise nations, ambitions and ideas, and creating trade-routes which had hardly existed before. They could connect the peninsulas, archipelagoes and islands of the Pacific basin with a web of routes which made them into neighbours; and by the seventies many Pacific airlines were catching up all but the biggest Americans or Europeans.

It was a poignant turnabout. In the post-war decade the Americans had helped most of the Asian countries to establish their own air services. TWA, as it was pushing to keep up with Pan Am, had seen its links with developing countries as the means to achieve its global ambitions after it was refused its own round-the-world service. In 1945 Howard Hughes was persuaded to try to link up with the new Philippine Airlines, which had been set up in 1941 by a Filipino industrialist Andres Soriano, but which had been suspended during the war years. Manila airport had been a Pan Am stronghold ever since the China Clipper had first triumphantly landed there in 1935, and it was only with some difficulty that TWA, helped by the Philippine government, established its rival service. Thirty years later Philippine Air Lines (PAL) is now a key instrument of the Philippine economy, run by Roman A. Cruz—a favourite technocrat of President Marcos who also runs pension funds and the Manila hotel—and one of the thirty biggest airlines in the world.

South of the Philippines the scattered islands of the old Dutch East Indies provided an obvious challenge to air transport, and a tantalising loss to the Dutch. KLM had resumed its flights to Jakarta soon after the war, as the key to their Far Eastern route. But the Indonesian nationalists fought for independence and in 1949 they formed their own airline-in-exile based on Rangoon in Burma. After independence the airline was reconstituted as Garuda Indonesian Airways, at first partly owned by KLM who gave it technical help; and the airline was given the unkind acronym: Goes All Right Under Dutch Administration. But in 1954 KLM gave up its share, and two years later Garuda got rid of all Dutch employees; KLM's eastern empire dwindled to a base at Biak, off the coast of West New Guinea, which suddenly achieved a new significance as a stepping-stone from Europe to Australia, or from Alaska to Tokyo. But without Indonesia, KLM had lost its most valuable diplomatic counter in the bargaining game. And in the meantime Garuda was developing into a semi-global airline, offering cut-rate fares between Europe and Australia.

Further west the Thailand government had set up its own national airline in 1947 which extended further abroad in 1959, with the help of the Scandinavian airline SAS—untainted by any imperialist past—which took a thirty per cent share in the new Thai International. It was a good deal for SAS, which sold off its old propeller-planes to the Thais and got landing rights in Hong Kong; but in 1977 the Thai government became sole owners. Bangkok airport was now rivalling Singapore as the chief stopping-place on the way from Europe to Oceania, which gave the Thais their own leverage in obtaining landing rights elsewhere; and by 1982 Thai International was number twenty in international traffic, only three places behind SAS itself.

THE CITY-STATE AIRLINES

The size of airlines in Asia has no relationship to their countries' populations: two of the smallest territories have two of the most wide-ranging airlines. Cathay Pacific, based on the few hundred square miles and five million people of Hong Kong, has eighteen jumbo jets which fly as far as Tokyo, Vancouver, Australia and London. Its story is full of oddities. It is British-owned, but largely staffed by Chinese. It can appear a Hong Kong company when it wants to, and a London company when it doesn't. It is privately owned, still part of the Swire's trading group, surrounded by state airlines. Most extraordinary, it has made a profit every year except one for the last thirty-six years. Its romantic image conceals a very canny and disciplined management; and while most airlines have built up their own expensive bureaucracies Cathay (as their ex-chairman John Bremridge described it) has "borrowed halves of men" from Swire's.

Cathay Pacific was in the midst of Asian upheavals, but after its earlier battles with BOAC (see Chapter 5) it gradually fought its way into the key Far Eastern routes, using the growing strength of Hong Kong as its lever. It faced setbacks from Asian nationalism as it was cut out of Burma and Cambodia and restricted by Malaysia, while the British government could still exert its own national pressure: when in 1966 the British wanted BOAC to fly to Australia via the Pacific—because they were worried that Indian troubles would disrupt their Eastern route—they had to allow the Americans to fly into Hong Kong in return, thus stepping up the competition for Cathay Pacific. Hong Kong airport became still more desirable, with no fewer than twenty-two airlines flying into it by 1968, while the route from Hong Kong to Tokyo was even more competitive than the North Atlantic. But Cathay Pacific could nevertheless double its size every five years, benefiting from Hong Kong's growing role as an entrepot and banking centre, and from the family links between the overseas Chinese: by 1979 they were flying right across to Vancouver, to link with one of the biggest Chinese colonies abroad. Cathay's final triumph came in 1980, when they were at last allowed to fly to London itself, and by the next year they were flying daily to London including a non-stop flight taking fourteen hours. It was a symbolic triumph, the colonial's homecoming; it was also typical of airlines to thrive more at the other ends of the world.

The most extraordinary of all the success stories belongs to Singapore Airlines (SIA), which grew from being the fifty-fourth biggest in the world in 1972 to being seventh in 1982—ahead of TWA or Qantas—from a base of only 2.4 million people and only one airport. The airline owes much to its unique base on the crossroads between East and West, North and South—the strategic advantage which first persuaded Sir Stamford Raffles to buy Singapore for the East India Company in 1819. But its dynamism and ambition came from the people and government who were determined, as their prime minister, Lee Kuan Yew, put it, "to plug into the world grid".

SIA had several predecessors, dating back to Malayan Airways which was founded in 1936 and reconstituted after the Japanese occupation, jointly controlled by BOAC and Qantas: it was run for a time by Keith Hamilton, now the head of Qantas. But SIA only took its present form in 1972 when Lee Kuan Yew decided to break the airline away from the Malaysians, with a small fleet of Boeing 707s displaying the new yellow and blue colours. Its beginnings were tricky, set back by the first oil shock; but it was boldly piloted by its chairman Joe Pillay, an engineer educated in London who was a confidant of the prime minister and also a permanent secretary in the finance ministry. A slight man with large eyes and expressive gestures, he seemed like an irreverent pixie among his stolid western rivals: the airlines, he complained, believed that they were at the centre of the universe, and their illusions had been fed by "systematic and prolonged cosseting".

Pillay realised that Singapore was in a strong bargaining position. Long-range jets from Europe might be able to miss out India or the Middle East on their way to Oceania, but they still needed Singapore or its rival airport Bangkok: and his airline could thus insist on reciprocal landing rights round the world. SIA had ordered Boeing 747s from the outset, and with quiet pressure Pillay and his deputy Lim Chim Beng built up their own world network. By 1975 it was flying to Seoul, Hong Kong and Taipei, linking Singapore with the rest of the "gang of four" newly industrialising countries. It established a thriving trade with Tokyo, helped by the "meat-flights" on which Japanese bought cheap meat back from Singapore. In 1976 it flew into Paris, Dubai and New Zealand. In 1977 it began flying the supersonic Concorde to Bahrain to link up for a time with British Airways' Concorde to London. By 1979 it achieved its great ambition to fly across the Pacific—with 747s complete with upstairs beds and the words "California here I come" across the fuselage—and SIA soon linked up with TWA (who had abandoned their own global service) to provide bargain round-the-world flights.

Singapore could obviously pay lower wages, but Pillay insisted that the airline's real secret was the more efficient use of planes and manpower, and superior service—including four more cabin staff in its 747s than most of its rivals. It remained state-owned but claimed to be consistently profitable, filling an average of three-quarters of its seats, and Pillay insists that it has never been subsidised—"only weaklings run to their governments for subsidies and protection". SIA, like other Asian airlines including Korean, has refused to join IATA: so it could dole out free drinks and free gifts as it liked and even for a time hired Filipino singers to provide live entertainment flying to Australia. Above all it projected an image of productive service, advertising the "Singapore Girl" in a sarong with shameless sexism, showing her through a soft-focus haze with a singer chanting "I want to stay up here with you for ever."

Through the seventies Singapore Airlines expanded by thirty per cent a year. It has now levelled out to two or three per cent a year, but it is still aggressively expanding with the help of the first "Big Top" Boeing 747s with stretched upper decks. By 1980 SIA was employing more than one in eighty of all workers in Singapore and providing scope for many more. Singapore now aims to double its hotel capacity in three years, to reach 36,000 rooms by 1986. It is now more like a huge extension of an airport than a country: the palatial new airport at Changi, with its tall fountains, instant baggage tracks and cosmopolitan style, is designed to lure still more tourists on their way west or east: and Singapore's easy access attracts money and businessmen from less reliable centres like Manila or Jakarta. Singapore has shown more strikingly than anywhere how mastery of the skies can integrate a distant country into the world economy.

Inevitably SIA came up against objections from western airlines
—most of all from Qantas which had helped to establish it and
which it had now overtaken. In 1979 the Australian government
introduced a new International Civil Aviation Policy (ICAP) which
aimed to protect Qantas from Asian competition by providing
"point-to-point fares" to London and elsewhere to protect its
market. The Singaporeans were furious at this protectionism. "We
don't believe," complained Lim, "that any airline owns a specific
market." Their prime minister launched a general diplomatic offensive with the help of his fellow members of the Association of
South-East Asian Nations, ASEAN, while the Australian media
and public opinion joined in attacking the policy which had put up
the fare to London by sixty per cent. Eventually the Australian
government climbed down and Qantas faced up to the competition
with more competitive fares; as Lim put it, "Qantas flew into SIA
and the other airlines like a whirlwind, but when the dust settled
we found we were all better off." The two airlines now have more
relaxed relations, helped by Qantas' Keith Hamilton with his dual
experience, and the Singapore stop-over is now again part of the
Australian way of life.

THE WORLD'S OTHER FAVOURITE

Japan Air Lines over three decades became the biggest of all. In
1951 it had chartered a single plane from Northwest Airlines; in
1982 it overtook Pan American to top the list of the world's airliners
in terms of international tonne-kilometres flown—which threw
some doubt on British Airways' claim to be "the world's favourite".

The Japanese like the Germans had been forbidden any involve-
ment in aviation in the first post-war years, by decree of the supreme
commander General MacArthur, and the Americans could freely
award landing rights in Tokyo to their airlines, led by Pan Am and
Northwest. It was not until 1951 that a small private company
Japan Air Lines was able to set up its office in the Ginza district of
Tokyo, in a building so small—according to its first president,
Seijiro Yanagito—that the directors sat on straw hats. (JAL, which
dreads ostentation, has occupied dingy buildings ever since.)
Yanagito had been a vice-governor of the central bank, and could
mobilise his old network of bankers and backers: he vowed with his
chairman not to play golf—a supreme Japanese sacrifice—till the
airline made a profit, which it did five years later. By 1954 a JAL
DC-6 took off from Tokyo on its first international flight to San
Francisco via Wake Island and Honolulu.

At first JAL was preoccupied with attracting American tourists and trying to neutralise Japan's image as a ferocious ex-enemy. The airline carefully emphasised the romance and peace of the Orient: the hostesses were reluctantly persuaded to wear kimonos (soon adapted to a three-piece version which was easier to put on in the lavatory), and they handed out "happi" coats, delicate Japanese gifts and the little damp towels or *oshiburi*, which other airlines soon copied. But by 1964, when the Tokyo Olympics attracted a rush of American tourists and Japanese exports were already earning surplus dollars, the Japanese government allowed the first tourists to travel abroad. The next year the airline sent its first JALPAK group on a two-week tour of Europe, and the great Japanese migrations had begun. The Japanese compared this sudden re-entry into the world, after fifteen years' isolation, to the historic year 1853 when Commodore Perry's "black ships" arrived in Japan and first opened it up to the West.

By 1972 two million Japanese were going abroad and during the difficult seventies JAL increased its international passengers by an average of twenty per cent a year. It was still a private company, consistently profitable, while the government gave it "guidance" to ensure that it provided routes in the national interest, and in return gave diplomatic support to extend its landing rights. JAL was very conscious that it lacked lucrative routes after the post-war carve-up: it reckoned that routes were responsible for ninety-five per cent of its performance, and sales efforts for only five per cent. But as other airlines wanted to fly into Tokyo, JAL was allowed to fly further away from it. To the West it flew along the "silk route" via Hong Kong and Bangkok to Europe; and after patient negotiation it persuaded Aeroflot to share crews on joint flights to Moscow, until by 1970 the Soviets allowed JAL to fly its own planes across Russia —after they realised that American satellites could photograph all their territory anyway. To the North JAL followed the Alaskan route to America and Europe, and by 1976 was flying non-stop to New York. Southwards it began flying to New Zealand via Australia —as far as from Tokyo to London—bringing a new relationship between Japanese investment and the resources of Oceania. To the East the flight across the Pacific became commonplace for Japanese businessmen connecting up with the technology and markets of California.

JAL was a key instrument in the westernisation of Japan, both through its passengers and its own organisation. It deliberately employed both American and Japanese captains, leaving behind any associations with wild wartime kamikaze pilots; and its safety record was well above average. (Yet it was not totally predictable:

in February 1982 a JAL pilot in a DC-8 suddenly put two engines into reverse and crashed straight into Tokyo bay, killing four passengers. In the subsequent inquiry it turned out that the pilot had behaved very oddly on previous flights, but after being demoted had been reinstated. In the uproar the new President of JAL, Yasumoto Tagaki, apologised to the Japanese Diet, but refused to resign.)

The oil shocks of 1973 and 1979 brought an end to easy profits and compelled JAL ruthlessly to cut down its costs: but it continued to grow, encouraged by a new surge of American tourists in the "Shogun boom" of the eighties—stimulated by James Clavell's bestseller and the subsequent television series—and by the completion of the Tokyo Disneyland, which attracted 6 million visitors in its first six months in 1983, of whom nine per cent came from abroad. But JAL feels itself increasingly threatened. "We have rivals both in front and behind," their director for corporate planning, Mitsunari Kawano, told me in Tokyo. "Northwest, Pan American and United are competing from America. Singapore, Thai and Philippine Airlines—all promoted by their governments—are competing from Asia." As the biggest international airline JAL is very aware that it now has the most to lose.

DEREGULATING ASIA

By the early eighties the western invasion of Asia was going into reverse: for every American that visited Asia in 1982, two Asians visited America. Of the thirty biggest international airlines in 1982, nine came from Asia. The chart overleaf shows the leaders in 1982 and 1972.

Both tourism and business travel within Asia were expanding much faster than in Europe. In spite of the two oil shocks Asian air traffic grew on average by seventeen per cent a year through the seventies; and even during the recession of the early eighties it went up by ten per cent a year. But the Asians still have plenty of room for growth: even now only four per cent of the Japanese travel abroad, compared to about thirty per cent of the British or West Germans.

The western airlines frequently complain that the Asians pay lower wages and exploit their submissive women to provide obedient cabin service. But their success has deeper roots, for they have deliberately developed their airlines as the instruments of global competition. "Japanese cars, VTR's and TV sets have been able to penetrate western markets because of quality, reliability, the application of modern technology and price," said the chairman of Cathay Pacific, Duncan Bluck in 1984: "so will Asia-Pacific airlines continue to win customer support, not by low prices but by quality of service." They have built up much of their new trade through the air. They were not cluttered with rail or steamship networks, restrictive interests or defensive pacts. They saw their air-routes more as Europeans and Americans first saw the railroads, as the spearheads of their industry and growth, as the new arteries of trade, carrying goods, people and ideas across the vast distances of the Pacific Basin and making neighbours and competitors of

THE BIGGEST INTERNATIONAL AIRLINES

Airline	Rank 1982 (1972)	Tonne-kilometres international* 1982	1972	Average annual growth
Japan Air Lines	1 (7)	4,318m	1,432m	11.7%
Pan American (US)	2 (1)	4,205m	3,412m	2.1%
British Airways	3 (2)	4,190m	2,380m	5.8%
Air France	4 (6)	3,624m	1,442m	9.7%
Lufthansa	5 (5)	3,526m	1,516m	8.8%
KLM (Netherlands)	6 (8)	2,540m	1,196m	7.8%
Singapore IA	7(54)	2,466m	59m	45.2%
Korean Air Lines	8(38)	2,110m	154m	29.9%
Qantas (Australia)	9(13)	1,913m	670m	11.1%
TWA	10 (4)	1,799m	1,600m	1.2%
Northwest (US)	11(24)	1,657m	276m	19.6%
Alitalia	12 (9)	1,561m	1,043m	4.1%
Swissair	13(12)	1,527m	728m	7.7%
Flying Tiger (US)	14(18)	1,484m	437m	13.0%
Iberia	15(14)	1,437m	646m	8.3%
Aeroflot	16(16)	1,252m	501m	9.6%
SAS (Scandinavian)	17(10)	1,219m	773m	4.7%
Air Canada	18(11)	1,171m	759m	4.4%
Air India	19(22)	1,091m	350m	12.0%
Thai International	20(44)	1,061m	112m	25.2%
Varig (Brazil)	21(19)	1,002m	420m	9.1%
UTA (France)	22(21)	998m	375m	10.3%
Sabena (Belgium)	23(15)	967m	511m	6.6%
Saudia	24(58)	948m	52m	33.7%
SAA (South Africa)	25(25)	877m	268m	12.6%
PAL (Philippines)	26(43)	769m	116m	20.8%
British Caledonian	27(42)	754m	118m	20.4%
El Al (Israel)	28(20)	706m	407m	5.7%
PIA (Pakistan)	29(40)	684m	124m	18.6%
Air New Zealand	30(33)	665m	176m	14.2%

(Source: ICAO) * Scheduled traffic, including passengers, freight and mail.

countries thousands of miles apart. Juan Trippe had seen himself fifty years earlier as bringing the American air age to Asia. Now the Asians—at least in terms of their international relations—were the most air-minded of all.

Thus the impact of the American deregulators on Asia has had a special edge. The Americans still have some overwhelming advantages: their internal airlines carry more passengers than the rest of the world put together and their aircraft manufacturers, led by Boeing, still dominate the world markets (see overleaf), contributing more to American exports than any other industry.

But the American airlines' share of *international* passengers has plummeted over four decades from over fifty per cent just after the Second World War to less than eighteen per cent in 1980; while many of their competitors have bought American planes with the help of American cheap loans. Many Asians suspected that the Americans wanted to use deregulation to extend their airlines across the world; yet any thorough-going deregulation, liberalising access on both sides, could well benefit the Asian airlines more than the Americans.

In the global contest the United States still has the advantage of its sheer size: even without Alaska it is bigger than all Asian countries outside China while the deregulators demanded that the Asians liberalise their air routes, the American airlines retained their exclusive rights to "cabotage" or "beyonds": they alone could pick up or drop passengers on flights inside the United States— which stretch from Hawaii to Boston, from Miami to Alaska. Roman Cruz of Philippine Airlines complained that Pan American could carry passengers on each stage of a flight from New York to San Francisco to Honolulu to Manila; while PAL flying eastwards could not pick up anyone at Honolulu or San Francisco, which were thus "dead legs". To the Asians it seemed an outrageous form of protectionism. "We cannot sit idly by," complained Takayuki Hashizumi of JAL, "when this policy is being shoved on the international market . . ."

As the deregulators moved into Asia to sign up more liberal deals they came up against a spectrum of attitudes. The Middle East, including the oil countries, was opposed to liberalisation; and only El Al agreed to deregulate their fares when they signed a bilateral treaty with the Americans. But most East Asian countries felt they had to agree to more liberal terms if they wanted to keep their share of flights across the Pacific to America; and they dreaded new competition from other countries. Korea, Thailand and Taiwan all signed more liberal agreements, followed reluctantly by the Philippines. Joe Pillay of Singapore Airlines, who was at first wary,

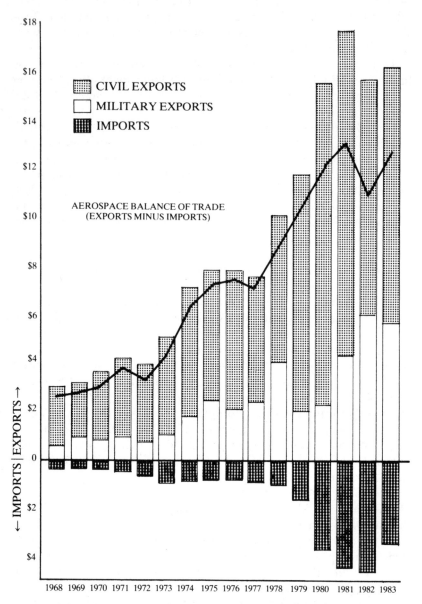

US AEROSPACE EXPORTS, IMPORTS AND TRADE BALANCE
(Billions of Current Dollars)

Source: SPEEDNEWS 17 February, 1984

later became a champion of deregulation: SIA had generated a huge increase in travel to the Far East which was growing by seventeen per cent a year after 1978, and Pillay enjoyed teasing the Europeans—particularly Lufthansa, which tried to stop SIA from discounting—for their defensiveness. "The industry must ask itself," he told an IATA seminar in 1983, "why it should not be exposed to the winds of competition like other economic sectors."

Japan, the most advanced country, was the hardest nut for the deregulators to crack. "I had an awful time with Japan," Alfred Kahn said, "considering the state of their trade. They seriously complained that the balance of trade in aviation was against them —without considering their other exports." The Japanese had for long complained that the United States had exploited its diplomatic strength and its size. "The US repeatedly used its overwhelming strength to frame treaties entirely to its liking," said Takayuki Hashizumi of JAL, and he warned that the "open skies" preached by Americans "are in effect not as open as the US would have you believe". The debate became angrier as Washington pressed for United Air Lines to fly into Tokyo—which Japan reluctantly allowed in 1983: "in anyone's books," said United's Vice-President for the Pacific Colin Murray, "this region is *the* market." JAL complained that they could not carry passengers on "beyonds" between American cities, while Pan American and Northwest pro-tested that the Japanese discriminated against them in Tokyo, through noise pollution and other regulations. And the Americans, with all their divided interests, were very conscious of confronting a highly organised government committed to wholehearted support of a single overseas airline. Juan Trippe's warnings were still reverberating from his grave.

As the deregulators pressed on, many Asians had second thoughts about accepting their doctrine. "I've always criticised it," said Roman Cruz of PAL, "as the product of the innocent vision of theoretical economists." It was unrealistic, said Duncan Bluck of Cathay Pacific, to contrast competition with regulation, particularly in the Far East which has the most competitive routes in the world: between Hong Kong and Bangkok or Hong Kong and Tokyo fifteen airlines were already competing. "You can and do have regulation *and* competition—and very effective it can be." There was no point in arguing about American-type deregulation in Asia, Bluck went on; for nearly all the airlines (though not his) were owned by governments, which would never allow them to be liquidated.

To give free play to market forces was never very credible to ambitious young nations whose governments were so closely in-volved with their exports and airlines, who were so conscious of their own sovereignty and threats from abroad. "Can the thorough-going freedom which America claims to want," asked Hashizumi, "really exist in the world's air transport industry? The shooting down of Korean Air Lines flight 007 was a brutal reminder of airspace sovereignty."

13

The European Cartel

For too long cosy cartels and protectionism have been the order of the
day.

Anglo-Dutch statement, June 1984

A recession is when you have to tighten your belt; depression is when
you have no belt to tighten. When you've lost your trousers—you're in
the airline business.

Sir Adam Thomson, April 1984

"WE are like a champion boxer who has been knocked out for the
first time," said Umberto Nordio, the eloquent chairman of Alitalia,
at the IATA meeting in 1982 where he was enjoying his role as the
speaker of home truths. "We used to ignore the gross national
product because we were always ahead of it. Now we're dependent
on the economy like everyone else. Some of us can't come to terms
with that." It was the thirty-eighth annual conference of IATA,
held that year in its home town of Geneva, and most European
delegates agreed that the prospects were gloomier than at any
previous meeting. Recession and competition, sharpened by American deregulation, were providing new threats to the European
airlines; and the ghosts of Laker and Braniff stalked through the
hall.

The annual conference had grown beyond recognition since
IATA had been reborn four decades earlier. English was still the
only language, but the delegates who crowded into the Geneva
convention centre now came from 120 airlines from a hundred
countries who between them employed 900,000 people. A spectator
could well take it for a meeting of a United Nations agency rather

than a trade association: the delegates were royally entertained
as if they were diplomats, and the commercial arguments were
continually overlaid with political tensions. The airlines were called
on to speak as if they were nations—"Thank you KLM; I'll ask
Air France to speak"—and when they put up their paddles to vote
they usually stayed in continental blocs—Latin American, East
Asian or African. Many of the member airlines came from outside
the conventional western world, including Jamahiriya Libyan Arab
Airlines or Air Niugini which came (as it sounded) from the newly
independent New Guinea. The Polish airline LOT, which had
belonged to the pre-war association, was still a member of IATA.
But other Communist airlines, including Aeroflot from the Soviet
Union, Interflug from East Germany and Malev from Hungary,
were only represented by observers at the back of the hall, together
with other non-members like Korean and Singapore Airlines. IATA
represented about two-thirds of the world's civilian aircraft; but in
geopolitical terms the IATA meetings were always lopsided, for
they did not include the Soviet Union, China or most of Eastern
Europe, who saw IATA's crisis as part of the crisis of capitalism.

The director-general Knut Hammarskjöld sat on the platform
with his impassive style: a tall, athletic Swedish ex-diplomat, he
had held the job ever since Sir William Hildred had retired in 1966,
and he now appeared as an elder statesman of the air. He believed
firmly in a regulated world for both airlines and countries, much
influenced in his world-view by his uncle Dag: and always seeking
new openings and reconciliations —whether between Koreas, Ger-
manys or superpowers. In successive speeches he had not concealed
his fears about deregulation, and he repeatedly warned the airline
chiefs of the dangers of uncontrolled competition in the midst of a
recession. "The problems facing the airline industry as an integral
part of the world economy," he said in the annual report for 1982,
"are staggering . . . on the basis of current trends the industry,
overall, could have a negative worth by the end of 1983." In other
words, it would be technically bankrupt.

The Swiss hosts, who always stood for orderliness, were appalled
by the nightmare of free competition and uncontrolled discounts.
Armin Baltensweiler of Swissair, the current President of IATA,
warned that the next years were a make-or-break period which
called for a return to rationality and effective sanctions against
airlines which broke the rules. Leon Schlumpf of the Swiss transport
department insisted on "pricing discipline and tariff integrity" and
a "return to serious values". Werner Guldiman, who used to run
Swiss civil aviation, explained how air transport was no longer a

closed system but caught up in "an immensely complex web of relations" in which "everything depends on everything else". Some other European airlines echoed the Swiss conviction that IATA must maintain strict controls. "It's tragic," said Pierre Giraudet, the inflexible head of Air France, "that an organisation which has done so much for the consumer should have been so misunderstood."

But there was not much sign of unity or serious values in the airlines' behaviour, as they had to admit to each other; for they were nearly all busily discounting tickets, to surreptitiously fill up their seats. They all hoped that by selling tickets through "bucket-shops"—the unofficial travel agents in back streets—they could get more passengers without spoiling the market for regular fares. It was as if Harrods or Macy's were employing street traders to peddle exactly the same goods which they sold inside. But the practice was spreading so fast and visibly that regular business travellers were now insisting on discounts, and the airlines were losing revenues which they reckoned at $1.5 billion a year.

The airline chiefs eventually passed a resolution to stop discounting and to establish a Fair Deal Monitoring Group with a team of inspectors to roam round the bucket-shops and look for malpractices. But it was not enough for airlines to clean up their own national market which—as Sheikh Mattar of Saudia explained—would only drive traffic across the borders. At the back of the conference hall there were rows of observers, from Moscow to Seoul, to remind them that even if IATA agreed on total discipline, many others would not. "Try asking Aeroflot how much it costs to fly from London to Singapore via Moscow," said one delegate. "They'll ask how much money you've got on you." In the next months IATA did succeed in diminishing the discounting in some parts of the world. But so long as half-empty jumbos were flying round the world, the temptation to fill them up with cheap tickets was impossible to resist.

Only two weeks after that IATA conference the British Magazine Business Traveller—the champion of the bucket-shops—organised a "cost-saver symposium" in London which was really an anti-IATA conference, to explain to travel agents and others how to avoid paying the full fares. Air-travel freaks described every kind of cut-price fare: how it was cheaper to fly the wrong way round the world than to buy a return ticket to the Middle East; how you could save money on long trips with "cross-border ticketing", pretending you had started your journey at Amsterdam; how to save thousands by ingeniously exploiting tourist offers. The heroes of the conference were the bucket-shop operators who explained how they could never be cleaned up, because some airlines were always desperate to grab a bigger slice of the market. "Do they really want it?" asked an Australian operator, Garry Lawson. "These clean-up campaigns come and go—and we're still in business." "Remember that it's the airline itself that does the discounting," said Frank Barrett, the magazine's resident expert. "They just need the cash flow."

The airlines, it turned out, were thoroughly hypocritical in their attitude to the bucket-shops: not least British Airways, which had been engaging in "jugular marketing" with massive discounting. Some months later in London the staff of Deluxe Travel of Soho were prosecuted in court for having conspired to defraud British Airways by backdating an advance APEX ticket to Hong Kong. The judge convicted them, but in the meantime discovered that BA had knowingly allowed backdating to continue until only a few months before. "It is a sad day," he commented, "when a senior executive of this country's national airline has to admit that its practices in connection with regular breaches of IATA and CAA regulations were dishonest."

And the bucket-shops were gaining some political friends, who saw them as the equivalents of the deregulators in America, who were giving consumers the kind of competition which IATA denied them. "Stop kicking the bucket-shops," wrote the London *Times*. "They are a symptom of the problems affecting the world airline industry. They are not its cause." But the travel agents had their own worries. "Deregulation would be suicide for the industry," said John Slade, the head of a British mass-travel agency. And even bucket-shops worried that fares might drop so low that their profit would disappear. "I'm afraid there are too many believers in free enterprise in this business," Garry Lawson told me. "It may be good for the consumers, but it's a jungle for us." If the free-for-all was taken to its logical conclusion, with state-owned airlines undercutting each other further and further, no one could see the end of it.

THE PASSENGERS' REVOLT

While the European airlines were insisting on "tariff integrity" and maintaining high fares, the price wars across the Atlantic and the effects of deregulation inside America were making European passengers much more aware of the high cost of air travel within their own continent. The transatlantic contrast looked absurd: it was often cheaper to fly from London to New York, than to Rome or Stockholm, which were less than half the distance. When the

Federation of European Consumers planned a conference in 1984, they calculated it would be cheaper to fly all their delegates to Washington than to meet anywhere in Europe. The European airlines replied that their regular flights and fares were aimed at businessmen, and that tourists or students could use advance bookings, package holidays or weekend bargains which compared favourably with American cheap fares. But the pre-booked or weekend flights could never have the social benefits of spontaneous last-minute journeys, which had made America seem so much closer. And the European airlines had become expert at devising bargain flights which looked generous but turned out to have impossible stipulations—like having to spend four days away including a Saturday, which ingeniously excluded both businessmen and weekenders.

The high cost of air travel was particularly exasperating to the outlying European nations, including Britain, Ireland and Scandinavia, which could not easily travel by car or train to the rest of the continent. It was an ironic outcome to the first expectations: after Blériot had first flown the Channel the Europeans had assumed that air travel would bring the nations closer together, and that Britain was no longer an island. But it was the Atlantic which turned out to be the spectacular "air bridge", with a journey that was both faster and cheaper than the ocean liners; while within Europe the outlying countries found themselves relatively more distant from their neighbours. If the Atlantic (as TWA had claimed in its advertisements) had dwindled into a river, then the Channel had enlarged into an ocean. The table overleaf shows some comparisons: the "business fare" in Europe is usually the only one available without special pre-payment or other conditions, and is thus comparable to the economy fare to New York.

The high fares were still more disappointing to Europeans who had looked to the Common Market to allow easier exchange between neighbours, which was part of its original ambition; for in practice it had totally failed to unify air transport. After the proposed Air Union had collapsed in 1964 (see Chapter 6) each national airline had continued to pursue its own policy, each making its pools with its opposite number between cities; and passengers were made all too aware of the pools, not only by the price of the ticket, but by the lack of competitiveness and minimal service compared, for instance, to the transatlantic routes. While a score of transatlantic carriers advertised their competing merits across the Atlantic, British Airways and Air France felt no need or incentive to encourage

FARES IN WESTERN EUROPE, APRIL 1984

Journey and kilometres		Business fare (return)	per km	Lowest bookable (return)	per km
London–Paris	418	£168	40.2p	£ 71	17.0p
London–Brussels	422	£156	37.0p	£ 84	19.9p
London–Amsterdam	460	£156	33.9p	£ 87	18.9p
London–Frankfurt	800	£214	26.8p	£103	12.9p
London–Zurich	960	£266	27.7p	£122	12.7p
London–Milan	1,168	£332	28.4p	£151	12.9p
London–Copenhagen	1,222	£332	26.4p	£122	10.0p
London–Nice	1,270	£344	27.1p	£180	14.2p
London–Oslo	1,460	£356	24.4p	£133	9.1p
London–Madrid	1,530	£382	25.0p	£218	14.3p
London–Rome	1,784	£430	24.1p	£174	9.8p
London–Stockholm	1,816	£432	23.8p	£159	8.8p
London–NY (Club)	5,504	£898	16.4p	£299	5.4p
(Economy)		£398	7.2p		

(source: SAS, *Business Traveller*)

travel across the Channel, and the London–Paris route which was still the busiest of all international routes was also, in the cost per mile, one of the most expensive. (Nor was the contrast confined to international flights; when the consumer councils in Britain investigated fares in 1983 they found that the 349 mile journey from London to Glasgow cost £58, while the equivalent distance from Los Angeles to San Francisco cost £36.)

The high fares within Europe had a special political significance for the British, who had always been pulled between the United States and the continent of Europe. When de Gaulle had vetoed Britain's entry into the Community in 1962 he had warned that Britain would always prefer *le grand large*—the open sea. When Britain eventually joined the European Community in 1973 the British "Europeans" felt an obvious need to strengthen the social and political links with the continent. The Channel which had always been a psychological as well as a physical barrier could now be far more easily bridged by air than by ship (and the rail journey between London and Paris had actually become slower over the previous century). But after Britain joined Europe, when the transatlantic airlines were competing more fiercely, the United States became more accessible than most parts of Europe, and English families began flocking by Laker and other cheap airlines to Florida or California, while the flights to the South of France were more expensive than ever. And when Freddie Laker threatened to bring cheap flights to the continent the European airlines set about bringing him down.

The European airlines, despite the Common Market, were becoming still more interlocked with their own governments and their ambitions. Whether nationalised like Air France or Alitalia, or half-private like Lufthansa or KLM, they were all dependent on government agreements and restrictions which gave little scope for the innovation and competition which had stimulated American travel; and the national bureaucracies added to their costs. The navigation and landing costs in Europe (according to British Caledonian's calculations) were four times the world average; while the airlines' costs were rising almost twice as fast as the world average costs. Military restrictions added to both the time and expense of air travel by requiring planes to fly along dog-legs instead of along straight lines: the flight from Zurich to Brussels, for instance, takes forty per cent longer than the direct route.

The airlines not only depended on governments: they helped to reinforce their centralised power. The growth of hubs and spokes which had changed the American air map had still more significance in Europe, where many of the hubs coincided with the capitals (though not in West Germany, where Frankfurt or Munich were powerful rivals to Bonn/Cologne). Governments, airlines and labour unions all tended to favour a single centralised hub, and to resist regional pressures; and while cars had given greater scope to the provinces, the national airlines were becoming natural centralisers. Sophisticated new industries, including computers, electronics and any business concerned with communications, gravitated towards an international airport which could provide easy contact with the rest of the world and attract overseas clients —particularly when it was as close to an exciting metropolis like London or Paris. Advanced industries and airports create their own conspiracy to attract jobs while less accessible regions are left out. Complaints from the regions are heard all over Europe: from Lyons against Paris or from Hamburg against Germany's air capital, Frankfurt. In Britain the depressed areas are far from the two major international airports, Heathrow and Gatwick, and Manchester airport, which is 193 miles north of London and close to areas of high unemployment, has campaigned vigorously for more international flights; but the British government has insisted that Manchester cannot take flights at the expense of London.

The Europeans had extended their political barriers into the sky more thoroughly than any of Blériot's contemporaries could have imagined. Britain was more an island than ever; the concentrations of power and money were reinforced; air transport, far from providing new freedom to take off from roof tops and land in open country, was regimenting passengers more strictly than trains. The hubs and spokes of Europe's air map were not fundamentally different from an old rail map whose lines converged on Paris or London, or an ancient road map with all roads leading to Rome.

Had Europe ever come to terms with the opportunities of air travel? Certainly the railroads, which had first helped to build industrial Europe, are still determined to fight back. The British have high-speed trains which can travel the 400 miles from London to Edinburgh in four and a half hours. Lufthansa now links its growing hub at Frankfurt with its own fast trains along the Rhine connecting with Dusseldorf or Cologne. The French have linked Paris and Lyons with the spectacular *trains de grand vitesse* (TGV), covering 370 miles in just over two hours on special tracks. The TGV not only competes with the plane, but looks and feels like one, with air-conditioned compartments, serving pre-cooked meals in airline-type seats, gliding over the country like a Boeing 707 which never quite takes off.

The European cities which had first grown up round cathedrals and railway stations were reluctant to adapt themselves to airports which rivalled the city centres. As the flying time between airports went down, the driving time to reach them went up. It was, says R. E. G. Davies "a remarkably constant inverse ratio": the journey from the centre of London to the centre of Paris took four hours in 1920, including an hour spent in cars to and from Croydon and Le Bourget, and three hours in a Handley Page bi-plane. Today the flight from Heathrow to de Gaulle airport takes forty-five minutes, but each airport is fifteen miles from the centre and subject to traffic jams. The big European airports, with their customs, immigration, and "brown army" of security checks, convey a greater sense of strain than any railway station, and the airport ordeals —particularly for old people—of anxiously waiting and lugging luggage along endless corridors can be much greater than the strain of flying. "In the old days it was the flight that was tense and exhausting," as one veteran traveller said, "today it's the airports that wear you out, while the flight is relatively relaxing."

But the overriding objection to the European airlines has been the cost of their tickets, and by the early eighties the movement to bring down air fares was gaining some political momentum. The old arguments between cartels and free enterprise which had raged for so long through European industry found a new battlefield in the skies. Deregulation in America had coincided with the election of right-wing governments first in Britain, then in West Germany, who were committed, at least in theory, to more vigorous competition. The Dutch, who since the days of Plesman had always favoured freer trade, were becoming more conscious of consumer agitation. "Users are beginning to discover that the existing system may have a built-in system to increase costs," said Dr Raben, the Dutch director-general of civil aviation in 1983. "The industry will never be able to answer satisfactorily the relevant questions unless they come to grips with the degree of protection versus competition they can operate under."

But the strongholds of state control, led by Air France, insisted that deregulation and liberalisation would only worsen the already dangerous financial problems. Air France continued to follow its own confident flight path: while other airlines including British Airways had been firing thousands of workers in the early eighties Air France was actually increasing its workforce, under pressure from the Mitterrand government; and the airline maintained a legendary bureaucracy. (When I asked for an interview with its president, Pierre Giraudet, I was told that I must not only submit a formal list of questions, but state full details of my proposed book, including "publisher, title, size, selling price, expected date of publication, etc".) Giraudet was appalled by the "chaotic, un-bridled competition" in America which had been caused by over-capacity and compounded by deregulation, and was shocked by attempts to pull IATA to pieces. "Is it in the best interest of consumers," he asked in 1983, "to set up tariffs with excessively divergent levels that are detrimental to small-town services and the poorest countries? Can the consumer expect to get good service from airlines that are constantly in financial difficulty and are incapable of making investments?"

IATA itself, which had so often been attacked as the heart of the airline cartel, was now visibly liberalising its own approach, and becoming more sympathetic to the European consumers. "IATA used to insist that they weren't a cartel, when they were," said one British civil servant in aviation. "Now they're not a cartel, but people don't believe them." Hammarskjöld himself remained con-vinced that a framework of regulation and discipline was essential for a healthy industry; but he was more sensitive than many European airline chiefs to the pressures from passengers, and from America; and he wanted to expose his members to the debate. In 1983 IATA organised an international seminar at the Lufthansa training headquarters at Seeheim—a luxurious hostel built at the height of the air boom, dedicated to efficiency and order, with its courtyard adorned with a Boeing jet engine mounted like a sculpture and a giant chessboard. Lufthansa's chief executive Heinz Ruhnau —formerly State Secretary for Transport—welcomed guests in front of a parade of immaculate Lufthansa chefs and hostesses. "No wonder the fares are so high," said one ungrateful American guest, looking round at the Lufthansa splendour.

Two contrasting joint-chairmen presided over the debate— Michael Dargan the veteran chairman of the state-owned Aer Lingus, and Lord Marsh the former chairman of British Rail and now a forceful advocate of free enterprise (whose father-in-law Lord McFadzean had been chairman of British Airways). Most American participants were sceptical of the European tradition of cartels and controls, but they argued both for and against deregulation. Mike Levine, who was then running New York Air, described the achievements of deregulation but stopped short of trying to export it to Europe. Secor Brown, the former chairman of the CAB, advocated re-regulation and insisted that the industry was still heading for "intelligent oligopoly". The airline expert from Citibank in New York, Fred Bradley, was still unsure whether deregulation was working: the airlines, he quietly pointed out, were nearly all deep in debt, and the banks could no longer act as Santa Claus. "The first question I ask an airline who wants to borrow is: how much money do you have in your till?"

The Europeans were at odds. Ruhnau of Lufthansa advocated "vigorous competition in an organised framework" and insisted that Lufthansa did not need deregulation to make them efficient. Giraudet of Air France did not attend but wrote a forceful submission to explain why deregulation was so dangerous. Had not Adam Smith himself excluded public transport from the full force of competition? The airline industry must extend their "organised competition and multilateral concertation".

The Dutch and the British lay halfway between the American and European extremes, as they did in other fields of business. Professor Wassenbergh, the outspoken International Vice-President of KLM (who was once Plesman's secretary) insisted that the American experience was no more relevant to Europe than the Soviets'; but that competition should be encouraged by allowing new entrants to fly on new routes. The British were the most concerned to liberalise routes and cut fares, and the Tory campaigner Lord Bethell complained angrily about the cost of his air ticket and arranged for a BBC helicopter to record the scene of the meeting from the air, making play with the sinister cartel associations.

The delegates from overseas were sceptical about European protectionism. Joe Pillay of Singapore Airlines portrayed Europe as the last bastion of tight regulation, which must free itself to stimulate growth and create a true common market. "I sometimes thought," said Keith Hamilton, the chief executive of Qantas, "that inter-national airlines were an extension of NATO." But the Latin Americans and Africans had their own reasons to be protective; and Dr Pellegrini, the small and combative President of Aerolineas Argentinas, blamed American deregulation for precipitating the whole aviation crisis.

The airlines and experts at Seeheim agreed that American-style deregulation, in the words of their press statement, "while firmly en-trenched, did not provide a suitable model for application abroad"; but that nevertheless "some liberalisation could be achieved in Western Europe". And elsewhere in the meantime the movement to break up the airlines' cartels was beginning to gather some momentum—particularly in Britain. Sir Adam Thomson of British Caledonian had long been pressing for cheaper fares and had tried in vain to introduce "mini-prix" fares back in 1979. "You would have thought we had fomented revolution," he said later, "such was the antagonism from across the Channel." But he began trying again in 1984, as part of his challenge to British Airways; and at the same time the new Conservative Minister of Transport Nicholas Ridley, a right-wing individualist, began to take up the cause more militantly, with the support of his prime minister, Mrs Thatcher, who called for deregulating European airlines at the Fontainebleau summit. In Germany the Kohl government was putting some pressure on Ruhnau at Lufthansa to adopt a more flexible policy, while in Holland Dr Raben argued for allowing greater freedom for new routes, with some support from KLM.

In Brussels in the meantime the European Commission was trying stealthily to move the member governments away from their entrenched positions and cartels. Already in 1981 it had made proposals to apply the rules of competition, which had been stipu-lated in the Treaty of Rome, to agreements between airlines, while the European Parliament had been protesting against the cartels and Lord Bethell, a member of the parliament, had sued Sabena, without success, for contravening the treaty. But in March 1984 the commission published a "Memorandum No.2" which was much bolder than its earlier proposals. It accepted that "American-style deregulation would not work in the present European context"; but it insisted that the Community's long-term objective must be to create a common air transport policy, and it advocated more flexible and competitive systems which would allow "the efficient and innovative airline to benefit, encourage expansion and thus employ-ment, and better meet consumer needs". The memorandum exoner-ated the airlines from some of the blame for the high fares: it reckoned that sixty per cent of the total costs—including fuel,

airport and landing charges—were beyond the airlines' control.
But it proposed that air agreements should be more flexible, that
pools should become more competitive with less government intervention, that smaller airlines should be permitted on scheduled
flights, and that all restrictions should be lifted on flying planes
with less than twenty-five seats, to encourage the development of
thinner routes. The freedom for small planes to open up new routes
and airports had an immediate attraction; and it was quickly taken
up by the small Plymouth airline Brymon which proposed flying
short-take-off planes from London's dockland which, it argued,
could be the basis of the first genuinely European airline.

Behind its cautious Eurospeak the memorandum had a clear
strategy: to avoid confronting the governments, but systematically
to eliminate their vetoes and obstructions, to give the airlines scope
for more aggressive competition. And already by June 1984 there
was the first sign of some new freedom, when the two most liberal
governments, the British and the Dutch, reduced the restrictions
between them. They agreed that in future an airline would only
need permission from its own government, not both—which thus
abolished the veto and opened up new competition. And the British,
with surprising generosity, agreed to let KLM match the lowest
British Airways fares—so that KLM could for instance fly passengers from London to Singapore via Schiphol at the same price
as BA's direct flight to Singapore. The agreement did not have
immediately sensational results: BA and KLM offered a cheap
return fare between London and Amsterdam of £49 which was
hedged in with restrictions, while the normal return fare remained
absurdly high. The British airlines were soon protesting that Schiphol would lure passengers away from London while Lufthansa
warned the British and Dutch that their revenues would "melt
like snow in the sunshine" and Alitalia still opposed any further
competition.

But the Anglo-Dutch deal nevertheless marked an important
step towards greater competition and the beginnings of a liberal
European policy which would bring pressure on other airlines,
particularly Lufthansa. And the breakthrough clearly revealed that
the governments, more than anyone else, were obstructing air travel.
"Don't just look to the airlines," said Sir Adam Thomson, "look to
putting pressure on Euro politicians, some of whom pay only lip
service to the cause." Cheaper air travel would depend in the end
on the political will to break down national barriers; and as in the
Far East the air in Europe was impregnated with politics.

X.   STILL LOSING MONEY IN 1994!

14

The Flight of the 007

We were once told that the aeroplane had "abolished frontiers". Actually it is only since the aeroplane became a serious weapon that frontiers have become definitely impassable.

George Orwell, 1945

THE land-mass of the Soviet Union still loomed as a vast obstruction between Europe and the Far East, a blank space in the middle of the globe. Japan Air Lines, Air France and others were allowed to fly along the narrow route through Moscow; Japanese students could take cheap Aeroflot flights to Europe stopping at domestic Soviet airports. But the Soviets remained almost as defensive about their airspace as when Lenin had first laid down their rules of air sovereignty. In theory the strategic position of the Soviet Union, lying astride the direct routes from Europe to the East, should have given it a valuable bargaining position in airline politics. As Professor Thornton has put it:

Because of the size and geographical location of the USSR, air transport from Europe to the Orient can avoid flights over that country in only two ways: by flying westward around the globe with an interim landing at Anchorage, and thus paying a severe penalty in distance; or by going south of the Soviet Union through the Middle East, and entailing an even greater penalty.

But the Soviet Union was never prepared to open up its frontiers to exploit its advantage. Aeroflot, though far the biggest airline in the world, had fewer international flights than the Japanese or even

Singapore Airlines. Russian tourists had little scope to fly abroad, and however much the Soviet government wanted foreign exchange they were unlikely to attract mass tourism. And Moscow remained terrified of any "violation" of Soviet airspace, which brought back all the memories of past incursions.

The by-passing of the Soviet Union had become so accepted that the whole territory—together with most of China and Indo-China—seemed to have been cut out of the airlines' maps. Pilots and passengers flying to the Far East via Alaska had become accustomed to flying close to the Soviet Union without thinking about it. But in the summer of 1983 a sudden disaster revealed the fragility of the assumptions of civil aviation, including the new polar routes, the expansion of third world airlines, the co-existence between civil and military aviation and the basic communications between the superpowers. It was the more alarming because the airliner, like the *Marie Celeste*, left no clue as to the basic cause of the catastrophe.

ROMEO TWENTY

The scheduled route from Alaska to Korea is now commonplace. After the first pioneer flight of the Lindberghs the legendary north-west passage had soon achieved a growing commercial importance. By 1946 Northwest Airlines based on Minnesota was already flying to Asia via Alaska on the "top-of-the-world" route. By 1957 SAS was flying DC-7s from Copenhagen to Tokyo via Anchorage; and by the early seventies other airlines had caught up on the polar route, flying from the European capitals to California or to Tokyo. By the late seventies this North Pacific route (NOPAC) was established as one of the world's major air-routes. But it still had a fundamental difference from the others: for three hours planes flew along the edge of the Soviet Union.

When Lindbergh had first opened up the north-west passage Russia presented no special peril. Even during the cold-war years of the fifties, pilots flying DC-3s down the coast could make landings on the Russian islands without much danger. But from the sixties onwards the Soviet Union had become much more concerned about its eastern outposts—firstly because China had begun to represent a serious military threat, and secondly because the Pacific coastline was becoming strategically more crucial, providing bases for missiles, nuclear submarines and aircraft.

By the early eighties, as the Americans were preparing to deploy Pershing II and cruise missiles in Europe which could reach the Soviet Union in six minutes, the Soviets became more active in the North Pacific which provided the means for an equally swift counter-strike against the United States. The peninsula of Kamchatka which had seemed so friendly and innocent to the Lindberghs was now a crowded arsenal of sophisticated weaponry. "An extraordinary array of Soviet electronic targets," as Major General George Keegan put it, "made up of air-defence radars, missile-guidance radars or missile-tracking radars, of research and development radars, worked on by the Soviets for anti-ballistic missile purposes . . . "

On the other side of the Bering Sea the Americans were watching these developments with increasingly elaborate technology. They equipped the Aleutian Islands with powerful radar and listening systems; and the island of Shemya became a much more important base for watching missile-landings and other military developments on Kamchatka only 500 miles away. The North Pacific—the only common frontier between the United States and the Soviet Union—was becoming much more tense in the early eighties while Japan further south, uncomfortably close to the Russian island of Sakhalin, was more concerned with its own defences against Russia; and in the summer of 1982 the Japanese defence ministry decided to equip its fighters with air-to-air missiles. In September 1982 the Americans deployed two aircraft carriers in exercises off the coast of Kamchatka, and the following April they conducted more extensive exercises which clearly alarmed the Soviets.

The commercial airliners on the busy polar route were thus now flying on the edge of a heavily armed and thoroughly surveyed battleground. But the development of civil radar and safety precautions was lagging far behind the military build-up. There was no ground radar station for commercial aircraft between Anchorage and Tokyo, which meant that aircraft had to rely for four hours on their computers—the same period as across the North Atlantic, but with a far greater hazard. In April 1982 the two authorities which controlled the route, the Federal Aviation Authority in Washington and the Japan Civil Aviation Bureau, introduced a new "composite system" of airlanes like that across the North Atlantic, designed to ensure that aircraft would be separated on parallel tracks at different heights. The most-used and shortest of the airlanes from north to south, called Romeo Twenty, flew only thirty miles from the Soviet Kuril Islands. The danger was spelt out on the standard chart with a notice headed NAVIGATIONAL WARNING: "Pilots flying Northern Route between the US and Japan avoid approaching or overflying territory under Soviet control, specifically the Kuril Islands." The hazard was self-evident: but the airlines, all concerned with the higher cost of fuel, still preferred to fly along Romeo Twenty than to take the parallel track, Romeo Eighty, which took twelve minutes longer and cost another $600 in fuel.

The pilots themselves, through their international federation IFALPA, carried out their own survey of the route and at their next annual conference in 1982 expressed their worry about the lack of flight safety. They asked for better radar monitoring, a special manual for the North Pacific and a systems planning group to keep check on the route. IFALPA's secretary Captain Taylor wrote to the then Administrator of the FAA in Washington, J. Lynne Helms, asking for a meeting of the countries using the route and for the enforcement of minimum standards for aircraft navigation as was done across the North Atlantic. Other groups also complained, including the Civil Aviation Authority in Britain which had a long experience of observing navigational errors and their causes across the Atlantic. But the American FAA told the British CAA that since the North Pacific traffic was still relatively light the airliners' computerised systems would be sufficient safeguard. "We gave way gracefully," said one CAA official. Replying to the pilots the FAA insisted that the system was working well and that there was "no indication" that the North Pacific needed a system of minimum standards. The pilots repeated their requests at their regional air navigation meeting at Singapore in January 1983, but without results. The airliners continued to fly this long night journey without radar for most of the route.

THE KOREAN SHOWPIECE

By the beginning of the eighties, as the Far Eastern countries extended their trade and tourism, the route from Anchorage down to Japan and Korea was becoming a critical international highway, with over thirty commercial planes flying in each direction every day—most of them jumbos, half of them carrying cargo. The biggest user of Anchorage airport was now Japan Air Lines, but the second biggest was a relative newcomer to the big league whose rise had been even more spectacular. Korean Air Lines had grown to be the world's seventh biggest airline outside the United States. Its rapid expansion—from the base of a third-world country of only 38 million people, which thirty years earlier was war-torn and destitute —aroused both admiration and jealousy from its rivals, both western and eastern. The Koreans offered discounts which lured Japanese tourists to fly to Europe or America via Seoul, and they gained the reputation of being second only to Aeroflot in their dis- counting of fares. KAL's expansion could be matched by Singapore's, but its chairman Harry Cho boasted to me in 1983: "SIA is a hundred per cent state-owned, but my airline is a hundred per cent free enterprise. I am not a politician: I am independent, a businessman from head to toes."

KAL was indeed a showpiece of Korean capitalism. It had been owned by the state until 1969 when it was sold off, in keeping with the free-enterprise policy of President Park, to the Hanjin transportation company, owned by the two Cho brothers who had made a fortune with their trucks during the Korean war. When Harry Cho bought the airline it was a domestic carrier which made only a few overseas flights, to Japan; but as the Korean economy raced ahead the airline raced still faster. By 1971 KAL was crossing the Pacific, by 1975 it was flying to Paris, by 1979 via Anchorage to New York. After the oil shock of 1973 South Korea had begun exporting its construction workers and managers to pay for its oil imports, and KAL expanded accordingly, establishing regular flights to the Middle East; by 1981 they were even flying to Libya where Korean companies had won lucrative contracts.

KAL had a wider network than most European airlines, and it was the most visible symbol of the Korean miracle abroad. It had a semi-military pride: it recruited its pilots from the Korean air force—with a reputation for daring rather than steadiness—and to forestall hi-jacking some of its cabin crew regularly carried guns. The Cho brothers reinforced their military links when they began manufacturing Northrop Tiger fighters for their country's air force. The almost unique combination of airline and military manufacturer aroused suspicions abroad; but Harry Cho insisted to me that the plane-making company was kept quite separate, with altogether different personnel.

The airline had stretched round the world, but its local operations were narrowly constrained. KAL is very conscious, like Finnair on the other edge of the Soviet Union, of being "at the end of the line". To the north, an hour's drive from Seoul's international airport, is the fanatically Communist regime of North Korea which still manages to get support from both its giant neighbours. To the south and west is China, and to the north is the Soviet Union with which South Korea has no diplomatic relations. The South Koreans are acutely conscious of being a capitalist outpost alongside the Communist land-mass, and the Japanese, though they may despise and joke about the Koreans, are thankful to have them as a buffer-state. Korean children are instilled from birth with the fear of the Communist bogey.

It was all the more astonishing when in 1978 a Korean Boeing 707, bound from Paris to Seoul, strayed hopelessly off course, flying across the Soviet Union until it was shot at and made a forced landing on a frozen lake near Murmansk.

The Korean pilot of the 707, Captain Kim Chang Kyu, gave me his account—clearly well rehearsed—of that extraordinary incident when I met him in Seoul five years later. He was flying by night, relying on his navigator (who soon afterwards left the airline) who was using a gyro compass and a sextant: the plane was not equipped with a computerised system. When the plane should have been over arctic Greenland Captain Kim suddenly noticed the lights of a village and realised that he was drastically off course. Not long afterwards his co-pilot saw a jet fighter with a red star on its tail, alongside the left hand wingtip. He tried to get in touch with it by radio, switched his landing light on and off and reduced speed; but as the airliner began to descend it was hit by a missile which damaged the fuselage and killed two passengers. Captain Kim went on flying for an hour and a half before he found a lake where he landed with difficulty. The Russians arrested him, impounded the plane and eventually told him to write a letter to Brezhnev apologising for violating Soviet territory. He was then flown with his passengers to Leningrad and thence on an American plane back to Korea. The Russians, Captain Kim insisted, never accused him of spying: they did not even question him about his past or look at his personal papers. His crew and passengers were reasonably well treated and President Park later thanked Brezhnev for his helpfulness.

Korean Air Lines explained that the blunder was due to a navigational error: they hired more American pilots and soon afterwards began using Boeing 747s on their polar routes, equipped with full computer systems. But the intrusion of the Korean airliner had far more important consequences inside Russia. The Soviets were humiliated to find that the plane had been undetected for so long while the NATO surveillance system—which could follow it for most of its course—confirmed the incompetence of the Russian defences. The Soviets court-martialled several senior officers and later radically reorganised their air defences, giving more autonomy to the regional commands. With their traditional obsession with the sanctity of their airspace, they were determined not to be caught again; and the Americans helped to humiliate them. "There was a deliberate attempt to embarrass the Soviets," I was told by Admiral Bobby Ray Inman, who at that time was deputy-director of the CIA, "which only made things worse. After 1978 the Soviets became ever more paranoid about their airspace."

The inexplicable flight to Murmansk raised doubts about the standards of Korean Air Lines, but they gradually regained a qualified reputation as a reliable airline. The pilots of other airlines made jokes about the Korean "cowboys" and British pilots preferred not to fly by KAL. In 1980 a Korean Boeing 747 landed short of the runway at Seoul and burst into flames, killing sixteen people including the captain. But there was no negligence to compare with the case of the mad JAL pilot crashing into Tokyo bay. When I talked to the air controllers on the control tower at Anchorage airport they said they had great respect for the Koreans' skill in landing in bad weather conditions. The Korean accident rate was not high compared with most other airlines: at Lloyds in London they paid about half the insurance premiums of Japan Air Lines but twice those of Philippine Air Lines.

THE FATEFUL FLIGHT

On 31 August 1983 a Korean 747 took off from JFK airport in New York, from the terminal the Koreans share with American Airlines, on the regular flight KE007, which flies four times a week to Seoul via Anchorage. The passengers included seventy-five Koreans, thirty-five Chinese, twenty-eight Japanese and sixty-six Americans including the right-wing Congressman Larry McDonald, the head of the John Birch Society who was on his way to a conference in Korea. He signed his name flamboyantly in the visitors' book in the first-class lounge.

The plane was twenty-seven minutes late leaving New York and arrived equally late at Anchorage, at 2.37 local time. The airport record-sheet, which I saw, shows clearly that the plane refuelled at Gate 2—the usual gate for KAL which is close to their own first-class lounge—and spent one hour thirteen minutes at the airport, about average for that day. The departure was scheduled for 3.20 but it was delayed until 3.50 because favourable winds would reduce the flight-time to Seoul airport which did not open until 6 a.m. (When I followed the same flight later the plane arrived just before six, and the airport was only half-open.) At Anchorage four lucky passengers on the 007—an employee of Alaskan Airways and his family—left the plane together with the crew, two of whom stayed aboard to guard the airliner until they were replaced. A new Korean aircrew of twenty-nine took over, including six who were "dead-heading" (returning as passengers) to Korea. The new pilot Captain Chun Byung-in, aged forty-five, was one of the senior KAL pilots, who had recently been chosen to fly the Korean president on his journeys abroad. He had been a Korean air-force pilot for ten years before joining the airline in 1972, after which he had flown

6,619 hours on Boeing 747s. Before the fateful flight of the 007 he had flown a cargo plane from Toronto and had rested for eleven hours at the Korean airline hostel at Anchorage.

No one at Anchorage remarked anything odd, then or later, about Flight 007 while it was at the airport. The plane had reported some trouble with one of its VHF radios; but it was looked at by members of the five-man Korean maintenance team, and it was then checked (according to the airport staff) by Captain Chun himself. When the plane was cleared for take-off at 3.58 the air traffic controllers on the tower could hear the plane's radio (they told me) with no sign of a fault. Twenty minutes later another scheduled Korean flight, the KE015 from Los Angeles, also took off from Anchorage heading for Seoul, ahead of time, with American senators among its passengers.

The flight of the 007 appeared to continue without incident. The Anchorage radar showed that the plane had begun to deviate slightly, so that it was six miles too far north when it went out of range at 4.27: in fact it was already heading straight for Russia. But this was considered too minor to report to the crew. The Anchorage very-high-frequency radar (VOR) should have given the pilot fuller information; but by another worrying coincidence it had been out of action since 23 August, and came back into service the day after the flight. By the time the 007 reached Bethel, three hundred miles east of Anchorage, it was recorded by the military radar as being twelve miles off course; but this radar was not connected to the civilian aircraft control. And in the meantime the airliner was reporting passing the "waypoints"—the fixed points with made-up names, recorded on the computer—as if it were precisely on time. It reported passing NABIE at 5.32 Anchorage time and NEEVA at 6.58. By 8.07 it was in touch with Tokyo radio (at 2.07 Tokyo time), with the news that it was passing the next waypoint NIPPI.

THE RECEPTION

In the meantime a group of families, friends and diplomats— including the US political counsellor in Seoul, Harry Dunlop—was gathering at the shiny new Kimpo airport outside Seoul to wait for the arrival of the two planes at dawn. Flight KE015 from Los Angeles via Anchorage arrived on time with its senators aboard, but there was no sign of KE007 which was due to land twenty minutes earlier. The families became worried, and there was no explanation or announcement until the Korean Broadcasting

System issued a confident statement—never later explained—that the 007 had been forced down over the Soviet island of Sakhalin, and that all passengers and crew were safe.

But in Tokyo there was now frenzied activity. The radar at Narita airport outside Tokyo had expected to detect the Korean airliner as it passed north through Japanese airspace on its way to Seoul, since it had been consistently reporting its position at successive waypoints. At 3.15 Japanese time (the same as Korean time) the airliner had asked Tokyo for permission to increase its altitude—a normal request from a plane with less fuel—which was granted five minutes later. At 3.27 the plane called Tokyo radar station, but the signal was noisy and incomprehensible. By 3.30 a.m. the Tokyo air controllers were expecting to see the plane on their radar, but they saw nothing; and they reported the fact to the military radar station at Wakkanai, the huge "mast-farm" on the northern tip of Japan overlooking Soviet Sakhalin Island. At Wakkanai (according to intelligence sources I talked to in Tokyo) the Japanese quickly checked the video tapes of their radar screen, which had shown up a big plane which they first assumed to be a Soviet transport flying over Sakhalin. They played and replayed the video tapes and also checked the recordings of Russian voices which they had picked up over Sakhalin. They soon realised that the big blob must have been the Korean airliner, while three smaller blobs swerving round it were Soviet fighters. Then the voice recordings, listened to by a Japanese expert on Russian, revealed clearly the Russian word for "shoot". Putting video and audio together, the Japanese soon had little doubt that the Korean airliner had been shot down by the Soviets and had crashed into the sea at 3.38—just two minutes before it was due to reach Japanese airspace.

The Japanese defence ministry moved quickly. By 8 a.m. the Cabinet Secretary Gotoda was told the news while he was breakfasting. By 10.30, while the Koreans were still reporting that the plane had landed at Sakhalin, the Japanese Prime Minister Nakasone was told that it had been shot down. That afternoon Nakasone had an anguished meeting with his ministers discussing how much to reveal; the cabinet secretary insisted that they should reveal enough to make the Soviets face up to what they had done, even if they would never apologise. The Americans were duly informed. That evening at 8.20 the Japanese Foreign Minister, Shintaro Abe, publicly announced that the Soviets had shot down the plane.

At 9 p.m. in Washington George Shultz, the Secretary of State, also revealed that the plane had been shot down, and attacked the Soviets for their brutal behaviour. The next day a few grim details of the crash began to emerge: Japanese fishermen off the coast of

Sakhalin reported seeing two orange flashes in the night-sky, and others found bits of wrecked fuselage and the remains of bodies.

The Japanese base at Wakkanai had close links with American intelligence, which has its own sophisticated base at Misawa further south, directly linked with the National Security Agency outside Washington. But the Japanese cabinet were politically embarrassed by the question of how much to reveal to the Americans. A senior defence official insisted that they could not entrust their tapes of the Soviet pilots to the CIA, who would always act in their own national interests. But he was overruled, and the tapes were handed over—the "family jewels" as the Americans called them—on strict condition that Washington would not make use of them without Japanese permission, and would only use them together with their own information which (the Japanese were convinced) was extensive. "We could only trace the airliner for fifteen minutes," I was told by a well informed defence official in Tokyo, "while the Americans could trace it for two hours."

But the Americans could not resist making public the sensational tapes. On 6 September, five days after the disaster, the US ambassador to the United Nations Jeane Kirkpatrick revealed the transcript of the Soviet pilot's conversation with his ground officers. It appeared to prove clearly that the Soviets had not tried to warn the Korean airliner, and must have known that it was a passenger plane. The Japanese were embarrassed and angry to hear their intelligence capability being revealed by a foreign power which was concealing its own information. "We should have known from the name of the White House spokesman," a Japanese official commented bitterly. "The trouble with Larry Speakes is . . . he speaks!"

THE OUTCRY

The transcripts were made public at the UN in the full glare of television, made visually dramatic by converting them into Cyrillic characters with a Russian typewriter. The presentation acutely embarrassed the Soviets in front of the world, and gave the Reagan administration new support in Congress just when it was trying to push through the bill for the MX missile system. "Quite simply," said Jeane Kirkpatrick, "it establishes that the Soviets decided to shoot down a civilian airliner, shot it down, murdering the two hundred and sixty-nine persons on board, and lied about it." In the resulting uproar many western countries including Canada and Britain temporarily banned Aeroflot flights, while the US—which had already excluded the Soviet airline after the invasion of Afghanistan—refused to sell Aeroflot tickets.

But the certainty that the Soviets had knowingly shot down a civilian plane without warning became less certain in the following weeks. For it was soon revealed—not by the Russians, but by Michael Getler, the defence expert of the *Washington Post*—that there had been an American spy-plane in the region, a RC135, much like a Boeing 707. The spy-plane had at one time crossed the path of the Korean airliner before returning to its base at Shemya —a conjunction which might well have confused the Russians. The weather, which President Reagan had claimed was "a clear night, with a half moon", proved (in the words of the later official ICAO report) to have had "extensive coverage of low, medium and high level clouds over southern Kamchatka" and "mostly overcast low cloud" over southern Sakhalin. And a few days after the UN presentation Washington released a revised version of the transcripts with two very significant corrections: it now showed that the Soviet pilot had said "they do not see me" and also "I am firing cannon-bursts"—which made clear that he *had* tried to warn the airliner before firing a missile. The original mistakes in the transcript (according to the Japanese sources) were genuinely due to garbles which took time to clarify; but both the revised transcript and the presence of the spy-plane threw doubt on Jeane Kirkpatrick's account. And an intelligence analysis provided in Washington two weeks after the disaster reported that the Soviet fighter was below and behind the airliner, and probably did not know what kind of plane he was firing at.

The Soviets in the meantime had reacted quickly with a bombardment of careless lies and mounting accusations that the Korean plane had been deliberately spying against them. On the day after the disaster the news agency Tass had explained that Soviet planes had tried to warn the Korean plane by radio and then to force it to land on Sakhalin, but that it did not obey demands and tried to evade pursuit. The Soviet pilots, Tass insisted, "could not know that it was a civilian aircraft", and it was flying without lights. The Korean flight, said Tass, was "a major intelligence operation" planned by the Americans—which if it went wrong could be turned into a "major political confrontation". In Madrid on the day after the UN presentation the Soviet Foreign Minister, Andrei Gromyko, insisted that "as has become perfectly clear, the South Korean aircraft was on special duty for American authorities" and Washington had put out a "lying version" to disguise its responsibility for "this criminal activity".

Two days later the Soviet Chief of General Staff Marshal Nikolai

Ogarkov took the unprecedented step of holding a press conference in front of TV cameras in Moscow, equipped with a large map showing the alleged course of the Korean airliner, flying straight across Kamchatka, three hundred miles off course, and turning eastwards across Sakhalin before it was shot down. How, he asked, could the American radar systems not notice this huge aberration? Why, when the plane failed to report the correct waypoints on the route, did the Americans not sound the alarm? A highly qualified Soviet state commission, Ogarkov reported, had concluded irrefutably that the Americans had deliberately chosen a commercial plane for a thoroughly planned intelligence operation.

Over the following days Soviet papers elaborated on their account with detailed allegations: about how the plane had been delayed at Anchorage to take on special agents, how it had been carefully synchronised with the spy-plane and with another Korean airliner, how Captain Chun had boasted of his links with the CIA, how Korean Air Lines had close links with American intelligence and had been allowed to buy American planes cheaply, and how their flying over secret installations was in keeping with the previous Korean intrusion five years before.

An article by Air Force Marshal Kirsanov put great emphasis on the role of the American satellite Ferret-D, which was circling above Kamchatka, he said, just when the 007 was entering Soviet airspace. "The intrusion of the South Korean aircraft into Soviet airspace made our radio and electronic facilities increase their activity almost two times," Kirsanov explained, "and that was just the intention of the organisers of the provocation." And Kirsanov claimed that it "had been established beyond doubt" that the 007's departure from Anchorage had been delayed to synchronise with the flight of the American satellite.

How far do the Soviet leaders seriously believe these conspiracy theories? Certainly when I talked a few months later to Giorgi Arbatov, a member of the Supreme Soviet who is an expert on American affairs, he still seemed convinced that the two airliners were conspiring together. But perhaps, as Admiral Inman suggested, "the question of spying wasn't really relevant. The fact was that the Soviets are obsessed by violations of their territory; and the Koreans, twice in five years, had given them the opportunity to justify their paranoia."

Most of the Soviet allegations could be quickly dismissed as rather careless lies—as could be checked by anyone who retraced the plane's flight. The delay at Anchorage was easily explained by the favourable winds. The extra people taken on were merely another crew returning to Korea. No one in Anchorage noticed any special equipment or "blister" on the plane's surface—which would be essential for any surveillance, and hard to conceal. The other Korean plane was the scheduled flight from Los Angeles, which the Russians could have checked in the timetable. The fourteen Korean Boeing 747s and the five DC-10s had been bought quite normally with the help of American bank loans (which for a time seriously overextended the airline). The navigation lights and the bright strobe on top of the plane must have been visible, since the Soviet fighter-pilot referred to them in the transcripts. No convincing evidence remained to back up the Soviet allegation of espionage. "Their only real evidence," joked a Japanese defence official, "was that the flight was called 007."

Yet the fact remained that the circumstances of the disaster were bound to arouse deep suspicions—which the Americans did not allay. No convincing explanation had been given as to how the airliner, equipped with three computers, could have deviated from the route Romeo Twenty which the American FAA had pronounced as being safe. A Korean airliner had once again made a huge and inexplicable incursion across Soviet territory bristling with military secrets—first across Kamchatka, then across Sakhalin, then apparently heading for the key base of Vladivostok. Its mysterious flight had coincided with the close presence of an American spy-plane, together with American warships and a satellite; and three weeks after the disaster Washington sources added to suspicions by revealing that the spy-plane was specially engaged in watching for a new Soviet missile, the PL5, which was due to be launched that night, on a trajectory ending at Kamchatka, in violation of the SALT 2 Treaty. The coincidences were piling up. And Air Marshal Kirsanov's theory, that the airliner was being used to help the satellite gather information about Soviet reactions, attracted some support from observers outside Russia; ten months after the disaster, an anonymous writer "P. Q. Mann" in the British magazine *Defence Attaché* described how twenty years earlier two American planes had flown over East Germany just when a satellite was passing overhead. Mann's article was dismissed by the American Defence Secretary Caspar Weinberger as a repetition of "the total set of lies that the Soviet Union published"; but the earlier satellite incidents were not specifically denied.

In Seoul in the meantime Korean Air Lines had expressed continuous outrage against the Russians, but offered no convincing explanation of their airliner's blunder. Their chairman Harry Cho tried to make me believe the unlikely theory that the Soviets had deliberately lured the airliner into their territory by interfering with the computers. When I asked him why the airline had been so silent he explained. "We were brought up on Confucian principles: when victims are suffering we should not try to defend ourselves. But we feel ourselves the prey of the intelligence games of the superpowers." The Korean government appeared equally uninformed—and humiliated by their ignorance. "The foreign ministry kept on summoning us," said a western ambassador in Seoul, "but they turned out to have nothing to say." "It was humiliating for us to know so little," said a Korean journalist. "We spend four times as much on defence per head than the Japanese, and yet when the crisis came we had to find out from the Japanese what had happened."

Most of the Soviet allegations were easily rebutted, but some worrying questions remained unanswered. Why didn't the traffic controllers know that the airliner was wildly off course? Why couldn't the Americans—including the spy-plane—have warned it, and the Russians, before it was shot down? The fact that the plane had strayed off course on such a critical night of missile-testing and surveillance, and the fact that much information was still clearly being withheld, gave limitless scope for conspiracy theories from both sides. Was the airliner used as a decoy to conceal other espionage? Was it testing Soviet air defences, which the spy-plane could then observe? Was the satellite, or the space shuttle, recording information about Soviet communications?

While most conspiracy theories assumed a plot by American intelligence, others assumed that Korean Air Lines were simply too greedy for profits. Pilots from rival airlines, insurance agents and lawyers acting for victims all spread the story that Korean airliners had regularly been cutting the corner across the Soviet Union in order to save fuel, which would explain why the 007 had flown the direct great circle route from Anchorage to Seoul. KAL was said to be so keen to cut costs that they had promised pilots bonuses if they reduced fuel-consumption. If proved the allegation would be devastating to Korean Air Lines as evidence of their negligence, making them liable for huge insurance compensation.

Cutting corners to save time or fuel is not unknown among the most responsible pilots. But to fly regularly over obviously hostile Soviet territory would be a criminal act of folly; and it would also soon be detected. The Japanese radar would have observed that Korean airliners were regularly off course, and the ICAO report confirmed that "there were no records of such deviations." "And how could anyone standardise bonuses?" asked a traffic manager at Anchorage, "when winds, weather and altitude are always vary-ing?"

THE COMPUTERS

In the months after the disaster investigators began to favour a less sinister explanation as they looked more dispassionately into possible navigational errors. The American aircraft and computer manufacturers, Boeing and Litton, sent their experts to Korea. The American FAA and the British CAA conducted their own investigations. The International Civil Aviation Organisation from Montreal—the UN body which includes the Soviets—appointed its own team. And the experts seemed less surprised than the public by the airliner's huge deviation. "I've never yet met a pilot who hasn't made a mistake," an official of the American safety board said in Seoul, "—or one who will admit it."

The investigators increasingly concentrated their attention on the computers. The basic safeguards for the airliners on the long stretch without radar were the three independent computers of the "Inertial Navigation System" (INS) which were regarded as virtually foolproof; but if they were fed with the wrong information they could consistently mislead the pilot into thinking he was on course. The ICAO team published a detailed report in December 1983 which included their most favoured scenario: that the pilot had failed to connect the first computer on to the autopilot, and had kept the plane on the "heading" mode, linked to the magnetic compass on a course of 246 degrees. Allowing for the wind, and the extreme magnetic variation in the North Pacific, this would take it roughly on the course where it ended up, flying across Kamchatka and Sakhalin. After this original mistake the second computer could have continued showing what appeared the right time and distance between waypoints, while the third computer was known to be recording the winds for meteorological reports. The pilot must also have failed to check his position by looking down on the islands with his radar—an unforgivable negligence, but not unprecedented.

The pilots' federation was sceptical of this explanation and two months later the navigation commission of ICAO produced a dissenting report which "found it difficult to validate and endorse" any of the earlier scenarios and recommended a careful study of past malfunctions of INS systems. As it happened an important clue emerged the next month from the captain of a Northwest 747 flying from Osaka to Honolulu on 30 March 1984. He found his airliner suddenly making a left turn, following a heading course which had been put onto the autopilot earlier: he was convinced that it was the fault of the computer, and he wrote a careful report because, he said, "it presents another theory for the KAL navigational error". The report took three months to come to light, and some aviation officials suspected that this and other malfunctions had been deliberately covered up. Duane Freer, the chief navigational expert at ICAO, told me that the report provided "a new and important additional scenario": but he added, "there still had to be an inattentive crew".

Computer-flying generates its own boredom and complacency on regular runs. The most obvious test is the North Atlantic, with 100,000 planes crossing it every year, likewise relying on their computers along a long stretch without radar. Most mistakes never become public; but they all have to be reported—even mistakes by Aeroflot—and confidential analyses of North Atlantic flights show that about twice a month there is a "gross navigational error", which means flying more than fifty miles off course. (Significantly, the ratio of pilots' errors dropped sharply for a few weeks after the shock of the Korean disaster; but over the last two years they have been running higher than average; and some experts ascribe this to a new generation of pilots who rely too heavily on computers.)

There have been blunders even more careless than the Koreans'. The captain of an American Boeing 747 flying from New York to London showed off his computer in the cockpit to a senator, and temporarily set it to fly to the senator's home in Washington: he then forgot to change it back, failing to notice that the plane had slowly turned 180 degrees, until one of the crew noticed that the sun was on the wrong side. Only a few weeks after the Korean disaster a British airliner flying from Hong Kong to Australia made a very similar error to the one postulated for the 007. All such errors are investigated by the traffic controllers, but most of them remain unnoticed by passengers. The airlines can conceal most of the "Oh Christ activity"—as they sometimes call it—in the cockpit.

Along Romeo Twenty, where forty miles or four minutes can take a plane over Soviet territory, the dangers of any deviation are obvious. But a pilot can soon regard any regular flight as a "milk-run". A senior pilot can be more prone to boredom, while his seniority makes it harder for his co-pilot to argue with him. Across that weird timeless flight through the night from Alaska, it would not be astonishing for a pilot eventually to make a spectacular blunder; nor was it so unbelievable—since the Koreans are the second-biggest users—that two Korean airliners should make serious errors in five years. What was deadly was the conjunction with the military blunder.

Who was really to blame for the final tragic outcome? The evidence which gradually emerged suggested a succession of coincidences and blunders. The Soviets, after all their efforts to improve their air defences, had clearly lost track of the airliner as it crossed over Kamchatka and had only caught up with it as it was about to leave Soviet airspace. The transcripts showed that both the pilot and (according to Japanese intelligence) the ground station were preoccupied with the need to shoot down "the target", as they called it, without identifying it. The airliner's crew remained apparently oblivious of any danger; and when at 3.15 a.m. the Korean captain asked Tokyo for permission to climb, it was only two minutes after the Soviet fighter-pilot had reported, "the target isn't responding to the call"—when the Korean captain may still have been preoccupied. As the airliner began climbing the Soviet pilot evidently thought he was taking evasive action. He shot his two missiles, the first of which hit the No.4 (outer right) engine and caused sudden decompression. At 3.26 the Soviet pilot said, "The target is destroyed." The last words from the airliner, at 3.27, mixed with unintelligible sounds, were: "Korean Air zero zero seven . . . rapid compression . . . rapid compression . . . descending to one zero"—suggesting total bewilderment. The plane took nine minutes before it crashed into the sea, littering wreckage and bodies on the ocean.

Why could no one have warned the airliner in the course of its fateful two and a half hour flight? That question has never been satisfactorily answered; but the explanation clearly lies in the complete division between the civil and military monitoring. The sophisticated surveillance systems, including the American spy-planes, all had strictly military priorities. Two former crew-members of RC135s, Tom Bernard and Edward Eskelson, recollected that the spy-planes often deliberately penetrated Soviet airspace in order to test the air defence systems, and that they were quite capable of warning a civilian airliner if they wanted to.

Whatever the Americans may have observed from their radar base at Shemya was clearly not used to warn the airliner. American intelligence sources insist that Shemya was equipped primarily to monitor Soviet missiles and verify their performance in line with the SALT agreements; but the ICAO report confirms that Shemya had a powerful normal radar with a 200-mile range, which overlaps with the Romeo Twenty route—though not with the 007's actual route. "Had the military radar at Shemya been used to monitor KE007's progress," said ICAO, "the mere absence of its radar response would have been grounds for corrective action." It was not till after the disaster that the FAA began sharing radar information with the US Air Force along Romeo Twenty, through their long-promised "Joint Surveillance System", and pressed ahead with building a new radar site on St Paul Island in the Bering Sea. At last the airline pilots were getting the more effective monitoring for which they had pleaded two years earlier.

But the confrontation between the superpowers on this explosive frontier, which had contributed to the disaster, was made more dangerous by the political exploitation of it—as had happened after the Murmansk incident five years earlier. "Washington didn't help by politicising the whole incident," said Admiral Inman; "it only increased Soviet paranoia. And the Soviets who could have limited their political damage told lies without thinking them through: they've gone back to the crouching position." Both sides were still further withdrawing their contacts and communications—just where more communications were needed. The Soviets were still more obsessed with the sanctity of their frontiers: in later accounts they had to admit the shortcomings of their air defences, and the local commander at Kamchatka was reported first to have been moved, and then to have died. The escalation of tension and weaponry continued on both sides. It was a depressing sign of the lack of political progress over the previous decades. The north-west passage, which had been developed as a miraculous new air-route to link the East with the West, was now on the edge of an electronic frontier bristling with dangers.

The assertion of national sovereignty in the air was more ruthless than ever. It was not only Soviet airspace that threatened foreign aircraft. Every country including the United States and Britain reserves the right to shoot down unauthorised planes over its own territory. The South Koreans themselves forbid foreign planes to fly over central Seoul, where the president has his heavily-protected "Blue House"; and they once even shot at a TWA plane which had wandered off course. Over the last twenty years an average of one commercial plane a year has been shot at—though not always brought down—as a result of blunders. "The Korean case may look like an amazing coincidence," said one British CAA official, "but most disasters are the results of coincidences."

But the coincidences involving the superpowers were far more dangerous; and the political barriers across this remote frontier at the back of the world seemed more insuperable than ever. It was a pathetic outcome to all the hopes at the end of the Second World War that the airplane would eventually help to dissolve frontiers and bring nations closer together. When Anne Lindbergh had flown fifty years earlier above the Great Wall of China, she had reflected about the contrast between the plane and the wall. "I am a wall. You are a plane; you will be gone tomorrow. But I—I will be here forever—a wall."

15

Davids and Goliaths

We have to make you think it's an important seat—because you're in it.
Donald Burr, of People Express, 1984

IN June 1984 the newest and smallest of the transatlantic airlines was launched by Richard Branson, a thirty-three-year-old British showbiz entrepreneur who had built up his Virgin record business by appealing to teenagers with flashy shops and brilliant publicity. The Virgin Atlantic airline seemed to mark the consummation of the marriage between showbusiness and the air. Branson had bought a single 747—which had been returned to Boeing from Aerolineas Argentinas which could not pay for it—for £20 million. "The great thing about having only one plane," he told me, "is that you know what your airline *is*. It will either have the best safety record, or the worst." He did not pretend to know anything about airlines: for the inaugural flight from Gatwick he put on a blue and silver uniform, like a bogus airline captain, with the cap perched raffishly on his head; and baptised the plane "Maiden Voyager", with the help of a magnum of champagne and his two-year-old daughter. It was celebrated as if it were the first 747 ever flown. A battery of photographers and TV cameras recorded the brass band and the array of pop stars and personalities, while Branson splashed champagne over the fuselage and endlessly replayed his act for the cameras with an inexhaustible grin. ("We decided against a personality airline," he assured me on the flight.)

The "maiden voyage" was a kind of spoof of aviation, as if to proclaim that the air was now so safe and so boring that it could not do without entertainment. During the take-off a video film showed the cricketers Ian Botham and Viv Richards at the controls in the cockpit; a magician dressed up as a pilot pretended to be airsick, catching silver balls out of his mouth; the flashlights blazed as Branson chatted up passengers and told risky stories about how he had once taken flying lessons and crashed into a field; the young air hostesses, with the eagerness of aspiring stars, pushed trolleys of drinks and souvenirs. The plane was transformed from sedentary rows into a stand-up champagne party where the overcrowding was forgotten. The real captain's announcements about seat-belts and designated smoking areas sounded like spoofs themselves, and when the plane landed at Newark and the airport official asked for the ship's papers he was greeted with roars of laughter.

It was a brave attempt to defy the conformity of the air. But no amount of showmanship could conceal that this was just one more 747 crossing the Atlantic with the same plastic food, the same tiny lavatories, the same narrow rows of seats. And Branson, for all his cult of youth, knew quite well that his airline, like all the others, must appeal to every age group from grandmothers to babies: to make the point, he had his parents and grandmother as well as his daughter on board.

FOR YOUR COMFORT AND SAFETY

The distinction between airlines was inevitably blurred now that they all flew the same kinds of plane almost equally reliably. In the pioneer decades both passengers and managers had been obsessed with safety, and any airline which had a fatal crash might go out of business. But the coming of the jets had dramatically reduced the proportions of fatal accidents. The statistics of ICAO (which exclude the Soviet Union which provides only "incomplete data") showed that 802 people were killed on planes in 1983, excluding casualties from military intervention such as the 269 passengers of the KE007. The 802 deaths amounted to less than one death per billion passenger-kilometres, or one death per 400,000 aircraft landings. Even propeller-planes which had been markedly less safe than jet planes—partly because they were relegated to more remote routes—now showed an almost equal safety record—0.9 per billion passenger-kilometres instead of 0.8. The table on the next page shows the accidents and deaths for scheduled flights over the last twenty years.

The American airlines, which accounted for about half these passenger-kilometres, still had the most remarkable record of safety. In 1983 only twenty-five people were killed on American-certified planes, flying over 3 billion miles—which was fewer Americans

	Plane accidents	Passengers killed	Deaths per 100 million miles	Fatal accidents per	
				100 million miles	million landings
1963	31	715	0.78	1.46	4.6
1964	26	668	0.63	1.13	3.7
1965	25	684	0.56	0.98	3.3
1966	31*	1,001	0.70	1.11	4.0
1967	30	678	0.40	0.91	3.5
1968	35	912	0.29	0.92	3.8
1969	32	946	0.43	0.77	3.4
1970	28	687	0.29	0.64	3.0
1971	31	867	0.34	0.71	3.2
1972	42**	1,210	0.42	0.94	4.4
1973	36	862	0.27	0.77	3.4
1974	29	1,299	0.38	0.63	3.0
1975	20	443	0.12	0.43	2.1
1976	20*	734	0.19	0.41	2.0
1977	24	516	0.12	0.48	2.4
1978	25	755	0.15	0.47	2.4
1979	31	878	0.16	0.55	2.9
1980	21	812	0.14	0.36	2.0
1981	18	350	0.06	0.32	1.8
1982	23	732	0.13	0.45	2.6
1983	20	802	0.13	0.35	1.9

* includes one collision in mid-air, shown as one accident
** includes two mid-air collisions, shown as two accidents
Source: ICAO Bulletin, 1983 & 1984

than were killed by bee-stings and about one-thirtieth of the number killed in cars. There were still worrying signs that deregulation and cost-cutting were making American planes less safe. In a report in April 1984 the US Department of Transportation would only give the American airline industry an "A-minus" for safety. Some smaller airlines had been suspect—including Air Florida, Air Illinois and Global International (all of which later went bankrupt). But the overall figures showed no significant upturn since deregulation, and American airlines were still the safest in the world.

Air travel in Europe is roughly twice as risky as in the United States; in Latin America three times more dangerous, in Africa four times more. But the figures for fatalities remain tiny, even in the third world, compared to other causes of death including driving cars and crossing the street, and they have as much to do with airports as with planes. British statistics produced by Sir Peter Masefield in 1983 showed that if an individual is reckoned to travel 10,000 miles a year, before he was likely to be killed he would have to travel for

938,000 years by scheduled airlines
760,000 years by buses or coaches
497,000 years by train
220,000 years by charter or non-scheduled airlines
109,000 years by commercial road vehicles or trucks
 78,000 years by private car
 19,000 years by private plane
  4,500 years by motorcycle
    900 years by bicycle

But even these figures underestimate the comparative safety of planes compared to cars, which cause at least ten times more serious injuries than deaths. (The figure for bicycling is misleading, since few people cycle 10,000 miles a year.)

Some experts maintain that aviation accidents are now so rare that comparisons between airlines are statistically meaningless. There is evidence from individual crashes that a few airlines still go through dangerous phases. In 1983 an Avianca 747 came into Madrid airport too low, hit the ground and killed 181 people; and a 727 belonging to Turkish Airlines—already with a bad record—landed short of the runway in the fog at Ankara airport and killed forty-seven passengers. But over 500 deaths on scheduled airliners in 1983 appear to have been primarily due to political or military causes; the Korean airliner was shot down by the Russians; a Gulf Air 737 crashed near Abu Dhabi, killing 111 people, which was later blamed on military manoeuvres; and an Angolan Airlines 737 which killed 126 people after it took off from Lubango in Angola was thought to have been shot down.

Flying in the third world can still be unpredictable, but it is much less dangerous than western pilots had predicted, and some African and Asian airlines, including Iran and Ethiopian, have an outstanding record. Computerised systems have taken over much of the burden, and the risk of accidents comes as much from boredom as from lack of training. "Is the flight deck becoming such a pleasant ivory tower, with technology reducing the perceived workload towards a point where crews relax too much?" asked *Flight* magazine, reviewing the previous year's figures in January 1984. "Systems fail so rarely that the adrenalin is not even on standby, perhaps. And if that is true of the seventies cockpits, what will the flight deck of the eighties do to pilots, to their adrenalin supply, and to their sense of responsibility and usefulness?" It was an ironic turnabout: in the old days pilots tried to get away from the tension of "seat of the pants" flying; now—as the transcripts of the "black box" suggest—they are much more likely to be too relaxed.

The airlines, though they continually stress "comfort and safety", have long ago ceased to emphasise their own safety in their advertising. They have an unwritten law not to arouse passengers' fears or to suggest that other airlines are dangerous; and they know that the fear of flying is largely irrational. "If no amount of education will cure the phobia," as the authors of *Destination Disaster* put it, "what is the point of even talking publicly about safety?" The airlines content themselves with more general claims of reliability, like Pan Am's "you can't beat the experience"; but as they maintain their self-imposed silence about safety—which is still what worries most passengers—they find it all the harder to distinguish themselves from all the others flying the same planes. The contest comes down to seats, service—and smiles.

THE SMILING CONTEST

The ruthless competition and extravagant advertising of airlines are now increasingly focusing on a few facial muscles: the whole intricate industry, like the Cheshire cat, seems to be dissolving into an all-embracing smile.

It was the Asians who first set the new pace of smiling, as they staked their appeal to westerners on their reputation for charming, long-suffering girls. But the reputation was based more on hard drill and discipline than on the natural Oriental courtesy which the advertisements suggested. When Anthony Spaeth investigated the three training centres of Cathay Pacific, Singapore and Korean Airlines in 1984 he found that they all imposed rigorous conditioning. In Korea, Confucian education had taught girls not to smile, but to keep poker faces; so Korean Air Lines insist that their stewardesses keep smiling throughout their six weeks' training, even during reprimands. Cathay Pacific, which recruits their trainees from ten countries, have formidable training standards which were built up by a strict Australian bachelor: the girls are now required to have daily eye-contact exercises, staring into each other's eyes for ten minutes. The "Singapore Girls"—many of whom in fact are Malaysians—are taught to chant the four rules—smile, attitude, humility and co-operation.

Faced with this young smiling army the western airlines have been hard pressed to fight back, hedged in with women's lib movements or labour unions which stop them from firing hostesses who get married or grow old: while western passengers are quick to complain about ageing women who smile only with their mouths, not with their eyes. The Asian airlines have no such obstacles to their smiling offensive; and the competition in the air has dramatised a critical Asian advantage—the submissiveness of their women.

WHAT IS AN AIRLINE?

Deregulation, recessions and competition have forced all airlines to think harder about what kind of business they are in. They have all had to cut costs, reorganise routes and step up their marketing and salesmanship. Some airlines have even had to agree to new kinds of labour relations in return for concessions from their unions, including profit-sharing and participation. And the harsher conditions have thrown up a new generation of dominating entrepreneurs who have called into question the old assumptions of managerial revolutions and the "technostructure".

Within America the Big Four are still the same four which were put together in the twenties and which had been granted their "grandfather rights" across the continent in the thirties. United Airlines based on its giant hub of Chicago is still the biggest airline in the world including domestic passengers (but excluding Aeroflot). It remains remarkably profitable in spite of deregulation—largely thanks to its mastery of marketing and its computer booking system linked to the travel agents, which smaller airlines bitterly resent. It has concentrated on marketing ever since it was taken over by Eddie Carlson and Dick Ferris from Western hotels—"At Western I was selling empty hotel rooms," Carlson explained, "here it's empty airplane seats"—and it has successfully proved that airliners can be treated like flying hotels.

But the other three have each suffered from the rigours of deregulation. American is still the second biggest domestic airline, but it had to become much more aggressive. In 1979 it even moved its headquarters from New York to Dallas, explaining that "it belongs in Mid-America"; but its president, Robert Crandall, faced rough competition in Texas including the deadly battle with Braniff; and he had to pursue a drastic programme of firing, cost-cutting and bargaining with unions for lower wages before he could ensure his airlines future with a huge order from McDonnell Douglas. Eastern Airlines, the third-runner based on Miami, continued to face the worst problems as leaner competitors including People's and New York Air nibbled at its routes and pushed it further into debt. Its astronaut chairman Frank Borman moved to a new hub in the west, invading TWA territory in Kansas City; but Eastern came perilously close to bankruptcy before its unions agreed to a deal which included representation on the board.

TWA faced a harsher twist of fortune. Twenty years earlier in 1965 its chairman Charles Tillinghast had begun buying up subsidiaries—including Hilton hotels, Canteen Corporation and Century 21 Real Estate—to ensure that TWA had "the strongest capital structure". But in 1983 a group of three Wall Street investors moved to split up the business, since the airline was cutting into the profits of the others. "The attempt to connect the business of an airline," they complained, "with that of real-estate broker, a fast-food operator and a hotel chain will never be recognised by the investment community."

In February 1984 TWA was duly spun off from the parent Trans World Corporation, and its chief executive Ed Meyer had to survive without the capital structure which had been meant to fortify him. Facing much tougher competition at its Kansas hub, TWA once again looked for more overseas routes to offset its losses at home and spread out to more European cities—Amsterdam, Brussels, Zurich and Munich—as part of "the biggest single route expansion in TWA's history".

Up on the forty-sixth floor of the Pan American skyscraper, where Juan Trippe once autocratically ruled over his empire, the new chairman Ed Acker has an almost equally dominating style. He still retains some Texan drawl, with intimidating silences. He conveys the impression that he is merely camping in the great building, and he even contemplates moving out of it altogether. ("It's not important where we hang our hat and coat," he told me. "There aren't many people left here anyway.") When he first took on the job he joked that he had thought of applying to be captain of the *Titanic* and decided on Pan Am instead; "but the job was much worse than I had expected", he said in mid-1984. "I couldn't foresee how the high dollar would add to our problems. We're more hit by it than any other big American corporation because so much of our revenue is in other currencies."

Pan Am still lives in the long shadow of Juan Trippe and the accretions of imperial splendour, and Acker has had to live with his predecessors' mistakes. When Pan Am bought National Airlines in 1979 it was seen as providing a valuable domestic network, and the means at last to encircle the world; but in an era of deregulation it now appears as an extravagant mistake. "There was little basis for taking that decision," Acker now says. "It meant that National's wages rose to the level of Pan Am's." But Acker has relentlessly cut down the airlines' costs, firing vice-presidents, rationalising the routes and fighting back against his more flexible rivals, including his own former company Air Florida which Pan Am and others pounded into bankruptcy: Pan Am under Acker seemed to combine

the size of Goliath with the combativeness of David. Acker now sees
Pan Am becoming more of a businessman's airline, with half its
revenue soon coming from Clipper and first class. And it remains
above all an international airline, with forty per cent of its traffic
passing through the Worldport at Kennedy—with much congestion. The difficulty of actually *reaching* American airports, Acker
thinks, will be the industry's greatest problem. But he still expects
another technological breakthrough in the nineties, to a new age of
supersonic travel, with planes bigger and faster than Concordes,
providing a special service for businessmen, while the jumbos cater
for the masses. He is determined that Pan Am will again become
the pacesetter for other international airlines.

All the traditional airlines, carrying their heavy baggage from
the past, are still threatened by more nimble rivals travelling light;
and the most successful and the most unorthodox remains People
Express, which challenged not just the fares of established airlines,
but their whole style of business. Donald Burr's management methods are so unconventional that he himself is almost impossible to
find: anyone who rings him is told that he has no secretary—no
one at People has a secretary—and no proper office. I eventually
heard he was coming to London to run in the annual Marathon
and managed to pin him down to a long breakfast at the Savoy,
where he discussed his ideas on management. "You can't assume
that United and American are just sleeping monsters waiting to be
raped," he explained to me. "To compete seriously you need
alignment between the individual and the enterprise, to make everyone feel responsible. The old airlines were brought up in different
space and time, with a different value system. Pan Am and the others
are in a we–they situation, which is beginning to be supplanted. Ed
Acker is a fighter, and I admire his courage. But he believes in
confrontation. He won't do anything great with his airline because
he insists on telling people what to do—or be fired." Acker, not
surprisingly, takes a different view: "I don't think Donald Burr
knows anything about labour relations that I don't know," he told
me. "It's just that he runs a non-union airline and the unions don't
choose to take him on—for the time being. But at Pan Am I'm one
of the few people who don't belong to a union." Burr's British rivals
are still more sceptical. "We had a look at People's," said one
executive of British Caledonian, "and really their employees are
just like Moonies—they're all identical. We could never get away
with it in Britain." "Bullshit," said Burr. "We get the best recruits
because we can offer them every kind of job, and they can become
a team manager in a fast-growing company in two years. Who
wouldn't want that?"

Certainly People's has had a spectacular growth: it has doubled its size every year, and by the time it was three years old in 1984 it was 400th in Fortune's list of big companies. Burr has still more ambitious plans for expansion, both in America and Europe, where he aims to multiply his cheap flights to Britain, embracing Heathrow, Manchester and Stansted; and already People's dominates the brand-new international terminal at Newark. Burr insists that he can handle his rapid growth, only because People's has its own concept of self-management and shared responsibility. His own holding in the airline has gone down to six per cent, and will soon be only two per cent, while several of his employees own shares worth over a million dollars. But People's is now worth over $300 million and Burr says: "I'd far rather have two per cent of a growing business than a hundred per cent of World, like Ed Daly [the late chairman of World Airways, whose World has now been reduced to America, London and Frankfurt]." Burr insists that his airline is efficient because his employees are highly motivated by being shareholders earning above-average salaries; and that this must be the pattern of the future.

Richard Branson of Virgin Atlantic has an even more unorthodox management style than Donald Burr; he conceals his shrewd business mind behind a casual Bohemian façade, running his company from a photogenic barge in Little Venice in London, surrounded by his young daughter's teddy-bears and rocking-horses. He had seen how Laker and Burr generated their own publicity and considered he could also enlarge his market for records and films with a plane. "I decided there must be room for another airline when I spent two days trying to get through to People Express," he explained on his barge. "That was the sum of my market research." He also, like Burr, thought he could motivate people, with the help of some showbiz glamour, much more effectively than the big airlines: "I can't face the idea of smiling courses: it's much easier to let them actually *enjoy* it."

Virgin and People, competing for "backpackers" across the Atlantic, each in their different way present a new face for an airline, run by younger people without unions and with minimal costs. The big airlines, mindful of their mistakes in confronting Laker—and wary of anti-trust suits—profess not to be worried by this competition. "We can match them if we need to," said Acker of Pan Am: "I'll only worry if they're allowed extra routes which we want." "They come and go," said Lord King of British Airways. "I hear that People Express had some trouble with a polecat which escaped; and Virgin had a flight full of drunks who troubled the captain." But the contest remains basically unstable: and if these maverick airlines try to expand rapidly, as Laker did, they may once again provoke a fight to the death.

SWEDISH SMILES

The new pace of competition, smiling and fare-cutting was even beginning to have some impact on the character of the European airlines, as they faced a tougher political mood and more critical passengers. For years the national carriers appeared to be run by anonymous managers following immutable rules. But the recession prepared the way for new entrepreneurs with no respect for paternalism or hierarchies who asked their own questions of what an airline should be, and created turbulence all the way from the boardroom to the cockpit and sales desk.

Perhaps the most remarkable individual impact was in Scandinavia where the tri-national airline SAS had declined in the late seventies until in 1980 it lost $16 million. Then the board appointed a flamboyant new boss, Jan Carlzon, a forty-year-old super-salesman with an un-Swedish enthusiasm who had first made his name running the tour company Vingresor. He made the usual economies, selling off planes and cutting down staff; but he also quickly increased revenue by upgrading SAS as "the businessmen's airline" and produced an improved "Euroclass" to justify the high fares—some of the highest per mile in the world. He then concentrated on punctuality, watching all arrival times on his monitor until he could advertise SAS as "Europe's most punctual airline". He hired a Californian company to redesign everything: he repainted the old DC-9 planes white to make them look bigger and refurbished them inside. ("Most passengers never notice it's not a new plane," he assured me, "provided the paint is fresh.") Then he moved into Copenhagen airport—the air-hub of Scandinavia—cutting down waiting-time, rearranging the gates to suit passengers rather than planes and providing a "Scanorama" lounge with secretaries, telexes and a silent corner. The cosseting worked, and with the help of Euroclass Carlzon made a profit of $71 million after his first year. The success of Euroclass influenced other airlines to upgrade their businessmen's service, but in early 1982 Carlzon clashed head-on with Giraudet of Air France, who wanted to impose a surcharge on the Euroclass service into Paris: the row raged for three months until it was settled by the two foreign ministers and Air France climbed down with its own business class. Carlzon claims that his revenues from executives have enabled him to offer more tourist bargains—though SAS' standard economy fares are still exorbitant. "The cartel between SAS and BA is one of the strongest in Europe," complained a British Caledonian executive who had tried to cut into the route, "but SAS could hardly survive without it."

Carlzon's most basic achievement was in motivating his staff. "Turning around SAS," he explained afterwards, "was all about changing people's responsibility and authority." He decentralised the structure to give staff more initiative in handling passengers: and like Donald Burr he spread his own evangelical zeal. He called himself an "itinerant preacher" and gave all his staff a Red Book called, *Let's get in there and fight*, proclaiming his own maxims like "the difference betweeen good and bad service is two millimetres". He went into partnership with a Danish company called Time Manager to provide courses to train staff in "customer contact". "We call them the smiling courses", one rebellious Norwegian ex-trainee told me. "It's the usual stuff: call all the men sir, look them between the eyes, keep your mouth half open. It's pretty degrading." SAS insist that their training is totally different from the Asians' strict discipline: "In Asia it's a question of smile—or else," said a SAS executive. "We could never say that. All we can do is to motivate people." There was some protest from Swedish women's libbers about Carlzon's sexism; but with high unemployment Sweden was in a very different mood from the sixties, and Carlzon became a new style business hero to many Scandinavians. Yet what he had done was very simple; as one Swedish politician said, "He realised that SAS had become a technological monster, and he turned it round to face the consumer." He knew that airlines, with their cabin crews and ground staff dispersed round the world, depend even more than other industries on the atmosphere at the top, and he showed that one man can transform it.

THE WORLD'S FAVOURITE?

British Airways, the biggest European airline of all, was undergoing the most extreme character change. In April 1984 its chairman Lord King attended a banquet of veterans at the Savoy to commemorate the sixtieth anniversary of the founding of BA's predecessor, Imperial Airways. He paid tribute to the great tradition of service and enterprise of the old airline; but in truth there was not much continuity. Over the six decades Britain's "chosen instrument" had undergone every kind of metamorphosis: it had been a pioneers' airline, an imperialists' airline, a pilots' and engineers' airline, and now it was a marketer's airline. It had been split up, reunited, and redivided between its European and overseas flights. It had been a private enterprise airline and a nationalised airline and it was now being prepared for privatising again. "People like me who used to think they were part of a great public service," said one Imperial veteran, "find it a bit odd to see BA selling itself with film stars."

British Airways was now undergoing the most drastic transformation of all. During 1981–2 when it made its huge losses, in the midst of its fare-war with Laker, the contrast with the bankruptcy of Laker the folk-hero made a powerful political point. The overmanning of British Airways seemed incurable, for no chairman—not even the aggressive oilman Lord McFadzean—had managed to cut it down to size. Its two components BEA and BOAC had never really coalesced, and Laker's brief triumph showed up all the flabby overweight of his giant rival.

The losses of British Airways were an obvious challenge to Mrs Thatcher. She had already promised to privatise it, but its mounting debts made it hopelessly unattractive to investors. In 1981 she appointed as the new chairman her friend Sir John King—soon Lord King—the kind of buccaneering entrepreneur who was coming back into political fashion. With his bluff foxhunting extroversion, striding the room or peering sceptically over his half-spectacles, he soon dominated the airline from his office in St James's— from which he also chaired his engineering company Babcock International—and kept clear of BA's headquarters at Heathrow: he was like a throwback to Eric Geddes who had run Imperial Airways from the Dunlop offices in a similarly autocratic style. He was expert at the art of the put-down and snub: at one BA banquet he deliberately mistook a waiter for his fellow director Sir Peter Parker. King's detachment and ignorance of airlines made it easier for him to cut down BA ruthlessly to prepare it for privatising, and he charged into it like a bull in a china shop. He had a few simple basic ideas—about firing staff, creating profit centres or putting more lavatories into planes. Like Acker or Burr he was never in awe of the mystiques of pilots or engineers.

BA's previous chief executive Roy Watts had already begun to slim down the airline, but King took the credit and sped up the process, firing senior managers with gusto and publicity. He hired the Tory party's advertising agency Saatchi & Saatchi to launch a £25 million campaign, based on the slogan "The World's Favourite Airline". (It was a misleading claim: Aeroflot and American Airlines carry more total passengers and JAL and Pan Am—see Chapter 12—carry more tonne–kilometres internationally.) The smooth commercials showed Omar Sharif and Joan Collins receiving perfect service from BA, and the "world's widest airline seat"—another questionable claim—descending into a BA plane to heavenly music.

King appointed a new chief executive, Colin Marshall, who likewise knew little about airlines but a lot about aggressive marketing and financial controls: he had made his name with Avis Rent-a-Car in the harsh school of Harold Geneen, the master-manager of ITT, and he afterwards became deputy-chief of Sears, the British shoe-and-shop combine. With his tense dedication to hard work Marshall complemented King's casual, bombastic style. He knew that the industry was becoming much more competitive: "I cannot agree with the precipitate rate at which deregulation was accomplished in the United States", Marshall said in 1984, "but as an industry we must face the facts that, long term, regulation will continue to wane steadily." Like Carlzon at SAS he wanted the airline to be "market-led", not "product-led". "Our customers take safety and reliability for granted," he explained, "even though twenty-five per cent of the passengers on almost any aircraft show white knuckles on take-off. The things they will rate us on as an industry are how we both serve them now and anticipate what they want in the future." He saw his passengers (he told me) as much the same market as his Rent-a-Car customers, and from Avis he knew something about their complaints—about airports, baggage delays or rude cabin-crews. "Customers make elephants look absent-minded," he said, "in terms of their ability to remember the slightest mischance." He made his staff wear buttons, saying "I fly the World's Favourite Airline", and hired SAS's subsidiary to provide courses in "customer contact" called "Putting People First" which taught cabin-crews and check-in staff how to cope with passengers who snapped their fingers at them.

Like other new airline bosses Marshall was conducting his own kind of social revolution. He criticised the British educational system for not turning out proper managers and with his American experience he had no inhibitions about salesmanship. British Airways, which had a reputation for bossy, unsmiling air hostesses, was soon joining the smiling contest. "We give 'em five year contracts," King told me, "and after that we take a look at 'em and see what they're like." BA now put great emphasis on their beauty expertise. "Passengers checking in at the airport," said BA's magazine in 1984, "can't fail to have noticed the warmth of the welcome from the smiling BA girls behind the desks, and the freshness of their looks, their complexions smooth, their make-up alive with colour and gloss. If—heaven forbid—there should be a delay or baggage hold-up, the girls are all smiling efficiency and sympathy." The airline was again a pointer to changed social attitudes. "Ten years ago we could never have told people to wear lapel buttons," said one former executive, "but with three million unemployed it's much easier to tell people to wear them—or face the consequences." King and Marshall certainly transformed British Airways. In two years (beginning under the previous team) the employees had gone down from 58,000 to 37,000—though the airline was still overmanned compared for instance with TWA. By 1983 BA was able to show a profit of £294 million, which made it less unattractive to future investors. "We've got a success on our hands," King said in July 1984. "Our routes are the envy of the world, and we're now applying the methods of a commercial enterprise—not a town hall. The staff understand that, and we've brought back a sense of pride, which is what Britain needs everywhere." But British Airways' profits, as Lufthansa complained in its own annual report, were "exotic"; for they ignored the huge debt of £900 million from previous losses. And as King prepared the airline to be sold he faced a political onslaught from its free-enterprise rival British Caledonian which brought back all the old arguments about regulating airlines and chosen instruments.

At British Caledonian Sir Adam Thomson had been chairman since 1970, and he had seen BA's bosses come and go. He had shrewdly cultivated political support, with the help of the Scottish lobby and his MP consultant Robert McCrindle, and he had made more political friends by ordering European airbuses while BA was ordering Boeings. His airline was always more enjoyed by passengers than BA, and it nurtured its image with brazen commercials showing male passengers chanting: "We wish they all could be Caledonian girls". In 1983 the British Guild of Travel Writers voted it "the world's best airline" (they voted Iberia and oddly Air France as the worst airlines and Heathrow the worst airport). As Lord King prepared to privatise BA, Thomson complained that it would become a private monopoly protected by lucrative routes, and he issued a persuasive "blue book" proposing "a complete restructuring of the UK air transport system under which the British Airways monopoly would be broken". It coolly suggested that B Cal should be allowed to buy thirty-three of BA's routes, thus doubling its size.

Lord King was furious that Thomson's demand got a sympathetic political reception; and that the Minister of Transport, Nicholas Ridley, had left the question in the hands of the Civil Aviation Authority, under Ray Colegate, which was conducting its own review. King called Thomson's proposal "a smash and grab raid". "I don't mind competition," he told me, "but I object to transferring routes. Why does Thomson get any support? Because the British are brought up on stories of Robin Hood, or David and Goliath.

But I haven't seen any clamour in the streets, or demonstrations in Trafalgar Square. It's just a lobby in parliament."

King protested to Ridley that any loss of his routes would be a breach of faith, and would scare away potential American investors; and he even hinted that he might resign; "but I don't intend to lose".

BA became still more aggressive, and their ex-chief executive Roy Watts, in connivance with King, counter-attacked with a letter suggesting that, to compete effectively with foreign airlines, BA should really have *all* the international routes, to become a single "chosen instrument". But the CAA was undeterred, and in July 1984 it published its review which did not conceal its fear of the British Airways monopoly and proposed transferring some routes to smaller airlines including British Caledonian, which would cut BA's revenues by at least seven per cent.

The battle between the British rivals—the "world's favourite" and the "world's best"—brought back all the old problems of the "chosen instrument", of reconciling free enterprise with state regulation. The profits of shareholders depended on the decisions of governments, which was why Lord Reith had advocated nationalising Imperial Airways forty-five years earlier; while a private semi-monopoly of the size of British Airways would be difficult for any regulatory authority to control, as the British CAA feared, and as Roosevelt had found with Juan Trippe at Pan American. Governments were still the arbiters of routes, and hence profits. The most apparently free-booting airlines, from Virgin to British Caledonian, still depended on licences; and the fiercer the world competition, the more they all looked for support to their governments.

16

Freedom of the Air?

whhheeeEEEEEEEEEEEEEEEE! The scream of jet engines rises to a
crescendo on the runways of the world. Every second, somewhere or
other, a plane touches down, with a puff of smoke from scorched tyre
rubber, or rises in the air, leaving a smear of black fumes dissolving in
its wake. From space, the earth might look to a fanciful eye like a huge
carousel, with planes instead of horses spinning round its circumference,
up and down, up and down. *Whhheeeeeeeeeee!*

David Lodge, *Small World*, 1984

IN 1522 Magellan's ship *Vittoria* returned to Spain after having
circumnavigated the world for the first time, in just under two years.
In 1936 Juan Trippe flew round the world by flying boats and a
Zeppelin in thirty-eight days. In 1947 Trippe again flew round the
world to inaugurate Pan Am's round-the-world service, taking
thirteen days with only 103 hours' flying-time. In 1980 David
Springbett, a London re-insurance agent who is the current record-
holder by scheduled airlines, circled the globe in forty-four hours
six minutes.

Tens of thousands of people now fly round the world every year
—though never on the same airline. Twenty years ago Pan Am,
TWA, BOAC and Qantas all competed with global services, but
none now link up completely: they all have to pair up to complete
the circle—TWA with Singapore, Pan Am with Cathay Pacific,
Northwest with Garuda, British Airways with United, Air France
with UTA. It is easy enough to do the round trip in a week, but
even the most confident travellers still have a sense of dislocation,
as if they are defying natural laws. In the early years of air travel
many fliers used to complain: "your body goes by air, your mind
by sea"; and most long-distance travellers still feel they have left

part of themselves behind. Most doctors now roughly agree on the remedies for jet-lag—that you begin to change your body-clock before you leave, that you fly from West to East, that while airborne you eat and drink nothing except water, that when you arrive you never go to bed before 9 p.m. wherever you are. But neither passengers nor airlines take much notice. Cabin-crews continue to serve meals at every opportunity, so that eastbound travellers across the Pacific can find themselves having three dinners in succession. Politicians and businessmen insist on getting down to work as soon as they fly in, even if they make disastrous blunders like confusing Brazil with Bolivia.

Whatever the physical effects, the psychological effects of jet travel have imposed their own limitations on these impatient travellers' view of the world; for the sense of both discontinuity and sameness in airliners and airports has made it harder to make connections and comprehend differences across the globe. The whole routine of jumbo jets—films, food, music, lack of landscape — conspires to remove passengers from the experience of travelling. Any rapid traveller is likely to be more struck by the world's sameness than by its variety. You can fly by a succession of exotic-sounding airlines—by Indonesian, Malaysian, Singapore or Colombian—and still find yourself on a Boeing 747 with the same rows of seats, the same kind of music through the headphones, the same "non-dairy creamer", the same announcements "for your comfort and safety" while the pressurised cabins all produce the same atmosphere and temperature.

The planes land at airports which all appear to be insulated from any known city or land. While the great railway termini took their architecture from temples or cathedrals which soared above the tracks, the airports took their origins from the hut and the hangar, and grew into cavernous metal barns, looking not on to a track but on to the great nowhere of the sky. The vast echoing airports like Honolulu, Anchorage or Pago Pago, where the jumbos stop to refuel and disgorge their transit passengers in the middle of the night, have all established the same kind of non-identity, as the flutterboards announce the names of every city but their own, and the duty-free shops sell imports from other airports. The transit lounges, cut off from both time and space, can generate a unique sense of numbness and not belonging—the feel of not to feel it. It is not surprising that many passengers, when they return to their same narrow seat, the same music inside the same cylindrical space, feel that, however cramped and eccentric , it is yet a kind of home.

Many travellers including myself can still feel a sense of exhilaration and stimulation when flying at 35,000 feet if the seat is wide and the plane is half-empty. But writers have said little about air journeys, compared to rail or sea journeys, and when they describe them they are apt to depict them as some kind of limbo, if not hell itself, with a disembodied detachment and discontinuity which cut off any association with normal life. And however safe the airliners the travel *angst* is still visible in the faces in every transit lounge—the white knuckles, finger-biting and strained cheekbones which have deeper causes than the simple fear of the air. Air travel can still provide a unique and devastating combination—of boredom and terror.

The airlines themselves willingly connive in a pattern of childish dependence as they herd their passengers like sheep between pens and only reluctantly tell the truth about delays or faults. They have trained air hostesses and ground staff how to deal with passenger neuroses—encouraged by Thomas Harris' bestseller about transactional analysis, *I'm OK—You're OK*, which in the seventies became the basis for training staff in American Airlines, and later in others including Lufthansa and Swissair. The courses told their staff how to handle awkward customers who revert to childish insecurity, feeling themselves inferior to those in positions of authority. "If a passenger goes for you with an unjustified amount of aggression," explains Swissair's company history, "don't take it personally; trouble in the office, nervousness about the journey or something else has woken the 'not OK' child in him and so he's gripped by the need to feel strong and superior with the aid of his 'parent ego'." And Swissair like to quote the story of an ideal response to the neurotic passenger:

Passenger: You're one of the stupidest people I've ever met.

Swissair employee: And you're one of the nicest gentlemen I've ever come across. But perhaps we're both wrong.

But all the elaborate training, from the "OK courses" to the "smiling courses" in Scandinavia and the Far East, only underline the limits which air travel has set on individuality. No doubt the paternalism of the airlines themselves, which refuse to treat their passengers as adult individuals, contributes to the childish regression. But that is only a reflection of a more fundamental phenomenon: that air travel, which had once seemed so liberating and so individualist, has become the most constrained form of mass transport since the slave-ships.

THE CONQUERORS

The regularity and efficiency of air travel, however commonplace, remains a staggering achievement by the airlines and manufacturers. As the veteran Senior Vice-President of Boeing, "Tex" Boullioun described it in 1983, commemorating the twenty-fifth anniversary of the first Pan Am jet service across the Atlantic:

> Great cities and great resorts stand in places where neither ship nor train could have caused them to be. Six thousand jets now fly daily between cities and towns and resorts. More than three million people switch places daily as if they were part of some giant chess game. Taken as a whole, however, the scene below suggests the world community has been woven into a single fabric by the jet. Air transport is the silver lining. Business depends upon it. Vacationers plan on it. Families retain their unity by using it . . .

Yet the silver lining, as Boullioun went on to warn, had become "stained with red ink" as the airlines faced a succession of crises. The world recession, made crueller by the extension of deregulation, brought the long air boom to an abrupt halt; and while 1984 brought an upturn in American passengers, the combination of deregulation, the high dollar and the Asian competition still threatened the American airlines. There were still no obvious technological miracles in sight to provide still cheaper or faster travel. Some airline executives, it is true, still look forward to a new supersonic breakthrough: "We'll shrink the world again," says Ed Acker of Pan American, looking towards future supersonics. "I don't think man will relinquish so easily his pursuit of speed," says Geoffrey Lipman of IATA. But for the time being the supersonic adventure has contracted into a few half-empty Concordes making prohibitive losses, while the 747s which were first seen as stop-gaps on the way to the supersonic age have become the world's workhorses. All the airline chiefs face a less exciting future, as they compete like hotel-keepers or department stores for each other's customers or act as wholesalers or middlemen, leaving travel agents to fill up their planes. Their new challenges have much less to do with aircraft technology, much more with marketing and showmanship, and with the mundane problems of how to connect the sky to the land. It came as an anti-climax after the early ambitions of the Conquistadores del Cielo. They had indeed conquered the sky, circumnavigated it and overflown its poles; only to find it so full of planes that it was hard for anyone to make a profit out of it; while they were forced back to the much more intransigent problems of congestion and politics on earth.

Would the airlines follow the fate of the railroads a century earlier? In 1830 the first railway, between Liverpool and Manchester, was opened by the Duke of Wellington: and in the same year the first American railroad was begun. By 1869 the Union Pacific and Central Pacific had joined the two sides of the American continent. But by the 1880s the American railroads were falling rapidly into the hands of financiers and bankers, as the world depression brought expansion to a halt; and by 1893 half the railroad mileage in America was in the hands of the receivers. In sixty years the railroads had progressed from birth to bankruptcy.

The earliest serious airlines such as KLM and Avianca dated back to 1919; and over the next decades they achieved a technical progress more astonishing than the railroads'. But sixty years later the airlines too found themselves in the midst of a recession while they saw little prospect of great technological advances. The long boom in civil aircraft, which had brought so much employment and profit to the west coast of America, was subsiding while military orders began to loom larger—a worrying parallel to the arms race which followed the railroad slump a century earlier.

In this historical perspective, were the deregulators offering a real prospect of economic revival, or only fighting a last rearguard action before the airlines became still more controlled or subsidised by governments? Certainly deregulation has brought some innovations and benefits to American passengers: more entrepreneurial leaders have challenged the old bureaucratic companies, made airlines more flexible, given new motivation to cabin-crews and ground staff, and reminded them that planes are for people. In Europe by contrast the rigid agreements between airlines and governments have too often conspired against the interests of passengers, who are only now gradually stirring themselves into protest, and have flagrantly defied the principles of the European Community.

But the laws of free enterprise can never be applied simplistically to the airline which must always require both competition *and* regulation. As long as nations feel dependent on airlines as the lifelines of their trade they will not deregulate the international system; and no airline operating abroad—not even an American airline— can escape from its dependence on the government in the critical bargains for landing and traffic rights. However enterprising the airlines' contests across the frontiers in the air, they can never escape the iron laws of sovereignty on the ground.

THE AIR CHANGE

How far has air travel changed the political map of the world? Certainly there is not much left of the rhetoric of unification—about abolishing frontiers or creating one world—which prevailed after Blériot's first cross-Channel flight, or in America during the Second World War. The opening up of the air gave as many opportunities for destruction as for peaceful communication, and frontiers and sovereignty were soon extended upwards. The hopes and promises behind the concept of "freedom of the air" soon faded as governments enforced their controls over airspace, landing rights and flight paths: the limitations on freedom were signalled on the political side by the Soviet destruction of the Korean airliner, and on the economic side by the national responses to the American deregulators; as they tried to spread their policy abroad the deregulators succeeded only in mobilising nations against them, and showing the power of co-ordinated mercantilist states.

The vast expansion of tourist passengers undoubtedly had huge social consequences, which are still too recent to be fully assessed. Cheap flights transformed the Atlantic; the emigrants who had left the European shores a few decades earlier, apparently for ever, could now rediscover their families after an overnight flight. As one airline executive put it: "No one nowadays says 'will ye no' come back again?'" Other far-flung peoples, including the Overseas Chinese, have acquired a new cohesion through the airplane, while the Islamic countries, from Nigeria to Pakistan, have used their airlines not only for mass pilgrimages to Mecca but for more practical political collaboration. But mass tourists without ethnic or political motivation in the first place have not noticeably improved relations between countries and continents. "I can't say that aviation has done anything to promote friendship and understanding," says the nonagenarian Sir William Hildred, looking back on his time as director of IATA. "The nations still compete as much as ever, and I'll tell you why: when human beings are crowded like rats, they fight like rats."

Airlines have always remained interlocked with their nations, and they remain so. Between the two world wars they all needed a subsidy—whether overtly in the case of Imperial Airways or Lufthansa, or more discreetly in the case of Pan American's "Empire of the Air". The links became less obvious after the Second World War, when airlines could be commercially self-supporting; but no government could afford to neglect its diplomatic support for an industry so valuable to trade and the balance of payments. While entrepreneurs from Burr to Acker relish their rugged independence, and Laker loved to attack the civil servants as "bums and gangsters", they all know that they depend on their governments.

It has been the governments in Asia which have realised the full importance of supporting their new airlines, as they press for global routes and each try to make their home base a critical world hub. The pattern of hubs and spokes threatens to produce a more extreme trend towards centralisation and concentration than was ever generated by seaports or railroad termini; and a handful of ambitious cities are now competing for high stakes to be the world's crossroads. The aggressive policies of Singapore, the Philippines or Hong Kong, with their governments and airlines working in tandem, can outbid western airlines as well as the sleepier developing countries. The city states, like brains without bodies, are playing a quite disproportionate role as they are "plugged into the world's grid" while far bigger countries are left out of the circuit.

While airlines ostensibly compete with smiling air hostesses, reclining seats or four-course dinners the ultimate contest is between governments fighting with every diplomatic weapon for their nation's interests; and the young nations, however mocked for their ambitions, have sometimes understood better than the old how vital their national airline can be in a real crisis—as the Lebanon found with Middle East Airlines. No country—not even free enterprise Chile—can safely leave its national interest to foreign airlines and open skies. And even the American airlines, as they have been spurred abroad by the deregulators, have soon realised how much they needed the support of a co-ordinated government.

The Asian and western airlines are likely to compete much more tensely in the next decade; and the airlines will be in the forefront of a much broader confrontation, and a central dilemma. How far can the western nations indulge in domestic policies to encourage competition and to forbid collusive agreements, when they are confronted abroad by nations determined to co-ordinate all their industrial and political efforts in their battles to capture world markets? The dilemma will face governments, particularly the United States government, in a whole array of industries. But the airlines—which depend from take-off to touch-down on the permission of governments—reveal it in the most visible form. Can Pan Am continue to compete with United, while both are competing with JAL? Can British Caledonian encroach on British Airways, while they both fight Lufthansa or KLM? Or will the dominant airlines find themselves still more closely associated with their nations? Already in nearly all countries the airlines, whether nationalised or private, have tended to play on patriotism as they "fly the flag" and spread their country's name, colours and language across the world. Only a few notable exceptions like SAS, Air

Afrique or Gulf Air have succeeded in representing several nations. And the pressures of deregulation outside America are likely to encourage national responses.

But the links between airlines and nations can all too easily be forged into cartel agreements which work against the passengers' interests and restrict rather than stimulate communications; and Europe, the old home of cartels, has paid a heavy price for its national rivalries and constraints. The contrast between Asia and Europe is revealing. In East Asia the airlines opened up the whole region and almost invented the idea of the Pacific Basin as they competed across a whole web of routes, with a score of rival airlines flying between Hong Kong and Taiwan. But the Europeans, after their first thrilling contests to fly across the world, soon retreated inside their own continent, into their own murky pools. The European agreements were not a cartel in the sense of ensuring steady profits; and the airlines could not keep out the charter companies, who still account for fifty per cent of European air travel. "A real cartel," as Geoffrey Lipman of IATA puts it, "Would have made sure its members made money." But the pools between airlines effectively kept up fares and restricted competition, discouraging the kind of casual travel on which European integration depended.

The European airlines must take part of the blame; they lacked the leadership and enterprise to take real advantage of the European Community, and they were glad to cling to their governments' bilateral deals. But the roots went much deeper. The individual nations would not risk giving up any part of their sovereignty, while governments and unions conspired with the airlines to reinforce the existing concentrations of power in the capitals. The governments who ultimately controlled this critical new means of communication, could have used it in the post-war years to open up their continent. "It cannot be too strongly emphasised," wrote Sir Osborne Mance in the middle of the Second World War, "that the intensity of international commercial co-operation, in air transport as in other fields, will depend first and foremost on the extent that governments are able and willing to become internationally minded." But the governments were not willing, the airlines did not push them, and the pools between nations became stagnant, with no real incentive to innovate or even to increase traffic.

European passengers have paid heavily—whether in the form of high fares, lack of regional services or general contempt for the customer. But the greater cost has been to the integration of Europe as a whole; the crazy structure of air-fares encouraged the European countries to feel closer to America than to each other, while the

Pacific nations, which were less hidebound and more geared to the future, rapidly gained a regional cohesion.

Airlines have always been locked into politics; but they cannot be absolved from their own political responsibility. For while they depend on their governments they are themselves changing the characters and the contexts of their own nation states. Airline executives, caught between the constraints of their governments and their consumers, and whirled round the world in their own dislocated environment, may find the implications hard to recognise, but they evade them at their peril. With imagination and leadership they can play their own role in by-passing the old concentrations of capitals, opening up opportunities, and providing freer patterns of communication for a younger generation. The conquest of the air, however complete it may seem, is only at a first stage of its social potential. It has made everyone aware of the interdependence of the planet, for better or worse—whether by encircling it with ease, or by enabling nations to destroy each other from the sky. But it still remains for the air to be genuinely associated with freedom.

Notes

NOTES TO CHAPTER 1

p 23 St Exupéry quotation: Rumbold and Stewart, *The Winged Life*, Weidenfeld & Nicolson, London, 1953, p 47

p 23 "The flying apparatus will be . . ." Alphonse Berget, *The Conquest of the Air*, Heinemann, London, 1909; GP Putnam's Sons, NY, p 265 & viii

p 23 "Before five years are out . . ." London *Times*, 27 July 1909; see also *The Observer*, 29 July 1909

p 24 "The practice of the present . . ." see D. H. N. Johnson, *Rights in Air Space*, Manchester UP; Oceana, New York, 1965, p 32

p 25–6 Mermoz and St Exupéry, *The Winged Life*, pp 120–1, 151

p 27 H. G. Wells: "The British Islands . . ." see John Pudney, *The Seven Skies*, London, Putnam, 1959, p 17

p 28 "Private enterprise cannot . . ." Alfred Instone, *Early Birds*, Simpkin Marshall, London, 1938, p 105

p 29 "In the eyes of Imperial Airways . . ." R. E. G. Davies, *A History of the World's Airlines*, Oxford University Press, 1964, p 59

p 29 "We were both intent . . ." Lord Templewood (Sir Samuel Hoare), *Empire of the Air*, Collins, London, 1957, p 115

p 29 "Photographing the pyramids . . ." Alan J. Cobham, *My Flight to the Cape and Back*, A. & C. Black, London, 1926

p 31 "He accused me . . ." Lord Reith, *Into the Wind*, Hodder & Stoughton, London, 1949, pp 327ff

p 32 "He spoke accented English . . ." Gordon McGregor, *The Adolescence of an Airline*, Air Canada, Montreal, p 65

p 32 "Throw the mailbag . . ." Hudson Fysh, *Qantas at War*, Angus & Robertson, Sydney, p 59.

p 33 "The US aircraft industry . . ." *A History of the World's Airlines*, p 122 p 35 "Working in close liaison . . ." John Killen, *The Luftwaffe, a History*, Frederick Muller, London, 1967, p 43

p 36 "Rivalling the great engineering . . ." *Qantas at War*, p 86

p 38 "One Imperial pilot . . ." Pettifer and Hudson, *Diamonds in the Sky*, p 80

p 38 "The road of the air . . ." Sir Charles Burney, *The World, the Air and the Future*, Alfred A. Knopf, London, 1929

p 38 "The International Air Traffic Association . . ." see S. Ralph Cohen, *IATA: the First Three Decades*, IATA, Montreal, 1949

p 39 Disarmament conference, see Sir Osborne Mance, *International Air Transport*, Oxford University Press, 1943, p 76ff

p 39 "How could the governments . . ." Henri Bouché, *Economics of Air Transport*, Air Transport Co-operation Committee, League of Nations, Geneva, 1935

NOTES TO CHAPTER 2

p 42 Scott Fitzgerald: "I suppose there has been nothing like airports . . ." *The Last Tycoon*, 1941, Chapter 1

p 42 "I've never known an industry . . ." Robert F. Six, *Continental Airlines, A Story of Growth*, Newcomen Publications, Princeton University, 1959. Interview with author, 21 June 1984

p 43 "He packed the whole thirty-four hours . . ." London *Times*, 23 May 1927. For details of Lindbergh, see Leonard Mosley, *Lindbergh, a biography*, Hodder & Stoughton, London, 1976

p 43 "Since flight is not a natural function . . ." Anne Morrow Lindbergh, *North to the Orient*, 1935

pp 44f "Young chief executive, Juan Trippe." In this and later chapters I am indebted to two recent biographies of Juan Trippe. Robert Daley's *An American Saga: Juan Trippe and his Pan Am Empire* (Random House, New York, 1980) was based on extensive interviews with Trippe before he died, and provides copious details of his financial dealings. *Chosen Instrument* by Marilyn Bender and her husband Selig Altschul (Simon & Schuster, New York, 1982) provides much important international background and analysis of Trippe's operations.

p 51 "The early Queensland pioneer . . ." Hudson Fysh, *Qantas Rising*, Angus & Robertson, Sydney, 1965, p 237

p 51 "A more fearful, introverted man . . ." ibid, p 128

p 51 "Preferred writing . . ." ibid, p 269

p 52 "The establishment of an efficient . . ." ibid, p 262

p 54 "The equivalent in the US . . ." *Chosen Instrument*, p 249

p 54 "An electric fan . . ." ibid, p 293

p 55 "Watched by President de Valera . . ." *The Seven Skies*, p 144

NOTES TO CHAPTER 3

p 58 "The agents of the opposing airlines . . ." *A History of the World's Airlines*, p 235 p 58 "Adapting flying fortresses . . ." see Anders Buraas, *The SAS Saga*, SAS, 1979, p 35

p 59 "Emperor of the Air . . ." Matthew Josephson, *Empire of the Air: Juan Trippe and the Struggle for World Airways*, Harcourt Brace, New York, 1944

p 59 "Churchill admitted . . ." Winston Churchill, *The Grand Alliance*, Cassell, London, 1950, pp 627–8

p 60 "Profit of a quarter of a million . . ." *The Seven Skies*, p 190

p 60 "A man of all-yielding suavity . . . an unscrupulous person . . ." *The Secret Diary of Harold J. Ickes*, Simon and Schuster, New York, 1954, Vol 3, pp 459–60

p 60 "Cordell Hull . . ." *The Memoirs of Cordell Hull*, Hodder & Stoughton, London, 1948, p 496

p 61 "Trippe embodies . . ." *Empire of the Air*, pp 204–5

p 62 "Trippe persuaded to stay out . . ." *An American Saga*, p 346

p 62 "It rung up the curtain . . ." L. Welch Pogue, *International Civil Air Transport, Transition following WW2:* Flight Transportation Laboratory, Massachusetts Institute of Technology, June 1979

p 63 "The imagination of men's minds . . ." ibid

p 63 "It is perhaps not too much . . ." Mance, p 104

p 63 "I feel that aviation . . ." Adolf A. Berle, *Navigating the Rapids, 1918 –1971*, Harcourt Brace Jovanovich, New York, 1973, pp 482ff

p 64 "Beaverbrook set out to flatter . . ." A. J. P. Taylor, *Beaverbrook*, Hamish Hamilton, London, 1972, p 557

p 65 "In his diary . . ." *Navigating the Rapids*, pp 492–4

p 65 "An event of the utmost importance . . ." Winston Churchill, *Triumph and Tragedy*, Cassell, London, 1954, p 606

p 66 "A fine, fighting, non-highbrow . . ." Paul Gore-Booth, *With Great Truth and Respect*, Constable, London, 1974, pp 129–33

p 66 "Convinced protectionist . . ." J. A. Cross, *Lord Swinton*, Clarendon Press, Oxford, 1982, pp 247–8

p 66 "Arrogant and inflexible . . ." *Navigating the Rapids*, pp 497–503

p 67 "Airlines were beginning to call . . ." The notion of the five freedoms was first brought into the open at the Dominions Conference in 1943. See H. L. Smith, *Airways Abroad*, 1950, p 116

p 67 "Swinton tried to get through . . ." *With Great Truth and Respect*

p 68 "We got totally confused . . ." Sir Peter Masefield, interview with author, May 1984

p 68 "Other countries . . ." *Navigating the Rapids*, pp 505–6

p 68 and 69 Churchill and Roosevelt letters: Francis L. Loewenheim et al: *Roosevelt and Churchill: Their Secret Wartime Correspondence*, Barrie & Jenkins, London, 1975, pp 603–23

p 69 "That Britain could have . . ." Vernon Crudge, interview with author, April 1984

p 70 "Berle himself was privately humiliated . . ." *International Civil Air Transport, Transition following WW2*

p 70 "A. J. P. Taylor . . ." *Beaverbrook*, p 557

p 71 "Vast, if silent, success . . ." *Navigating the Rapids*, pp 512–13 pp 71–2 "Everyone here is astonished . . ." *Roosevelt and Churchill*, pp 652, 673

p 72 "The British could not block it . . ." *International Civil Air Transport, Transition following WW2*

p 72 "We started poles apart . . ." Masefield, interview with author

p 72 "The annexe to the agreement . . ." Sir William Hildred, interview with author, April 1984

p 72 "Vast cobweb . . ." Bin Cheng, *The Law of International Air Transport*, Stevens, London; Oceania, New York, 1962, p 26

p 72 "A general philosophy . . ." Stephen Wheatcroft, *Air Transport Policy*, Michael Joseph, London, p 60

p 72 "The real competition . . ." *Consultation on Airline Competition Policy*, CAA, London, 19 December 1983

p 73 IATA as a hybrid: see Richard Y. Chuang, *The IATA, a case study of a quasi-governmental organisation*, A. W. Sijthoff, Leiden, 1972

p 75 "Leviathan of an airplane . . . two such planes . . ." *Empire of the Air*, p 210

p 76 "In 1944 the Brookings Institute . . ." J. Parker Van Zandt, *The Geography of World Air Transport*, The Brookings Institution, Washington, 1944

NOTES TO CHAPTER 4

p 77 "Unlike the boundaries of the sea . . ." *International Civil Air Transport, Transition following WW2*

p 77 "Inside of a boot . . ." Douglas Aircraft Company, *Flight Plan for Tomorrow*, Santa Monica, 1966, p 49

p 78 "Flight to the Orient . . ." see Stephen E. Mills, *A Pictorial History of Northwest Airlines*, Bonanza Books, New York, 1972

p 78 "They each had their man . . ." Robert Six, interview with author, June 1984

p 78 "Think of the English . . ." *Empire of the Air*, p 191

p 78 "Trippe wouldn't fight . . ." Sir William Hildred, interview with author, April 1984

p 81 "Truman's warm associations . . ." For this and other references to TWA I am indebted to Robert Serling's *Howard Hughes' Airline* (St Martin's/Marek, New York 1983) which includes much material from TWA sources. TWA challenged the legality of Truman's signature, but the Supreme Court upheld the merger.

p 82 Hughes and the Constellation, see *Howard Hughes' Airline*, pp 85–90

p 82 "In Shanghai, Chiang Kai-shek's finance minister . . ." *An American Saga*, pp 387–96

p 83 "Airline was like Belgium . . ." *Howard Hughes' Airline*, p 204

p 83 "Two-pants Charlie", *Howard Hughes' Airline*, p 230

p 84 "Emmanuel Celler . . . In the post-war years . . ." ibid, pp 422ff, 394ff

p 84 "Well recompensed . . ." *Chosen Instrument*, p 536

p 85 Sam Pryor and Hamburg prostitutes, *The Chosen Instrument*, pp 535–43
p 85 "Were true soldiers of fortune . . ." Ray Kline, *Secrets, Spies and Scholars*, Acropolis Books, Washington, 1976, pp 178–9
p 85 Continental Air Services, see Pierre Salinger, *Je Suis un Americain*, Editions Stock, Paris, 1975, pp 281–90. Also John Marks and Victor Marchetti, *CIA and the Cult of Intelligence*, Dell, New York, 1980, pp 129ff. Also Robert Six, interview with author, June 1984
p 86 "Mossad used El Al . . ." "The CIA abandoned most of its proprietaries . . ." see Jeff McConnell, *The CIA and Airlines*, Counterspy, Washington DC, December 1983

NOTES TO CHAPTER 5

p 87 "24,000 employees . . ." *The Seven Skies*, p 217. See also *A History of the World's Airlines*, p 301
p 88 "Cloying sense of lushness . . . just a political pawn . . ." Sir Miles Thomas, *Out on a Wing*, Michael Joseph, London, 1964, pp 333–5
p 88 "I never believed . . ." see Roy Jenkins, *How Not to Run a Public Corporation: Essays and Speeches*, Collins, London, 1967, p 185
p 88 "Public school airline . . ." London *Times*, 10 June 1983
p 88 "Avoid inter-Empire . . ." *Qantas at War*, p 204. See also *The Seven Skies*, p 217
p 89 "Come hell or high water . . ." *Qantas at War*, p 209
p 89 "You keep out . . ." Gordon R. McGregor, *The Adolescence of an Airline*, Air Canada, Montreal, p 1
p 90 "It is interesting that governments . . ." J. K. Galbraith, *The New Industrial State*, p 103
p 91 "A gradual escalation . . ." Charles (Chic) Eather, *Syd's Pirates: a Story of an Airline*, Durnmount, Sydney, 1983, p 35

NOTES TO CHAPTER 6

p 92 "Firm corset . . . finding it . . ." Sir William Hildred, interview with author, April 1984
p 93 "At last welded . . ." *IATA, the First Three Decades*, p 88
p 93 "One of the most hated . . ." A. Sampson, *The New Europeans*, Hodder & Stoughton, London, 1968, p 250
p 93 "We're the most competitive industry . . ." A. Sampson, *Anatomy of Britain*, Hodder & Stoughton, London, 1962, p 548
pp 94–5 "He was KLM . . ." IATA bulletin, October, 1965: and Sir William Hildred, interview with author, April 1984
p 97 "Helicopter protagonist's dream", see Kenneth R. Sealy, *The Geography of Air Transport*, Hutchinson Univ Library, London, 1957, p 102
p 97 "There can be no question . . ." *International Air Transport*, p 55
pp 98–9 For European negotiations see: *PEP: European Unity, Co-operation & Integration*, Allen & Unwin, London, 1968, pp 218–20. Also

Laurance Reed: *Europe in a Shrinking World*, Oldbourne, London, 1967, p 34

p 100 "People the world over . . ." Lorenz Stucki, *Swissair: a portrait of the airline of Switzerland*, Huber, Stuttgart, 1981

p 101 "They had first considered . . . Scandinavian co-operation", see *SAS: The Making of SAS*, SAS, Oslo, 1973, pp 15–22

p 102 "Bernt Balchen arrived in Oslo . . ." Anders Buraas, *The SAS Saga*, Oslo, 1973, pp 15–22

p 103 "Along the main arteries . . ." *The Seven Skies*, p 222

NOTES TO CHAPTER 7

p 105 "He was really only interested in money . . ." Sir Peter Masefield, interview with author, May 1984

p 106 "Bring down the cost of travel . . ." *An American Saga*, p 400

p 106 "Put the 707 . . ." Harold Mansfield, *Vision, the Story of Boeing*, Popular Library, New York, 1966

p 106 "Took a bet . . ." John Newhouse, *The Sporty Game*, Knopf, New York, 1982, p 8

p 106 "Shrunken the earth . . ." *Chosen Instrument*, p 533

p 106 "According to one account . . ." Johnny Guy of TWA, quoted in *Howard Hughes' Airline*, p 237

p 106 "He wanted so badly . . ." *Howard Hughes' Airline*, p 247

p 107 "Making him $547 million . . ." ibid, p 278

p 107 "Operating from a strong ownership . . ." *The New Industrial State*, p 92

p 108 "Imperial Airways had pioneered . . . some Hollywood producers", *Howard Hughes' Airline*, pp 11, 261ff

p 109 "There is much to be said . . ." *A History of the World's Airlines*, p 433

p 111 "A realisation was dawning . . ." *Vision, the Story of Boeing*, p 225

p 112 "A merchant was distinguished . . ." Iris Origo, *The Merchant of Prado*, Penguin Books, London, 1963, p 134

p 112 "The newest and most popular . . ." Daniel Boorstin, *The Image*, Pelican Books, London, 1963, p 102

p 113 "Has air tourism added . . ." Louis Turner and John Ash, *The Golden Hordes*, Constable, London, 1975, p 292

NOTES TO CHAPTER 8

p 115 "The most astonishing early achievement . . ." see Ian Driscoll, *Flightpath South Pacific*, Whitcombe & Tombs, Christchurch, New Zealand, 1972, pp 21–7

pp 118–19 "Spies in the sky . . . Breyten Breytenbrach", Gordon Winter, *Inside Boss, South Africa's Secret Police*, pp 546, 576

p 120 "The jumbo jet airliner enables emigration . . ." Hugh Thomas, *An Unfinished History of the World*, Hamish Hamilton, London, 1979, p 328

NOTES TO CHAPTER 9

p 124 "Plunged their companies . . . incredible as it seems . . ." *The Sporty Game*, pp 116–17

p 125 "He insisted that the most interesting part . . ." *An American Saga*, p 43

p 125 "Locked in a shrinking box . . ." *Chosen Instrument*, p 581

p 126 "I was the right man . . ." Najeeb Halaby, *Crosswinds: An Airman's Memoir*, Doubleday, New York, 1978, pp 253–4, also interview with author, October 1983

p 126 "Made deals . . ." *An American Saga*, p 447

p 127 Pan Am and Iran: *Chosen Instrument*, p 586

p 127 TWA and Iran: *Howard Hughes' Airline*, p 321

p 128 "Old sense of travail . . ." see *The Image*, p 93

p 128 "TWA's President . . ." *Wall Street Journal*, 7 March 1983

p 129 "Newly ambiguous points of arrival . . ." Daniel Boorstin: *The Americans: the Democratic Experience*, Vintage Books, New York, 1974, p 271

p 130 "Hoped to be controlling shareholder . . ." *Howard Hughes' Airline*, p 316

p 131 "There are those in the communications industry . . ." see Geoffrey Charlish in the *Financial Times*, September 1983

NOTES TO CHAPTER 10

p 133 "Refused to approve . . ." *Competition and the Airlines*, a Staff Report by the Office of Economic Analysis of the CAB, Washington, December 1982

pp 133–4 "Robert Six . . . friend of Johnson's" *Je Suis un Americain*, pp 283–6, also author's interview with Robert Six

p 134 "The airlines were not surprisingly anxious . . ." For testimony on Braniff and American see *Hearings before the Select Committee on Presidential Campaign Activities of the US Senate, 1972*, Book 13, pp 5483–521

p 134 "Is it not fair to say . . ." ibid, p 5512

p 135 "I never thought that the TWAs or Pan Ams", Alfred Kahn, interview with author by telephone, June 1984

p 135 "Maybe it's sex appeal . . ." interview with Alfred Kahn in *Wall Street Journal*, 4 October 1983

p 136 "Were uniquely suited . . ." John E. Robson, *The Move to Airline Deregulation, The Bureaucrat*, Summer 1982

p 137 Mike Levine: "There was a lot of scepticism . . ." Interview with *Airline Executive*, Atlanta, April 1984

p 137 Ed Acker: "Once you get hooked . . ." *New York Times*, 28 August 1981

p 141 "In the first three years . . ." see *Competition and the Airlines*, p 49

p 142 "Fifty hours per month . . ." Roy Pulsifer et al, *Regulatory Reform*, CAB, 1975, p 146

p 142 Typists' and cleaners' wages, *Competition and the Airlines*, p 123 p 142 "Painfully familiar . . . job-hopping is rare", see Henry Duffy, Statement to Aviation sub-committee, House Committee of Public Works and Transportation, 15 June 1983

p 142 "We're not country club boys . . ." *Wall Street Journal*, 2 November 1983

p 143 "Slushy runway . . . do you want me to do anything special . . ." see Malcolm MacPherson, *The Black Box: the Last Words from the Cockpit*, Granada, London, 1984, pp 13–21

p 143 "Henry Duffy warned . . ." *Frequent Flier*, October 1983

p 145 "If reality did not fit . . .", speech to Annual Air Transport World Awards, New York, 20 January 1983

p 145 "The rest of the world . . ." Christer Jonsson, *Sphere of Flying*, International Organisation, Vol 35 No. 2. Spring 1981, p 289

p 146 House sub-committee: Report of the Subcommittee on Investigations and Oversight of the Committee on Public Works and Transportation, August 1983

NOTES TO CHAPTER 11

p 147 "He was carried along . . ." Howard Banks, *The Rise and Fall of Freddie Laker*, Faber, London, 1982, p 12

p 152 "Was a very popular figure . . ." Affidavit of Dennis Kitching, 7 December 1982

pp 155–6 "Absolutely forbid . . . violent disruption", Warren Kraemer's telex to Sandy McDonnell, 2 February 1982

p 156 "Had not made any cash . . ." affidavit of Dennis Kitching, p 7

p 157 "No chance for Freddie . . . cash availability", Sedgwick's notebook, p 25

p 158 "Laker became the victim . . ." interview with Granada TV: *The Battle for the Atlantic*, 9 May 1983

p 159 "Laker has made a unique . . ." J. T. McMillan's account of Laker's career, prepared for his daughter's school project, p 3

p 160 "Defamatory, outrageous . . . without a shred of evidence . . . not necessarily couched . . . no form of agreement," report of meeting on 25 November 1982 by Touche Rosse. Affidavit of Antony Willis, 29 November 1982

p 160 "We needed no conspiracy . . ." affidavit of Dennis Kitching

p 160 "Laker's bones . . ." The *Economist*, 25 June 1983

p 161 "Laker did not directly . . ." *The Rise and Fall of Freddie Laker*, p 155

p 161 "Reckless price wars . . ." Acker, speech in Dubrovnik, 26 October 1982

NOTES TO CHAPTER 12

pp 163–4 Air India history and nationalisation: see Air India's magazine, *Magic Carpet*, October 1982, also Corbett, pp 303–23

p 165 "TWA flew out . . ." see *Howard Hughes' Airline*, pp 299–301

p 173 "In the subsequent inquiry . . ." *Asahi Evening News*, 15 May 1982 p 173 "Even now only four per cent . . ." see Yasumoto Takagi, President of JAL, *The Airline Industry—Present and Future*, JATA 28 November 1983

p 173 "Japanese cars, VTR's and TV sets . . ." Duncan Bluck, speech to the Chartered Institute of Transport, London, 12 March 1984

p 175 "Pan American could carry passengers . . ." speech by Roman Cruz at MIT, 29 July 1982

p 175 "We cannot sit idly by . . ." speech by Takayuki Hashizumi of JAL, Singapore, 16 January 1984

p 177 "Generated a huge increase . . ." speech by Lim Chim Beng, 20 February 1981

p 177 "The US repeatedly used . . ." speech by Takayuki Hashizumi, op. cit.

NOTES TO CHAPTER 13

p 184 "The consumer councils . . ." *Freedom of the Air*, report of the National, Scottish and Welsh Consumer councils, June 1983

p 185 "Navigation and landing costs . . ." Sir Adam Thomson, address to the American Chamber of Commerce, 11 April 1984

p 189 "You would have thought we had fomented . . ." Sir Adam Thomson, ibid

NOTES TO CHAPTER 14

p 191 "We were once told . . ." George Orwell, *You and the Atom Bomb*, *Tribune*, October 1945

p 191 "Because of the size . . ." R. L. Thornton, *International Airlines and Politics*, Michigan International Business Studies, Ann Arbor, Michigan, 1970

p 191 "But the Soviet Union . . ." *Sphere of Flying*, p 298

p 193 George Keegan: "An extraordinary array . . ." see BBC *Panorama*, 7 November 1983

p 197ff The details and exact times in this and following paragraphs are from the ICAO "Final Report of Investigation", ICAO, Montreal, 2 December 1983. The findings of this report were modified by the report of the Navigation Commission in February 1984.

p 201 "And an intelligence analysis . . ." *New York Times*, 7 October 1983

p 207 "Two former crew-members . . ." Tom Bernard and T. Edward Eskelson, in the *Denver Post*, 13 September 1983

p 207 "Pressed ahead with building . . ." See *Anchorage Daily News*, 27 September 1983

p 208 "I am a wall . . ." *North to the Orient*, p 117

NOTES TO CHAPTER 15

p 211 "Fewer than were killed by bee-stings", see *Newsweek*, 30 January 1984 pp 211-12 "British statistics in 1983 . . ." see paper by Sir Peter Masefield to the 50th National Road Safety Congress, Royal Society for the Prevention of Accidents, 3 November 1983

p 212 "Is the flight deck becoming . . ." *Flight International* (London) 28 January 1984

p 213 "When Anthony Spaeth investigated . . ." see *Wall Street Journal*, 26 April 1984

p 215 Acker: "But the job was much worse . . ." interview with author, June 1984

p 216 Burr: "You can't assume that United and American . . ." interview with author, May 1984

pp 218–19 SAS and Carlzon: see London Business School's case study, 1983. Also Carlzon's interview with author, March 1984

p 221 "Customers make elephants . . . Our customers take safety . . ." *Executive World* (British Airways magazine) May 1984

p 221 King: "We give 'em five year contracts . . ." interview with author, July 1984

NOTES TO CHAPTER 16

p 224 *"whhheeeEEEEEEEEEEEEEEEE"*: David Lodge, Small World, Secker & Warburg, London, 1984, p 271

p 226 "The courses told their staff . . ." Stucki: *Swissair*, p 134ff

p 227 "Great cities and great resorts . . ." E. H. "Tex" Boullioun, speech to the Aero Club of Washington, 25 October 1983

p 231 "It cannot be too strongly emphasised . . ." *International Air Transport*, p 101

Index